Managers of Modernization

Managers of Modernization

Organizations and Elites in Turkey (1950–1969)

Leslie L. Roos, Jr. and Noralou P. Roos

Harvard University Press, Cambridge, Massachusetts, 1971

60541

Contents

Tables

Preface

The writing of a book is such a long and painful process that any and all encouragement received must be gratefully acknowledged. This is particularly true for research conducted abroad where one is so dependent upon the goodwill and support of others. Three Turks — Fahir Armaoğlu, Mümtaz Soysal, and Metin Dirimtekin — were our major benefactors. Without their counsel and help, the surveys which form the background of our study could not have been coordinated. Arif Payaslıoğlu, Orhan Sertel, Hayrettin Kalkandelen, Sabahaddin Alpat, Halil Tanrıkulu, Cahit Tutum, Dündar Karaşar, Sırrı Kırcalı, Doğan Yalım, Cumhur Ferman, and Kemal Togay were also ever ready to submit to our entreaties for advice, contacts, information, and solace. Thanks are also due our research assistants: Mustafa Orhan, Mustapha Demiroğlu, Mehmet Demiroğlu, Doğu Ergül, Tanju Karasu, and Necati Erol. Not only did they stick with us over the long and tedious coding process, but they put up with our Turkish. Finally, a debt of gratitude is owed to those who took us into their homes, nursed us through illness and became our very good friends — İsmet, Katriya, and Ufuk Özbudak, Reşan Barutçu, Şeyhullah and Sakine Turan, Alev Bilgen, and Göksel Kalaycıoğlu.

Closer to home, we would like to thank Frederick W. Frey — thesis adviser, colleague, and friend. His support has come in the form of financial aid, personal contacts, access to unpublished data, insight into Turkish politics, and critical comments on our writing. Ithiel de Sola Pool, Frank Tachau, Bill Klecka, Herb Jacob, and Jim Caporaso provided advice at various points along the way.

As we moved into the final stages of analysis, writing, and revising we accumulated another whole series of debts. Accordingly, we would like to thank Sharon Perlman Krefetz, Michael Stohl, Sharon Symcak, and Alice Perlin for their help with the manuscript. Innumerable typing chores were smoothly carried out by Sally Lewis, Carol Anderson, and Betty Reed.

Finally, we are indebted to a number of institutions for financial assistance. American Research Institute in Turkey, Social Science Research Council, National Science Foundation, and Agricultural Development Council provided research support for data collection and analysis. The Woodrow Wilson Fellowship Foundation subsidized several long months of analysis and writing by the junior author, while fellowships from the Harvard Center for Middle Eastern Studies and the Ford Foundation aided the senior author. Computing was carried out with the aid of Project MAC at M.I.T. and the Vogelback Computing Center at Northwestern University. The survey data used in the study are available through the Roper Public Opinion Center in Williamstown, Massachusetts. The data were also deposited in Ankara at the Political Science Faculty and at the Public Administration Institute for Turkey and the Middle East.

Given so much help, we must take the blame for any errors of fact or interpretation which remain.

L.L.R., Jr.
N.P.R.

Managers of Modernization

1
Introduction

The literature on the modernization process is somewhat ambivalent regarding the role of the administrator. Some authors see transitional societies facing a bureaucratic dominance which threatens both the creation of independent political organizations and the expansion of the economy. A recent group of essays examining the role of the bureaucracy in the development process concludes that "by and large . . . we are witnessing in many places the emergence of overpowering bureaucracies." [1] La Palombara, for example, fears "bureaucracies of the developing areas will . . . hamper the growth of a private entrepreneurial class," and where bureaucracies are cohesive and coherent, "political parties tend to be ineffective, and voluntary associations, rather than serving as checks on the bureaucracy, tend to become passive instrumentalities of the public administrators." [2] In extreme cases of bureaucratic dominance — such as in Thailand — the bureaucracy is a self-serving mechanism uncontrolled by independent political forces. This leads to policies irrational for a country's economic development, but rational in terms of the administrators' own self-interest.[3] Bureaucratic domination also tends to inhibit social mobility. In a stable social environment, status systems may well "become ends in themselves instead of means to the fair distribution of abilities, responsibilities, and rewards." [4] This is particularly likely when there is an entrenched bureaucracy whose interest it is to prevent the emergence of other social groups.

"Bureaucratic polities," however, are not completely stable systems. Certain kinds of changes act to modify the influence of bureaucrats in politics. The development of competitive political systems seems to reduce bureaucratic power. When there is a change of government, new individuals representative of rural interests tend to move into positions

1. Joseph La Palombara, "An Overview of Bureaucracy and Political Development," in Joseph La Palombara, ed., *Bureaucracy and Political Development* (Princeton, N. J., Princeton University Press, 1963), pp. 23–25.

2. *Ibid.*, pp. 23–24.

3. Fred W. Riggs, *Thailand: The Modernization of a Bureaucratic Polity* (Honolulu, East-West Center Press, 1966), p. 131.

4. Suzanne Keller, *Beyond the Ruling Class* (New York, Random House, 1968), p. 242.

2

of authority, displacing politicians with administrative backgrounds and other members of the urban elite.[5] Huntington has conceptualized these electoral processes as "ruralizing elections"; such elections are characterized by the defeat of an urban-based modernizing elite, the mobilization of new rural voters, and the coming to power of a non-cosmopolitan, local elite.

Ruralizing elections and the declining cosmopolitanism of elites seem to be characteristic of many countries.[6] Although Huntington notes that "once in office, the new government's policies typically aimed to please and to benefit its rural supporters," he does not elaborate on the administrative changes likely to result from a ruralizing election.[7] An analysis of such changes is fundamental to an understanding of the larger problem of how developments in the political system affect the role of the bureaucratic elite;[8] the results of ruralizing elections constitute an important subset of the political changes likely to occur during the modernization process.

Contemporary theorizing on modernization has mentioned the "want–get" ratio, the gap between wishes and reality, as a particularly important psychological concept.[9] But more significant for this discussion is the "have–lose" ratio: the gap between an individual's past conditions and his present state. The "want–get" ratio has reference to such concepts as economic betterment and upward social mobility; for elites who have been ousted from power, the "have–lose" ratio raises the

5. See Frederick W. Frey, *The Turkish Political Elite* (Cambridge, Mass., M.I.T. Press, 1965), and Samuel P. Huntington, *Political Order in Changing Societies* (New Haven, Conn., Yale University Press, 1968).

6. William B. Quandt, "The Comparative Study of Political Elites," *Sage Professional Papers in Comparative Politics,* 1 (1970), 188. Quandt notes that democratic countries illustrating the declining cosmopolitanism of elites over time include the United States, India, the Philippines, Turkey, and Ceylon. Authoritarian countries may also show this pattern; Quandt lists the Soviet Union, China, Nazi Germany, Fascist Italy, Ghana, Burma, and Indonesia.

7. Huntington, *Political Order,* pp. 460–461.

8. For a discussion of this interaction between political system and bureaucratic role in Africa, see Richard L. Harris, "The Effects of Political Change on the Role Set of the Senior Bureaucrats in Ghana and Nigeria," *Administrative Science Quarterly,* 13 (December 1968), 386–401.

9. For a recent formulation of the "want–get" ratio and its application to contemporary history, see Daniel Lerner and Morton Gorden, *Euratlantica: Changing Perspectives of the European Elites* (Cambridge, Mass., M.I.T. Press, 1969).

specter of downward social mobility and deteriorating personal living standards.

Since they are already mobilized, elites who have lost much of their former status may be both susceptible to extremist appeals and likely to express their preferences forcefully. A number of countries have experienced coups during the years after a ruralizing election; the administrator's adaptability — or lack thereof — has obvious implications for a country's political stability. Identifying some of the dimensions of the processes of bureaucratic adjustment or bureaucratic frustration is of obvious importance. Which parts of a country's administration are most likely to be affected by a ruralizing election? What features of a nation's political culture might make it easier or more difficult for a bureaucrat to adjust to a loss of power?

The administrative systems of countries controlled by an urban elite often differ significantly from those of countries characterized by party competition. The concept of "ruralizing elections" is especially valuable because such elections provide one way of replacing a government dominated by an urban elite with a regime more sympathetic to rural interests. The rural politicization which accompanies political parties' efforts to gain mass support may tend to make bureaucrats more conscious of local desires. Frequently such developments lead to severe restrictions on bureaucratic power; representatives of the central government can no longer ignore the peasants' wishes with impunity. A possible consequence of such politicization is to make many administrative positions less attractive than they were before officials became subject to such pressures. The lower prestige which may be attached to many government jobs is just one indicator of the downward social mobility that threatens bureaucrats after a political system opens up to mass participation.

Rural political participation affects the bureaucracy's relationship to political leaders as well as to its clientele. Such participation is understandably likely to result in official dissatisfaction with politicians elected by rural support. Alienation on the part of bureaucratic groups has often resulted in military intervention, authoritarian rule, and/or continued political instability. Thus, an analysis of official reaction to this problem of rural politicization is of particular relevance to the study of modernization.

4

Organizational Change

This discussion of rural political participation and the bureaucracy addresses itself to one of the classical dilemmas of administrative research, "namely, whether bureaucracy is master or servant, an independent body or a tool, and, if a tool, whose interests it can be made to serve." [10] Another important theme in such research concerns the internal functioning of organizations. Bureaucracies, like other organizations, grow, stagnate, adapt, and decline, but the causal factors involved in such changes are unclear.

External pressures, such as those resulting from a ruralizing election, seem to precipitate many of the most significant organizational changes. Some pressures act directly upon the organization's power and authority structure; a change in organizational structure may take place independent of any action taken by the organization. Since few events occur in such circumstances, this type of change is difficult to predict. Organizational change through direct external pressure often occurs as a result of traumatic political events — assassination, military defeat, an overthrow of the national political system, and so forth.

A significant change in the organization's environment often results in more indirect pressures. Particular organizations may be respected for a considerable period and then fall from favor because of a change in the attitudes of the organization's clientele. Resources which have been previously available to an organization may be denied, creating substantial pressures for organizational restructuring. Technical innovations and social changes — both those occurring in the environment and those initiated within an organization — open up new possibilities for organizations to improve their internal controls and to expand their functions. Organizations which fail to adapt to such changes will, in the long term, be placed at a substantial disadvantage in competing for scarce resources.

An organization may also respond to other changes in its environment. Organizations seem particularly sensitive to innovations made by competitors performing similar tasks; imitation of successful competitors is one likely response. More generally, an organization may react by trying to change its environment or by trying to change itself.

10. S. N. Eisenstadt, *Essays on Comparative Institutions* (New York, Wiley, 1965), p. 179.

Such activities may have unintended side effects. An organization's original action may feed back and alter its environment in an unexpected fashion.

Although external and internal pressures can be separated analytically, a number of variables seem to operate both within individual organizations and within the society as a whole. Cultural factors may channel the nature and direction of change, acting both in organizations and in the environment. Our knowledge of cultural differences which might lead to differences in organizational behavior is limited, although the recent emphasis on comparative studies has produced valuable findings.[11]

Other kinds of internally generated change seem inherent in the structural nature of organizations. Katz and Kahn note that bureaucratic organizations move toward maximization, toward growth and expansion.[12] Goal displacement is a common phenomenon; organizations have been willing to alter their most fundamental goals in order to survive or improve their possibilities for growth. Such changes in function are encouraged because of the benefits which survival and growth promise for members of the organization.

Internally generated pressures suggest a focus upon the individual and his contribution to organizational purpose. The particular individuals occupying organizational roles are especially important when routinized activity is not sufficient. A discussion of the determinants of individual behavior is thus highly relevant for the study of organizational adaptation to change.

The Turkish Case

The general framework presented here is useful for understanding the major upheavals in the power and authority structure of the Turkish Republic. In Turkey an entrenched administrative elite, controlling a system resembling the ideal-type bureaucratic polity, was challenged by the pressures of political competition. The origins of the period of bureaucratic domination are not hard to trace. The Turkish Republic inherited not only a strong bureaucratic tradition and structure from

11. See, for example, Mason Haire, Edwin E. Ghiselli, and Lyman W. Porter, *Managerial Thinking: An International Study* (New York, Wiley, 1966).

12. Daniel Katz and Robert L. Kahn, *The Social Psychology of Organizations* (New York, Wiley, 1966), pp. 300–335.

6

the Ottoman Empire, but also the personnel who had staffed this far-flung structure.[13] The mental world of an Ottoman district governor (*kaymakam*) was summarized by a British traveler to Eastern Turkey in 1906:

> His idea of reform was the regular payment of *Kaymakams,* the provision of free illustrated newspapers for *Kaymakams* to read, the building of railways for *Kaymakams* to travel by, and eventually the restoration of all *Kaymakams* to (the capital), where they would be given places as highly-paid deputies in a Parliament of *Kaymakams,* who would collect and control the expenditure.[14]

Many of these Ottoman officials brought their administrative skills and their political and social viewpoints into the Republic's service.

During the first decades of the Republic the Ottoman district governor's utopia — a Parliament of *Kaymakams* — was for all practical purposes achieved. "Until 1950, there existed a sort of closed corporation of professional public servants who, acting as politicians, passed laws which they and their colleagues administered as bureaucrats." [15] Other observers have noted that, despite an initial tendency to encourage private enterprise, "the bureaucratic empire-builders who saw in etatism an opportunity for personal power eventually used this state machinery as a weapon against private competition." [16] Hostility toward business interests not directly under state control was understandable from a historical viewpoint. The most prominent business classes during the Empire were either alien minority groups (Greeks,

13. Rustow has noted that "among the graduates of the Ottoman civil service school (that is, the Political Science Faculty) who lived in 1960 only 15 per cent went to Syria or Iraq, of the graduates of the military college as few as 7 per cent." The rest remained or returned to Turkey. Dankwart A. Rustow, "The Development of Parties in Turkey," in Joseph La Palombara and Myron Weiner, eds., *Political Parties and Political Development* (Princeton, Princeton University Press, 1966), p. 128.

14. Mark Sykes, *The Caliphs' Last Heritage* (London, 1915), p. 65. Quoted by Roderic H. Davison, "Environmental and Foreign Contributions (Turkey)," in Dankwart A. Rustow and Robert E. Ward, eds., *Political Modernization in Japan and Turkey* (Princeton, Princeton University Press, 1964), p. 115.

15. Richard L. Chambers, "Bureaucracy (Turkey)," in Rustow and Ward, eds., *Political Modernization,* p. 326.

16. Richard D. Robinson, *The First Turkish Republic* (Cambridge, Mass., Harvard University Press, 1963), p. 110.

Armenians, and Jews) or foreigners exploiting the Empire's resources through one of the many "capitulations" arrangements.

Despite these predisposing factors, Turkey in the 1950's and 1960's was far from being a bureaucratic polity. Turkey's political system proved capable of supporting the development of a mass party (the Democratic Party) which successfully ousted the original governmental party (the Republican People's Party) from office. Grassroots politicians have acted as effective mediators between elite and mass and proved capable of putting real pressure on the elitist bureaucrats. Multiparty competition has led to debureaucratization — a tendency to relax hierarchical authority and rely upon more nonbureaucratic means of motivating cooperative effort.[17]

Similarly, in the economic sphere many developments cast doubt on the existence of bureaucratic domination. The parties (the Democratic and its successor, the Justice Party) which have been most successful in open electoral competition have been backed by private business interests. Given the support of Democratic and Justice party governments, the private sector generally prospered and expanded.

In view of the altered political environment, many members of the Turkish bureaucratic elite made efforts to change their style and adapt to the new circumstances. But change was psychologically difficult and personally distasteful, particularly for many district governors. New criteria for promotion and bureaucratic success added to the load upon the administrator. This stress placed upon the bureaucracy by the ruralizing election helped create a climate facilitating the military coup of 1960. Many observers say the coup reflected the official elite's response to its loss of power. Turkey is one of the few countries which have passed through the initial period of intra-elite conflict associated with the advent of rural participation in politics. Turkey thus provides an ideal setting in which to study the reaction of a bureaucratic elite to challenges to its power.

Administrative Systems — A Typology

Much of this book deals with the Turkish administrative system in two different political environments. Before 1950 Turkey was ruled by a predominantly urban elite group with strong official ties. With the introduction of multiparty politics, the government became more

17. Peter M. Blau and W. Richard Scott, *Formal Organizations* (San Francisco, Chandler, 1962), pp. 232–235.

responsive to local interests and less concerned with the opinions of the administrative elite. Such societal changes had a substantial effect on the functioning of the public administration. Table 1-1 highlights some features of the administrative system under these two types of political arrangements. Beyond their relevance for Turkey, it is hoped that these typologies might be applicable to cross-national comparisons. There are a number of countries still under the dominance of an administrative elite (such as Thailand) or characterized by party competition without having gone through a period of dominance by a native bureaucracy (such as India).

Table 1-1: Administrative Systems in Different Political Environments

	Administrative system under urban elite	Administrative system with party competition
Groups benefited	Urban, administrative elite	Rural areas and local elites
Bureaucracy's control over environment	Substantial	Moderate
Bureaucracy's Policy-making role	Wide	Narrow
National Level		
Bureaucratic representation in Parliament	High	Low
Representative's intervention in workings of bureaucracy	Relatively low	Relatively high
Bureaucracy's success with self-protective legislation	High	Low
Local Level		
Compliance structure	Coercive	Mixed
Direction of influence	Unidirectional	Reciprocal
Administrative dependence upon clients	Very limited	Moderate

Many of the terms presented here should be familiar, but some explanation is in order. When a political system is dominated by the urban elite, bureaucrats tend to participate in the important political decisions, controlling the environment so as to maximize their own influence. Under such conditions, the administrator's role set is wide;[18] senior bureaucrats tend to participate in many different activities of societal importance.

With the coming to power of the Democratic Party in 1950, the urban elite which had guided Turkey under the one-party system was ousted from office. The bureaucracy experienced a marked loss of control over its social environment; the role set of the bureaucratic elite tended to be narrowed as a result of this ruralizing election. Two propositions from Harris's work are supported by the historical data.

1. When the key leaders in a political system change, the extent of the similarity in backgrounds and values between the new leaders and the senior bureaucrats will determine whether the new leaders will seek to expand or restrict the number of functions performed by the senior bureaucrats in the political system.

2. When the key leaders in the political system change, the number of functions performed by the senior bureaucrats in the political system will be restricted if the new leaders conceive of their own role in expanded terms, and increased if they conceive of their role in more limited terms.[19]

After the 1950 Turkish election, the bureaucratic elite lost much of its representation in Parliament. Frey has documented the social background differences between the pre-1950 and the post-1950 Parliaments; perhaps the most conspicuous change is the decline in official representation from 34 percent in the Seventh Assembly (1940–1946) to 16 percent in the Ninth Assembly (1950–1954).[20] As might be expected, the bureaucrats' political influence was drastically reduced, while both national and local leaders conceived their own roles in expanded terms and came to intervene more freely in administrative matters.

The bureaucratic structure in a polity dominated by the urban elite is often characterized by a relatively great reliance upon coercion to

18. A role set is the "complement of role relationships which persons have by virtue of occupying a particular social status." Robert K. Merton, *Social Theory and Social Structure* (New York, Free Press, 1957), p. 369.

19. Harris, "Effects of Political Change," p. 399.

20. The representation of government administrators declined from 19 per cent in the Seventh Assembly to 10 percent in the Ninth Assembly (Frey, *Turkish Political Elite*, p. 181).

10

insure compliance to administrative decree.[21] The situation in rural Turkey under the one-party system illustrates a number of features characteristic of this type of system; for example, villagers were compelled to spend up to several weeks each year on labor projects. Despite local unpopularity this was generally enforced — by the gendarme, if necessary. Influence proceeded downward through the hierarchy in the Ministry of Interior and was communicated to the villagers; the possibilities for local participation were minimal. The successful bureaucrat had to be loyal to modernizing goals of Atatürk and the Republican People's Party and to avoid giving in to pressures from the traditionally oriented villagers. Administrative leadership was primarily instrumental and task-oriented; bureaucrats did not have to consider local opinion in carrying out their normal tasks or initiating special projects.

The administrative system under party competition reflects local political pressures to a markedly greater degree. Compliance with administrative directives is normally based upon factors other than coercive power. What Etzioni has called normative (or persuasive) power plays a greater role, while remunerative power is used to persuade villagers to participate in various development projects.[22] Under such a system there is reciprocal influence upward from the citizenry and its leadership into the administrative system. Local participation in decision-making with regard to new projects is substantial; politicians may also use their connections to influence bureaucratic careers. In this environment successful administrators may tend to be freewheeling, trying to please several different constituencies. Contacts outside the central ministries can be particularly valuable if there is a strong desire to change jobs. Within the Ministry of Interior, administrators have tried to bring centrally financed development projects into their districts while attempting to keep local leadership happy. In addition to being task-oriented, such administrative leadership must be concerned with keeping villagers and townspeople content.[23]

21. Etzioni's definition of coercive power is that adopted here; "coercive power rests on the application, or the threat of application, of physical sanctions." See Amitai Etzioni, *A Comparative Analysis of Complex Organizations* (New York, Free Press, 1961), p. 5.

22. "Normative power rests on the allocation and manipulation of symbolic rewards and deprivations . . ." while "remunerative power is based on control over material resources and rewards" (*ibid.,* p. 5).

23. This material on leadership is obviously influenced by the work of Bales. For a summary of studies concerning leadership in organizations, see Katz and

The Turkish Administrative Elite

This discussion will also focus upon how members of the administrative elite have reacted to modernization and their consequent loss of status in Turkish society. Many of the survey data used for this analysis were collected from graduates of Ankara University's Faculty of Political Science who answered questionnaires distributed in 1956 and 1965. Both panel and cohort data were available; 241 graduates answered both the 1956 and 1965 questionnaire, while 139 graduates responded in 1956, but not in 1965. Questionnaires were also answered by 69 younger graduates who received only the 1965 questionnaire. The methodology is discussed at some length in Appendix A.

Since the group studied are all graduates of Ankara University's Political Science Faculty, education provides the criterion of eliteness.[24] In terms of such indicators as father's occupation and lycée grades, Political Science Faculty students, compared with Turkish university students as a whole, constitute a very select group. More importantly, the choice of an educational criterion of elite status can be justified by comparison with more standard indicators. The relative success of Political Science Faculty graduates in obtaining high-level positions, both appointive and elective, reinforces the use of the educational criterion.[25] Frey simply defines the national administrative elite in terms of people who graduated from the Political Science Faculty (he calls it "the proper school") and consequently held positions in the central government.[26] Political Science Faculty graduates are an especially interesting group, since they have traditionally entered the three most powerful central ministries — Interior, Finance, and Foreign Affairs.

Longitudinal information from both 1956 and 1965 facilitates this study of the Turkish administrative elite's reaction to changing politi-

---

Kahn, *Social Psychology of Organizations.*

24. "Throughout most of Turkey's modern history, the fundamental social distinction has been that based upon education. Both the more impressionistic writings of traditional scholarship and the few studies of modern social science are in agreement on this point" (Frey, *Turkish Political Elite,* p. 29).

25. Dankwart A. Rustow, "The Study of Elites: Who's Who, When, and How," *World Politics,* 18 (July 1966), 701.

26. Frey, *Turkish Political Elite,* p. 117. We discuss the importance of the Political Science Faculty (*Siyasal Bilgiler Fakültesi*) in Chapter 2.

12

cal conditions. Such survey material gives a perspective on the recent history of a modernizing country which is unique among studies of the Third World. These occupational and attitudinal data help provide information on the state of the political system. They suggest how pressures are resolved and permit the study of changing patterns of recruitment to official positions. Moreover, comparing material from several points in time facilitates the understanding of any single period; when a society is undergoing rapid change, such aid is particularly helpful.

Despite wide agreement on the importance of systematic longitudinal studies, such studies have been generally lacking in both political science and public administration. Quinn and Kahn[27] note that "the measurement of change over time is axiomatic in science, but the axiom acquires a special importance in the study of organizations because it is so seldom possible to do conventional short-term experiments with properly chosen control groups." Since difficulties with experimentation are endemic to the study of government bureaucracies, the situation may call for a quasi-experimental design in which ongoing processes are measured at different points in time in an effort to isolate causal factors.

This research design has many aspects of the "most similar systems" design used in comparative research, but may be more efficient in singling out "experimental" variables.[28] By studying the same country at two or more points in time, the researcher examines systems that are similar along many dimensions. Such a design helps minimize the number of system-level factors which vary outside of the researcher's control. This technique makes it possible to introduce explanatory factors which refer to characteristics of the Turkish political system at two points in time, 1956 and 1965. Differences in the frequencies of — or relationships among — particular attitudes may be due to changes in the political system over this nine-year period or to changes in an individual's life circumstances.[29] A combination of panel and age-level analysis aids in isolating causal factors.

27. Robert P. Quinn and Robert L. Kahn, "Organizational Psychology," *Annual Review of Psychology*, 18 (1967), 460.

28. For a discussion of the "most similar systems" design, see Adam Przeworski and Henry Teune, *The Logic of Comparative Social Inquiry* (New York, Wiley, 1970), pp. 32–35.

29. See Gabriel Almond and Sidney Verba, *The Civic Culture* (Princeton, N.J., Princeton University Press, 1963), pp. 43–76, for a discussion of ex-

The research also has a specifically comparative aspect. Five types of organizations are followed over the nine-year period for which survey data are available; the questionnaire material is supplemented by historical information. Since the status of these organizations has been undergoing rapid change, this design facilitates comparing social processes in various different settings.[30] A particular focus will be upon organizational growth and decline.

The data present a number of possibilities for analysis. Recruitment to administrative positions — and circulation of individuals in these positions — will be studied. There will be a special concern for the factors which are associated with, and which may help to explain, various attitudes and behaviors. Several factors will be considered. The influence of social background variables upon the attitudes of our respondents is important both for its own sake and for its general relevance to elite theory. A number of authors have noted that political scientists cannot move directly from social background data to inferences about the attitudes and behaviors of particular individuals.[31] Thus it will be necessary to analyze systematically the relationships between social background and the hypothesized dependent variables. In addition, situational and psychological variables are important determinants of both attitudes and actions. We will examine some of the situational and psychological correlates of both job-related sentiments and ideological dispositions.

In addition, much of the orientation of this work will involve the study of the behavior of individuals in their specific roles as members of organizations. Career patterns and job satisfaction will be emphasized, although some attention will be paid to various group and organizational characteristics. This analysis of administrative behavior will include a consideration of bureaucrats in their interpersonal relationships.[32] In the course of their work, bureaucrats must relate to

planatory variables which are relevant to cross-national research. Much of this discussion is applicable to time-series studies as well.

30. Such research designs are discussed in Allen H. Barton, "Organizations: Methods of Research," in David L. Sills, ed., *International Encyclopedia of the Social Sciences,* vol. 11 (New York, Macmillan and Free Press, 1968), pp. 334–341.

31. See, for example, Rustow, "The Study of Elites," pp. 702–703.

32. Peter M. Blau, "Organizations: Theories of Organizations," in Sills, *International Encyclopedia,* p. 302. This discussion has also been influenced by the typology presented in Lewis Edinger, "Editor's Introduction," in Lewis Edinger, ed., *Political Leadership in Industrialized Societies* (New York, Wiley, 1967), p. 12.

14

both national and local politicians, to administrative superiors and subordinates, and to ordinary citizens. Extensive survey information aids the study of such relationships; of particular interest are the Turkish data on relationships among administrators. The linking of surveys from several sources permits us to investigate in some detail the interaction among district governor, village headman, and ordinary villager.

Frequent reference will be made to empirical research on attitudes and organizations in Western countries. Theories on motivation and work derived from the research of Maslow and Herzberg will be considered in another context.[33] The Turkish data help extend the generality of findings from other parts of the world, while propositions derived from organization theory can aid in structuring the material from Turkey. Work on organizations in a developing country is particularly relevant because of the possibilities for building links between various bodies of theory. An effort will be made to join three areas of research and theory. This study will draw freely from the literatures on modernization, on elites, and on organizations.

Several different vocabularies are involved. Table 1-2 attempts to make explicit some of the relevant political and organizational terms.

Table 1-2: Political and Organizational Vocabularies

Level of aggregation	Political vocabulary	Organizational vocabulary
Society	Polity	Environment
Group	Legislature or bureaucracy	Organization
Individual	Member of elite	Manager or employee

The literatures on modernization and elites use similar concepts, but variables pertaining to society, to groups, and to individuals are treated differently by political scientists and organization theorists. The substantive interests of these scholars have also differed. Much modernization theory deals with stability and change in forms of government, and this involves research on important macro-level problems. Elite research is clearly associated with the study of comparative politics and modernization, but such concepts as "circulation of elites," "status

33. A. H. Maslow, *Motivation and Personality* (New York, Harper, 1954), and F. Herzberg, B. Mausner, and B. B. Snyderman, *The Motivation to Work* (New York, Wiley, 1959).

incongruency," and "social mobility" are drawn from sociology. By comparison, organization theory, based in large part upon sociological and psychological research, generally ignores systemic changes to focus upon micro-level hypotheses and propositions. This study aims to link the discussion of macro- and micro-level problems. Certain hypotheses from organization theory are relevant to problems of mobility and social change. Particular kinds of system-level developments may modify organization theory propositions which have held true in other settings.

The ordering and structure of the different chapters reflect this concern with both macro- and micro-level. At various points we study system variables, organizational variables, and individual variables. The first several chapters concentrate upon system variables and organizational variables. Chapter 2 will discuss the Republic as founded by Atatürk: his goals for his country and the structure established to achieve these goals. Chapter 3 examines the consequences arising from the pursuit of these original goals; the measures taken by Atatürk eventually placed the authority structure under heavy pressure for change. Chapter 4 includes a discussion of the differential susceptibility of organizations to influence by environmental pressures and their responses to such pressures. Chapter 5 will focus upon organizational stratification, assessing the impact of social change upon various Turkish organizations. Chapters 6, 7, and 8 deal with individual variables, mobility and job satisfaction, within the context of these organizational and societal changes. In later chapters, the relationships between the administrator and other social groups are treated at some length. Finally, an effort is made to tie together the different kinds of variables; the findings are summarized in terms of their general implications for Turkish politics.

2

Authoritarian Leadership and

Bureaucratic Dominance

Turkey is one of the few developing nations whose political, economic, and social developments have been largely indigenous, influenced by foreign threats and foreign advice, but never by foreign domination. Although Turkey never went through a colonial period, the transition from Ottoman Empire to modern republic was a traumatic one. The Ottoman Empire tried to reform itself, but it proved unequal to the task. Atatürk's Republic was built on the basis of radical social and political change, but certain institutions — particularly the military and the bureaucracy — were of critical importance both before and after the Republic's founding.

During the decade from 1908 to 1918 the traditional Ottoman power structure had been undermined, first by the Revolution of 1908 and then by the wartime dictatorship of the Committee of Union and Progress. Over this period the army, in alliance with the Union and Progress Party, emerged as the dominant element on the political scene. In the chaos following the Empire's defeat in 1918 and the cowardly flight of the Union and Progress leaders, the military retained its critical role. In the provinces the army often became the only effective authority.

The direct external pressure under which the authority system of the Empire crumbled created the chaos conducive to the rise of charismatic leadership. Rustow has defined the Turkish situation in 1919 as characterized by "defeat and occupation, widespread desire for national resistance, and hence a need for a combination of military and political leadership." [1] With most of the other generals discredited by defeat, Mustafa Kemal, later to be honored with the name Atatürk (Father Turk) was the man to seize this opportunity. Atatürk imitated and responded to those external factors which he found useful. His own personal goals for national development shaped the future of Turkey for decades to come.

In addition to the war, other important external influences upon Turkey were international pressure for resolution of Greco-Turkish

1. Dankwart A. Rustow, "Atatürk as Founder of a State," *Daedalus,* 97 (Summer 1968), 797.

animosities, and the impressive example of authoritarian political and economic development set forth by the Communists in Russia. The population exchange between Turkey and Greece at the end of the First World War resulted in a more homogenous population and may have eventually eased tensions between these historic foes. But, perhaps more significantly, the exchange created a vacuum in Turkey's commercial sector. The implications of this vacuum will be discussed in Chapter 3.

The Russian example may have reinforced Atatürk's own predispositions toward an authoritarian political regime. The idea of a unitary structure also squared with Atatürk's desire to keep Turkey independent, free of outside entanglements and free of foreign help or obligations. Atatürk discouraged foreign business and committed the country to paying off the Ottoman debt in order to accomplish this goal. But, more importantly, Atatürk, having won the military battle against the Greek invaders, set upon an even more difficult task — the transformation of a stagnant Ottoman Anatolia into a modern Turkish republic. Atatürk's policy had two distinct goals — modernizing the Turkish elite and industrializing the country.

For Atatürk secularization and Westernization were almost synonymous with modernization. Reforms which helped Turkey identify more closely with Europe were marks of progress. Religious reaction against reform had hindered the Ottoman Empire's attempts to modernize, and Atatürk was determined to override such opposition. Atatürk had a similar commitment to industrialization. He created and expanded the industrial sector, demanding that the Turks endure long decades of economic austerity to finance ambitious development programs. The scope of this task is difficult to appreciate without a familiarity with the impoverishment of the Ottoman Empire. In the early 1900's Ottoman Turkey had only about 200 significant "industrial establishments," over two-thirds of which were concerned with food processing.[2]

The Empire's economic situation was aggravated by the influence aliens had exercised in the industrial sector: 80 percent of the Empire's finance, industry, and commerce was in the active control of Greeks and Armenians.[3] Ottoman Turks entered the bureaucracy, the mili-

2. These 200 plants employed about 17,000 workers, an average of 85 per enterprise. Z. Y. Hershlag, *Introduction to the Modern Economic History of the Middle East* (Leiden, E. J. Brill, 1964), p. 72.

3. Eliot G. Mears, "Foreign and Domestic Commerce," in Eliot G. Mears, ed., *Modern Turkey* (New York, Macmillan, 1924), p. 328.

tary, or the religious organizations, leaving commercial occupations to the infidel Greeks, Armenians, and Jews. Since the overwhelming majority of the industrial plants were owned by individuals,[4] when non-Turks were forced to leave at the end of the First World War, Turkey lost much of the human capital, including training and skills, necessary for economic development.[5] Great obstacles threatened the achievement of Atatürk's two goals of modernization and industrialization. A traditional, conservative population and a backward economy seemed impervious to change. But Atatürk was determined to create the allies and the authority structure necessary to push the country toward his goals.

The Political Science Faculty

Although Atatürk was a military man and authoritarian by nature, he endeavored to attract civilian as well as military support and to legitimize his actions through an elected parliament. Fortunately for him, experiments with Western education begun in the nineteenth century had produced an educated official class which could form the nucleus of Turkey's modernizing elite. Members of official groups — the military and the bureaucracy — were in particularly favorable positions for being coopted by Atatürk. Education was a scarce commodity, and these groups, along with the relatively small body of professionals, constituted a large percentage of the total number of Turks with higher education. Former military men and bureaucrats were drawn into the political party founded by Atatürk, the Republican People's Party, and became closely identified with his policies.

The use of European instructors in the military colleges and the reform of the army after the abolition of the Janissary corps in 1826 helped produce an officer corps which became "one of the most West-

4. Another source, which listed 269 industrial enterprises during this period, noted that 219 were owned by individuals, 28 by companies and 22 by the State. Cited in Hershlag, *Modern Economic History*, p. 72.

5. Total exclusion of minority groups was never accomplished and even in contemporary Turkey, non-Turks continue to hold a position in the commercial sector disproportionate with their numbers in the population as a whole. In a sample of private entrepreneurs in the six largest cities, 9 percent of the respondents were Jews and 7 percent were Greeks. See Arif Payaslíoğlu, *Türkiyede Özel Sanayi Alanîndaki Müteşebbisler ve Teşebbüsler* [Enterpreneurs and enterprises in the private sector in Turkey] (Ankara, Political Science Faculty-Financial Institute, 1961), p. 22.

ernized elements in the Ottoman Empire." [6] During Atatürk's conflict with the Sultan the legitimate source of civil authority, a number of officers followed the Sultan. But the clear majority (twelve out of seventeen) of the top-ranking front commanders from World War I joined Atatürk's nationalist cause.[7] Moreover, these generals were relatively youthful; they and their military subordinates provided critical support for Atatürk during the first years of the Republic.

The Political Science Faculty was the other source of trained, Westernized individuals to help formulate and carry out Atatürk's programs. This faculty had originally been established as what now would be called an "in-service training program." A one-year course of instruction was provided, and students were recruited from qualified *katibs* (clerks and secretaries) serving in various government bureaus. The inadequacy of such limited training was soon realized. In 1877 the curriculum was modernized and the study lengthened to two, three, or four years, depending on the educational background of the student.[8]

Students from quite diverse backgrounds took part in this innovative program. Although the school recruited primarily from an official, cosmopolitan upper class, social mobility was always possible. The Ottoman system of recruitment never systematically excluded the lower class. And at the Political Science Faculty it was not unusual to find the sons of farmers and small businessmen studying alongside the sons of generals and grand vezirs.[9]

6. Dankwart A. Rustow, "The Army and the Founding of the Turkish Republic," *World Politics*, 11 (July 1959), 511–522.

7. *Ibid.*, 526–534.

8. See Andreas M. Kazamias, *Education and the Quest for Modernity in Turkey* (Chicago, University of Chicago Press, 1966), pp. 87–88, for a good description of the establishment and early years of the Civil Service School (*Mülkiye*) which became the Political Science Faculty. Valuable additional material is presented in Joseph S. Szyliowicz, "Elite Recruitment in Turkey: The Role of the *Mülkiye*," *World Politics*, 23 (April 1971), 371–398.

9. Kazamias, *Education*, p. 89, presents data on the fathers' occupations of Political Science Faculty graduates from 1860 to 1909. Forty percent of the graduates' fathers were bureaucrats, 12 percent were businessmen, 12 percent were affiliated with religious institutions, 9 percent were in the judiciary, 7 percent were educators, and 20 percent were in other occupations. This includes only a sample of those who graduated from the Political Science Faculty during this period, since complete biographical data were not available for everyone. The social backgrounds of those attending other university-level schools during this period may have been similar. It is reported that 41 percent of the fathers of

20

Almost all of the early graduates assumed positions of importance in the Empire's administrative system. One analysis of the careers of those who graduated from the school between 1860 and 1909 is presented in Table 2-1. Clearly, the data would be more informative if we knew what percentage of people holding the highest positions during this period were Political Science Faculty graduates. Unfortunately such information is simply not available. By scanning the job histories of the graduates, however, it is possible to gain a better time-perspective on their occupational achievements. In the forty years after the school's founding (between 1860 and 1900) only one graduate, Ömer Sabri, reached the position of *vali,* governing one of the 27 regions into which the Ottoman Empire was divided.[10] This position was at the pinnacle of the provincial administrative system, and while graduates were very conspicuous at the middle levels (*as mutasarrïf* and *kaymakam*), very few reached the top. However, from the turn of the century on, Political Science Faculty graduates become increasingly prominent at the top levels of provincial administration. By 1916–17 and the years just preceding the founding of the Republic, probably about a third of the *valis* had graduated from the Political Science Faculty.[11]

The power and influence which such graduates commanded was considerable. The provincial government was modeled on the French

law school students enrolled in 1913–14 were bureaucrats (Osman Ergin, *Maarif Tarihi,* [History of Education] vol. III [Istanbul, 1941], p. 917).

10. Roderic H. Davison, *Reform in the Ottoman Empire 1856–1876* (Princeton, N.J., Princeton University Press, 1963), p. 159. This refers to the number of *vilayets* created in the period preceding 1876 to replace the old administrative unit, the *eyalet.*

11. This calculation was made by the authors and should only be taken as a very rough estimate. Information on the careers of graduates was obtained from Ali Çankaya, *Mülkiye Tarihi ve Mülkiyeliler* [History of the Civil Service School and its graduates], vol. II (Ankara Örnek Matbassï, 1954), pp. 5–17. It is interesting to speculate about the relatively slow progress of these "modern" administrators within the Empire's bureaucracy. Did they lack influential friends? Was their Westernized education resented by their immediate superiors? Szyliowicz has suggested that after 1877 Abdul Hamid began to take a personal interest in Faculty graduates, thus aiding their career progress. Szyliowicz, "Elite Recruitment in Turkey," 387–388. It should be noted that relatively few Political Science Faculty graduates achieved cabinet status. Of the 98 Istanbul Ministers in the 1918–1922 period only seven appear to have been from the Political Science Faculty. Dankwart A. Rustow kindly permitted a reanalysis of his data reported in "The Army and the Founding of the Turkish Republic."

Table 2-1: Highest Positions Achieved by 1860–1909 Political Science
Faculty Graduates

	%
Officials in the provincial government	
Provincial governor (*vali*)	5
Assistant governor (*mutasarrĭf*)	9
District governor (*kaymakam*)	28
Local government official (*nahiye müdürü*)	2
Officials in the central government	
Minister (*vekil*)	4
Diplomat, ambassador, etc.	2
Judge (*hakim*)	2
Other official (*memur*)	46
Number of graduates	792

Source: Andreas M. Kazamias, *Education and the Quest for Modernity in
Turkey* (Chicago, University of Chicago Press, 1966), p. 90.

system, with the *vali, mutasarrĭf,* and *kaymakam* appointed by and
responsible to the Sultan. They in turn were responsible for all activity
in the territory under their jurisdiction, including power over the
"police, political affairs, financial affairs, the carrying out of judicial
decisions, and the execution of imperial laws." [12]

Winning the loyalty of these trained administrators aided Atatürk
immensely. At the same time, Political Science Faculty graduates came
into their own with the founding of the Republic. The importance of
the Faculty to the administrative system of the Republic can be seen
through an examination of the careers of the twenty graduates of the
class of 1915. Seven graduates, over one-third of the class, went on
to become provincial governors (or acting governors). One graduate
served as the undersecretary in the Ministry of Finance, then went on
to become assistant general director of the Agricultural Bank. A number of the graduates went into education: one university professor, two
school directors, and a lycée teacher. Other responsible positions held
by graduates of the class of 1915 include: general secretary of the

12. Davison, *Reform in the Ottoman Empire*, p. 147.

22

Istanbul Stock Exchange, chairman of the Prime Ministry's general review board, chairman of the Ministry of Finance's review commission, and head inspector of the Ministry of Interior for the Istanbul and Izmir regions.

The twenty-seven members of the class of 1921 also made a distinguished administrative record. Within the Ministry of Interior, four graduates were appointed to jobs as provincial governors and one became the undersecretary of Security. Other members of this class became undersecretaries in the Ministries of Industry, Transportation, and Finance. Two graduates were appointed ambassadors, and four became university professors. Within the Ministry of Finance, one graduate was promoted to general director of Industry and another to head inspector. Another member of the class of 1921 became financial adviser to Etibank, a second became head reviewer for Sümerbank's purchasing department, and a third graduate became a member of the Prime Ministry's general review committee on State Economic Enterprises.

Not only did Political Science Faculty graduates serve in the highest administrative positions during the single-party period, but this Faculty also provided by far the largest group of administrator-politicians. As the administrators during the single-party period wielded disproportionate political power, so were Political Science Faculty graduates disproportionately represented among the administrators. Thus over the first ten Assemblies, 68 percent of the bureaucrats elected to the Grand National Assembly had attended the Political Science Faculty.[13] Since less than 7 percent of all university-educated bureaucrats had attended this Faculty, such prominence is especially impressive.

The Republic's reliance upon alumni of this school as high administrators makes the class histories read like a "Who's Who in Turkey." For example, of the 42 people who graduated in the class of 1908, five were elected to the Grand National Assembly, eight of the 47 graduates in 1910, and fully one-fourth (five out of twenty graduates) of the class of 1915 were elected to this important body.[14]

The higher one goes in the political hierarchy, the clearer it becomes that graduates of this school represented an elite among the elite. For example, one of the five Prime Ministers during the single-party period, Sükrü Saracoğlu, had attended the Faculty of Political Science. Four of

13. Frederick W. Frey, *The Turkish Political Elite* (Cambridge, Mass., M.I.T. Press, 1965), p. 116.
14. Çankaya, *Mülkiye Tarihi.*

the six Ministers of Finance had attended this Faculty along with two of the six Foreign Ministers, and two of the nine Ministers of Interior. Graduates of this Faculty served as ministers in almost all of the other ministries at one time or another.[15]

The disproportionate representation of Political Science Faculty graduates in the first seven Assemblies and Cabinets is another indicator of the status of this Faculty. Over the 1920–1946 period it produced only about 5 percent of Turkey's university graduates, but 21 percent of the Assembly members and 28 percent of the Cabinet ministers.[16]

Table 2-2: Percentage of Political Science Faculty Graduates in the First Seven Assemblies and Cabinets

Political Science Faculty graduates	I 1920– 1923	II 1923– 1927	III 1927– 1931	IV 1931– 1935	V 1935– 1939	VI 1939– 1943	VII 1943– 1946
Percentage of Assembly members	6	14	16	15	14	15	14
Percentage of Cabinet members	30	24	24	30	38	24	26

Source: Unpublished data furnished the authors by Frederick W. Frey.

The Authority Structure of the Single-Party Period

Atatürk's leadership in directing the transformation of Turkish society was not immediately accepted by all groups. This was particularly apparent in the First Grand National Assembly (1920–1923), where he lacked control over the nomination of the delegates. Strife and disagreements among the members were so bitter that two distinct factions developed, with the faction known as the Second Group opposing

15. These figures were taken from material furnished the authors by Frederick W. Frey.

16. These data were furnished the authors by Frederick W. Frey. The data must be considered approximate, since Frey was able to obtain data on all male Turkish university graduates only for the years 1938–1950. Information on the number of people with higher-level military education was lacking. Law, military, and medical school graduates were also disproportionately represented. See Frey, *Turkish Political Elite*, pp. 64, 280–281.

Atatürk and his supporters. This opposition was particularly threatening to the social aspects of Atatürk's reform program. Atatürk felt the need to consolidate his power and gain a firm control over the situation.

By 1923, when the elections to the Second General Assembly were held, Atatürk had made considerable progress toward establishing his control of the country. During the interim between the First and Second Assemblies, Atatürk had created a political party, later to be known as the Republican People's Party, to serve as an organizational base. He determined that this party had to give its approval to all Assembly nominations. Since Atatürk controlled the party, candidates who might be opposed to his policies were not approved, and as a result only three of the 118 members of the oppositionist Second Group were re-elected to the Second Assembly.

Atatürk was determined to carry out a broad, visionary program of social change even though conservative Turkish society would not easily accept such an ambitious program. Intent upon implementing his ideas as rapidly as possible, Atatürk turned to the existing centralized administrative structure, granting administrators whatever authority they might require.

A major aim of this campaign was to lessen the role which religious authority played in Ottoman society. Atatürk closed religious schools and imposed a new secular civil code giving the government responsibility in areas over which religious authorities had traditionally presided. He proscribed the giving of the Moslem call to prayer in Arabic and banned the wearing of the fez. In place of the fez, Atatürk required the wearing of the despised hat.

To obtain even minimal compliance with these directives, especially outside the urban centers, Atatürk had to rely upon his provincial military and administrative representatives. The structure of provincial government inherited from the Empire was admirably suited for this purpose. This included a network of provincial governors and district governors who were appointed by and directly responsible to the central offices of the Ministry of Interior. These men were part of a system in which control was highly centralized; much of their day-to-day activity was guided by directives from Ankara. On the other hand, the district and provincial governors were granted extensive authority over the local populace, and from this authority there was little hope of effective appeal. The bureaucracy could be coercive toward the mass without fear of political reprisals.

If the Kemalist reforms were to be implemented, the provincial bureaucrats would have to do the enforcing. This meant in turn that the peasants would come to associate the administrators with the policies of change which were being forced upon them. To the public, the Kemalists and the official elite were to become one. The enforcement of the unpopular "hat law" provided an example of this. In 1925 Atatürk decreed that it was illegal to wear anything on the head which lacked a brim or visor. This was very distasteful to Moslems, since it meant giving up their distinctive fez. But in villages which were in frequent contact with government officials, hats — not fezes — became the rule. In villages more distant from administrative supervision, the change was more gradual.[17]

At the same time, there was a recognized limit to the resources at the government's command. Much of village life changed slowly, if at all, during the period before 1946. The administration did not get involved in large rural development schemes; there were no efforts to mobilize villagers in support of particular programs. The aid of certain rural notables was enlisted; land redistribution and other reforms affecting these notables were not undertaken.[18] This decision to limit the financial and human investment may have been wise. Certain symbolic changes were forced upon the villagers; given the sociocultural environment of the 1920's and 1930's, perhaps that is all that could realistically have been accomplished.

Connected with the conscious decisions not to invest heavily in rural development were budgetary decisions which reflected on the power of various ministries. Riggs has noted that in politics characterized by substantial bureaucratic influence, "the officials responsible for police and territorial administration, ministries and departments of interior . . . being relatively well organized on a country-wide scale, do well in the competition for limited governmental funds."[19]

The Kemalists relied most heavily upon bureaucrats working in the Ministry of Interior. It is not surprising that this ministry was rated the most powerful during the Atatürk Era. In explaining the ranking of

17. Joseph S. Szyliowicz, *Political Change in Rural Turkey-Erdemli* (The Hague, Mouton, 1966), p. 49.

18. See the discussion of the influence of notables in the Republican People's Party in Michael P. Hyland, "Crisis at the Polls: Turkey's 1969 Elections," *Middle East Journal,* 24 (Winter 1970), 1–16.

19. Fred W. Riggs, *Administration in Developing Countries* (Boston, Houghton Mifflin, 1964), p. 305.

26

Interior above Foreign Affairs, Finance, and Defense, Frey noted that this was "in keeping with the profound domestic reforms of Kemalism." [20] The role of these officials was not confined to social reform. Bureaucrats in the Ministry of Interior were also intimately concerned with both economic and political matters.

Although Atatürk found little opposition to his goal of economic development, there was no indigenous structure upon which he could rely. His plans for development were less clear than his social ideas; the structure which evolved for achieving economic growth reflected an eclectic ideology. But the goal was clear: to change the economic environment through rapid industrialization.

The tasks seemed almost insurmountable. The Republic was debt-ridden; its industries were nonexistent or in a state of collapse, and much-needed capital was almost unobtainable. Since Atatürk was extremely jealous of the Republic's independence, he rejected the possibility of outside help. Turkey's own resources had to be exploited to the fullest extent possible. Toward this aim one very important tool was available to Atatürk — a centralized form of government. All major policy decisions could be made in Ankara, and then implemented in the provinces by officials directly responsible to the capital.[21] Thus, the provincial and district governors continued their traditional regulatory functions while at the same time taking charge of such activities as highway construction and credit institutions. New laws were passed requiring the provincial and district municipalities to provide certain services; the individual administrators were charged with seeing that the communities took appropriate action. Centralized control was reinforced while the functions of the bureaucracy were expanded.

With the founding of the first state economic enterprises, government officials became directly involved in efforts to industrialize. At first Atatürk had hoped to rely mainly on private enterprise for the development of the Republic's economy. Toward this goal, a rather liberal incentive plan called the "Law for the Encouragement of Industry" was formulated in 1927, while Atatürk pressed for the founding of the Business Bank (Iş Bankasî) financed by private capital. However, positions in the private sector continued to carry low prestige. Turkey

20. Frey, *Turkish Political Elite,* p. 234. Organizational ranking is treated in Chapter 5 of this book.

21. For a discussion of the importance of this centralized control to Atatürk's development plans see Malcolm D. Rivkin, *Area Development for National Growth* (New York, Praeger, 1965), pp. 51–53.

lacked entrepreneurial talent, and the incentives for private investment were not sufficient to overcome the risks and hardships of life in the Anatolian interior. By the early 1930's the Kemalists had become impatient with the meager progress shown by private enterprise. In an attempt to speed up the industrial development of the countryside, the first five-year plan was formed in 1934. The plan called for the creation of twenty new enterprises, and thus Turkish bureaucrats became involved in development as managers of industrial organizations. Almost all of these factories were located in the inhospitable interior, but a great effort was made to make these positions attractive to the managerial and supervisory personnel. This was not easy; even with liberal fringe benefits the state economic enterprises had trouble attracting and keeping capable personnel. Table 2-3 documents the creation of

Table 2-3: Founding Dates of Government Organizations[a]

Type of organization	1930 or before	1931–1940	1941–1950
State Economic Enterprise	2	11	8
Ministry	7	3	3

[a] The ministries which have existed since the early years of the Republic represent reorganizations, in varying degrees, of those ministries inherited from the Ottoman Empire. While there was a problem in the changing legal status of several of the organizations, the information as a whole is standardized according to the "founding date" (kuruluş tarihi) listed in T.C. Devlet Teşkilatı Rehberi [A guide to Turkish state organization], Ankara, Başbakanlık Devlet Matbaası, 1968.

state economic enterprises and the addition of ministries with new functions.[22]

22. In addition to the six ministries and nineteen state economic enterprises created after 1929, a number of new general directories were added as relatively autonomous units attached to the ministries. These figures do not begin to suggest the scope of the government's economic involvement, since several of the state economic enterprises were really investment banks. Thus, one of these state enterprises, Sümerbank, had major commitments in factories making textiles, paper, shoes, cement, building materials, pig iron, and steel. Kerwin notes that Sümerbank also participated in the operation of cotton gins, retail stores, insurance companies, and other banks and commercial enterprises (Robert W. Kerwin, "Etatism in Turkey, 1933–50," in Hugh Aitken, ed., The State and Economic Growth [New York, Social Science Research Council, 1959], p. 244).

28

Although etatism became a part of the official ideology of Atatürk's Republican People's Party and the state kept a tight rein on economic activities, the private sector was never abolished. The Law for Encouragement of Private Industry actually remained in effect until 1942. Protectionist import restrictions and the high prices set by state economic enterprises frequently guaranteed the private entrepreneur high profits. Moreover, private sector enterprise was staffed to a large extent by people trained at the state's expense. The strength of private enterprise, even during the height of the etatist period, is seen by the range of its operations. Private investment was involved in textiles, leather-tanning, building materials, food-processing, machine shops, chemicals, and pharmaceuticals.[23]

From a more general perspective, during most of the single-party period the strength of both state economic enterprises and private business increased. But neither state enterprises nor the private sector posed a serious threat to the power and prestige of bureaucrats in the central ministries (Interior, Finance, and Foreign Affairs). There was no general desire to enter either private business or state enterprises. Administrators in the central ministries enjoyed greater career possibilities and higher prestige.

Because of Atatürk's reliance upon this centralized administrative system, Turkish administrators were elevated to a level of responsibility they had never achieved, not even in the Ottoman Empire. While the traditional Ottoman administrator was largely concerned with maintaining order and collecting taxes, these were only part of the new administrative elite's concerns. For the first time, administrators became extensively involved in welfare and development activities. Moreover, bureaucrats were directly participating in the political process.

Bureaucratic Ascendance: Political Representation

Given the crucial role which the administrative elite was slated to play in the planned social and economic transformation of Turkish society, it was only natural that the Kemalists should court their support in various ways. Thus, the provincial party organization of the Republican People's Party was used to augment the power of the Ministry of Interior officials rather than to control and check it. The Minister

23. *Ibid.*, p. 246.

of the Interior became the party's secretary-general, and the governor of each province simultaneously served as the head of the provincial RPP organization. This link between party and government continued down the line, with the district governor heading the district party organization. Administrators were thereby provided with real political influence, since all political candidates had to obtain the approval of the provincial party organization.

An even stronger indication of the political power granted the official elite is the frequency with which members of the bureaucracy and military were elected to the Grand National Assembly. This was a significant honor, since these men "probably constituted a major portion of the wielders of disproportionate *real power,* not formal authority, in Turkish society." [24] Since after the First Assembly the Kemalists exercised a veto power over political nominations, the heavy representation of officials in all the Assemblies from the Second through the Seventh probably signified a conscious policy. Bureaucrats who had served in the Ministry of Interior were more likely to be elected and then reelected to political office than were officials without such experience. [25]

Over the entire single-party period, officials formed the largest occupational grouping in the National Assembly. [26] The higher one goes in the political system, the greater the Kemalist reliance on the official group. The peak of official power was obtained in the Fifth Assembly (1935–1939), when fully 61 percent of the cabinet members were former bureaucrats or officers. Only the free professions when grouped together (law, medicine, and engineering) approached the representation of either the administrators or military. A comparison of each occupation's share of assembly seats with its share of cabinet seats (Table 2-4 with Table 2-5) indicates that in the early assemblies the military and the members of the free professions were given a larger share of cabinet posts than their representation in the assembly would warrant, while bureaucrats were given less than their share. For example, the military had only 15 percent of the seats in the First Assembly but 29

24. Frey, *Turkish Political Elite,* p. 6.

25. *Ibid.,* pp. 117–118.

26. The extent of the officials' political power tends to be minimized by the classification scheme used in Table 2-4. During the early years of the Republic, lawyers, doctors, and engineers were much more likely to be government employees than to be in private practice. Thus, judges, government lawyers, public prosecutors, military and government doctors, were all put in the "free professions" category, even though they can be considered a part of the official establishment (*ibid.,* pp. 111–114).

Table 2-4: Percentage of Various Occupations in the First Seven Assemblies[a]

	I 1920– 1923	II 1923– 1927	III 1927– 1931	IV 1931– 1935	V 1935– 1939	VI 1939– 1943	VII 1943– 1946
Government	23	25	25	20	19	18	19
Military officials	15	20	19	16	18	16	14
	38	45	44	36	37	34	33
Professions	18	20	22	22	24	27	31
Business	13	8	10	12	11	13	9
Agriculture	6	6	6	10	8	6	7
Other	26	20	19	19	19	20	18
Unknown[b]	15	12	—	1	—	—	—
Total number of deputies	437	333	333	348	444	470	492

Source: Frederick W. Frey, *The Turkish Political Elite* (Cambridge, Mass., M.I.T. Press, 1965), p. 181.

[a] Frey's categories "trade and banking" have been combined to obtain the above "business" category, and his "education," "religion," "journalism," and "other" to obtain the above "other" category.

[b] The percentages have been calculated excluding the unknowns.

percent of the cabinet posts, while bureaucrats had 23 percent of the assembly seats and only 20 percent of the cabinet posts. Over the entire single-party period, business interests were discriminated against in appointments to cabinet level positions. During the first assemblies, members of the free professions may have been favored because of their official connections. As the free professions tended to lose their official status in the later assemblies, so too they seemed to lose the favor of the Kemalists. During this period the governmental administrator won increased recognition. Officials received preferential treatment in many other ways. Military men and bureaucrats had a higher mean election rate than did any of the other groups — save journalists.[27]

27. *Ibid.*, p. 84. Officials in the Ministry of Interior were especially favored by the Republican People's Party. Thus, 68 percent of the Political Science Faculty graduates elected to the Assembly had at one time served in the Ministry of the Interior. Graduates who had served in this ministry had a higher

Table 2-5: Percentage of Various Occupations in the Cabinets of the First Seven Assemblies[a]

	I 1920– 1923	II 1923– 1927	III 1927– 1931	IV 1931– 1935	V 1935– 1939	VI 1939– 1943	VII 1943– 1946
Government	20	16	19	30	35	23	26
Military officials	29	27	29	20	26	33	17
	49	43	48	50	61	56	43
Free professions	26	27	33	30	22	27	35
Business	3	3	5	5	4	3	4
Agriculture	6	8	—	5	4	7	9
Other	18	19	14	10	9	7	9
Number of cabinet members	35	36	21	20	23	30	23

Source: Frederick W. Frey, *The Turkish Political Elite*, p. 283.

[a] Frey's categories "trade and banking" have been combined to obtain the above "business" category, and his "education," "religion," "journalism," and "unknown" to obtain the above "other" category.

Atatürk and his successors needed the support of bureaucrats, especially those working in the Ministry of Interior, to put planned reforms into practice. Although the administrative elite might not have initially favored the radical reformation of Ottoman society, the wooing of this elite group was quite successful. The bureaucrats were major beneficiaries of Atatürk's policies, and they quickly learned to appreciate their political and economic power. In time, the official elite came to be identified with the Kemalist program in terms of both the policies advocated and the semi-authoritarian methods used to administer these policies.[28] Under the Kemalists, the official elite grew accustomed to

average election rate (2.95) than did those graduates who had not served in this ministry (2.36) — *ibid.*, p. 118.

28. This should, of course, not be interpreted to mean that all bureaucrats and military men were Kemalists. Both of these groups were prominently represented in all of the opposition movements which formed during the first seven assemblies. The only exception to this is the Independent Group which formed in the Sixth Assembly. No military men participated in this group, although 27 percent of its members were former bureaucrats (*ibid.*, pp. 301–347).

32

almost unchallenged power and to the social prestige which accompanied such power. The Republican People's Party was "bureaucratized"; bureaucratic and political power was largely fused "to create an apparatus to impose [the officials'] will on the public." [29]

To summarize, the authority structure of the Turkish Republic has been examined according to a framework emphasizing the sources of change in an organization's power structure. The main impact of external pressures upon the Ottoman Empire was to create conditions conducive to the rise of a charismatic leader — Mustafa Kemal Atatürk. External pressures continued to exert an indirect influence by providing models which Atatürk chose to imitate in an eclectic fashion.

The most profound influence upon the Republic's authority structure was an internal pressure — the personality of Atatürk. His personal goals for the Republic, social transformation and industrialization, became the goals of the Republic, and Atatürk's authoritarian biases (as well as historical precedent) shaped the governmental framework through which these goals were to be achieved. The groups which Atatürk brought into the Republic's authority structure were military men and bureaucrats. These two groups, particularly bureaucrats in the Ministry of Interior, were given responsibility for changing and controlling the conservative populace.

Atatürk did not anticipate conservative opposition to his goal of industrialization; thus, the organizational arrangements for economic development were more flexible than those used for social transformation. While the Ministry of Finance wielded a certain amount of overall control, and the Ministry of Interior was charged with collecting the heavy taxes to finance this effort, a good degree of decentralization existed. The state economic enterprises were created outside the central bureaucratic structure. Because of their unattractive locations and undistinguished public image, the state enterprises developed career lines quite separate from those of the central ministries. Similarly, the private sector remained quite independent; while it did not thrive, the existence of the private sector was never seriously threatened.

The power and authority structure of the Turkish Republic was created out of the shambles of the Ottoman Empire. Atatürk provided

29. Riggs, "Administration in Developing Countries," p. 265. Some very suggestive data on political and administrative roles in a "closed" polity are presented in Raymond F. Hopkins, "The Role of the M.P. in Tanzania," *American Political Science Review*, 64 (September 1970), 754–771.

the driving force in building this structure; military men and bureaucrats were given the opportunity to exercise this power. While other groups played important roles, particularly in economic development, they remained essentially outside the authority structure of the single-party period. This had major unanticipated consequences and eventually resulted in the erosion of the political framework constructed by Atatürk.

3

Industrialization and Social Transformation

The foundation of the Turkish Republic represented a major systemic change from the structure of the Ottoman Empire. In the decades following Atatürk's death, however, another significant change took place: power was redistributed as the political system was opened up for meaningful participation by the masses. As politics became competitive, the modernizing bureaucratic elite fell from power. Although external pressures from Western power cannot be disregarded, more important were internal pressures: unanticipated consequences of the successful pursuit of Atatürk's goals — economic development and elite modernization. Although the administrator's fall from power has been more relative than absolute, the official classes play a very different role in present-day Turkish society from that they played at the height of the single-party period.

The Kemalist bureaucratic elite governed the country by means of an exclusive, semiauthoritarian power structure. The policies pursued by this elite produced strong pressures toward structural change. In response to these pressures, the power structure was made more accessible and free elections were held. It seems to have been expected that democratization would proceed at a "rational" rate without disrupting the social and political structure. In fact, this opening up of the power structure produced major systemic change; the bureaucratic elite was displaced from its once preeminent position.

Consequences of Industrialization and Social Reform

By any standards of secularization and Westernization, the tutelage of Atatürk and his successor, Ismet Inönü, considerably advanced Turkey along the road of modernization. This economic and social progress led to a number of interrelated developments: the creation of different kinds of organizations performing similar functions, a changing demand for skills, and the rise of new social groups.

But these changes also added new elements of strain to the single-party authority structure. The establishment of new organizations led to increased competition among the various groups. On the one hand, the state economic enterprises — organizations founded by the Kemalists to speed up industrialization — aggravated the government's relationships with the private sector. On the other hand, the state enterprises became another center of influence largely independent of the central bureaucracy. Private businessmen became irritated with the economic power of the state enterprises, while the central ministries resented having to deal with competing organizations.

As Cyert and MacCrimmon have noted, "Rival organizations are those proposing essentially the same solution to possibly different problems, or different solutions to essentially the same problem." [1] The relationships between the state economic enterprises and the private sector were characterized by both kinds of rivalry. While the cement factory in the private sector is primarily concerned with the return on its investment, a similar factory in the state sector may have been brought into a region by a politician intent on creating jobs and cheap cement for his constituents. The two types of cement factories may be competing for workers, suppliers, and customers; their relationship is inevitably strained. Similarly, when a new bank is planned or when limited foreign exchange must be allocated, the two sectors have decidedly different viewpoints on how this should be done.

The state might have resolved this rivalry by driving the private companies out of business. A totally statist economic policy would have been quite appropriate to the Turks' historical experience. A Turk writing on the contemporary position of private business has noted:

> In Turkey, the notion of business is misunderstood. Often, the businessman is viewed as a speculator, if not a thief. Business in general, and retailing and wholesaling in particular, were for a long time downgraded and looked upon as occupations which no respectable Turk would enter . . . No great business heroes have emerged in Turkey, no entrepreneur has gained social recognition, and no business leader has ever held public office.[2]

1. Richard M. Cyert and Kenneth R. MacCrimmon, "Organizations," in Gardner Lindsey and Elliot Aronson, eds., *Handbook of Social Psychology,* (Reading, Mass., Addison-Wesley, 1968), I, 568–611.
2. Güvenç G. Alpander, "Entrepreneurs and Private Enterprises in Turkey," in Jerry R. Hopper and Richard I. Levin, eds., *The Turkish Administrator: A Cultural Survey* (Ankara, US AID Public Administration Division, 1967), p. 235.

36

But the Turkish economic ideology was more pragmatic and more tolerant, even when private business failed to measure up to Atatürk's original expectations. One economist has explained this tolerance in terms
of the liberal economic and political tradition in which the leaders of
the new Turkey were raised.[3] Moreover, even among the public at
large there is significant support for private business. When unlimited
freedom of speech was permitted in Turkey after World War II, heated
criticism of the state's etatist policy led to an extended debate over
public versus private enterprise during the 1950 campaign.

The state economic enterprises undermined the single-party authority structure from another direction. The central ministries, particularly
the Ministry of Finance and the Ministry of Interior, were the kingpins
of the single-party period. Through their various inspectorates these
ministries kept close control over other governmental organizations.
However, state economic enterprises were explicitly established to operate outside the direct control of the central ministries. While the
central ministries and the state economic enterprises have had a common interest in fighting an expansion of the private sector, the state
enterprises have also sought to preserve their own independence, frequently at the expense of the central ministries. Nowhere is this better
illustrated than with respect to the changing demand for skills.

As a country industrializes, technical changes occur which affect not
only the means of production and distribution, but also the structure of
organizations and the types of skills required. Skills that are in scarce
demand, and organizations which fulfill productive functions, tend to be
disproportionately rewarded by the industrialization process. Although
a country's overall level of resources tends to rise with progress toward
industrialization, it is extremely unlikely that the fruits of development
will be equitably distributed. Economic development may emphasize
one dimension of the stratification system — that of wealth — and
wealth tends to accrue to those actively involved in the productive sectors of the economy rather than to administrators in the public sector.

The Turkish bureaucratic structure greatly hampered the efforts of
the central ministries, particularly those of the Ministry of the Interior,
to keep their salary structures financially attractive. The salaries of
civil servants have long been tied to a rigid ranking system known as
the *barem*.[4] People enter the bureaucracy at a certain *barem* and salary

3. Osman Okyar, "The Concept of Etatism," in Hopper and Levin, eds., *The
Turkish Administrator,* p. 201.

4. The first *barem* system was adopted in Turkey in 1929 (Law No. 1452).
This was replaced later (in 1939) by another (Law No. 3646). The latter law

level, depending upon their education; they slowly advance every three years. Since the *barem* level attaches to the person, rather than to the position, a person's pay can be quite unrelated to the nature of his work. While ways have always been found to bypass some of the rigidity, and while civil servants under the *barem* system have enjoyed extensive social security benefits and job security, the salary scale proved unworkable in the more technical organizations. These organizations were unable to attract the professional and technical talents so necessary to the carrying out of their new functions. To surmount this crisis, these organizations began hiring personnel outside the *barem* system. Although such employees forfeited many of the social security benefits, they were able to start at a significantly higher level of pay (usually three *barem* levels higher).

The inflexibility of the personnel system hurt the more traditional ministries in several ways. Since the central ministries still enjoy a good deal of power and prestige, their ability to be competitive might well be assured by higher pay and better promotional opportunities. In the Turkish case, the central ministries' flexibility has been greatly limited by the excessively legalistic nature of the laws founding government organizations. Typically such laws have included the numbers, titles, grades, and salaries of the civil servants to be employed.[5] Because salary and position have been closely tied to seniority and education, rewarding and keeping ambitious young men has often proved difficult.

This rigidity was especially harmful to the administrator's financial position because of the inflationary conditions endemic to the Republic. If the cost-of-living index is set at 100 for 1939, by 1945 it had reached 345. During this same period, salaries of bureaucrats rose at a much slower rate, cutting their buying power by a factor of three.[6] Since the state economic enterprises operated under fewer salary restrictions and the private sector had almost none, these organizations

---

was subjected to many changes (over 100 amendments in 15 years). This system was copied from France, although the French no longer use it.

5. C. H. Dodd, "Administrative Reform in Turkey," *Public Administration,* 43 (Spring 1965), 78.

6. In 1939 the highest *barem* level received 600 TL while by 1945 the category of top civil servants received only 675 TL. See *Devlet Personel Rejimi Hakkında On Rapor* [A report on the personnel system] (Ankara, Başbakanlık Devlet Matbassı, 1962), p. 140.

were better situated to upgrade their salary structures to keep pace with inflation.

The inequities in salaries paid different types of governmental employees resulted in psychologically difficult situations. This has been particularly true for individuals working in the Ministry of Interior's provincial administration. Many employees in organizations legally under the district governor's control have been paid salaries several times those earned by the district governor himself. One district governor summarized his plight in this way:

> The Law of Provincial Administration gives the district governor the responsibility of inspecting and controlling the activities of all state economic enterprises under his jurisdiction. A simple secretary in such an enterprise earns more money than the district governor who is supposed to be supervising the organization. The directors and vice directors earn thousands more (than the district governor) and have private service cars, while the district governor is lucky to have a jeep which is already falling to pieces. It is obvious that such conditions will always lead to problems.[7]

High-level government officials suffered from other pressures which chipped away at the prestige of the central ministries. Traditionally, there has been a large gap between the salaries of higher officials and those paid lower officials. Thus, in 1939 the highest ranking bureaucrat earned thirteen times as much as did the lowest. Between 1939 and 1945 the salaries of lower-ranking officials were raised more rapidly than those of their superiors; by 1945, higher officials earned between nine and ten times as much as did lower officials.[8]

As economic development has proceeded, people with technical skills have become in scarce supply. The private sector, which in Turkey has been of lower prestige, could only hope to recruit the needed employees by offering high salaries. As the private sector began to attract former state employees, pressures were created to keep state employment competitive. Because the private sector was particularly interested in technical skills, the state was forced to upgrade the positions of its technical and professional personnel. Since most of these people were in the state enterprises and more technical organiza-

7. This quote is taken directly from the answers to the 1956 survey of district and provincial administrators. This survey is described in Appendix A.

8. *Devlet Personel Rejimi,* pp. 141–142.

tions, the upgrading took place at the expense of the person who had long been at the center of the Ottoman-Turkish government — the generalist administrator.

The 1923–1930 exchange of population between Turkey and Greece was initially seen as a step toward resolving a historical source of conflict between the two countries. But the removal of the Greeks and the wartime massacre of the Armenians also meant the disappearance of the entrepreneurial groups which had traditionally served the Ottoman Empire as merchants and artisans. The Turks themselves had to perform these economic tasks. While this was in keeping with Atatürk's desire for national development by and for the Turks, it also meant that native Turks, not second-class citizens, were acquiring money and status — the independent sources of prestige derived from a thriving private sector.

As Turkish entrepreneurs became more established, they grew increasingly resentful of interference by a government of bureaucrats. Throughout this period the People's Party made little attempt to bring private businessmen into the government. Without representation, private business feared the possibility of cutthroat competition between state and private factories. State enterprises with their far superior financial and political resources would be the inevitable victors.[9] Although there was never a direct attempt to eliminate the private sector, during World War II stringent controls were placed on the textile and cement industries. The private sector was a testimony to progress made toward Atatürk's goal of indigenous industrialization, but private businessmen remained outside the authority structure created to achieve this goal.

Similar things can be said, although to a lesser degree, about the free professions. During the early years of the Republic there were relatively few professionals, and almost all of them were government employees. Over the decades the numbers of lawyers, doctors, and engineers grew; they increasingly turned to private practice. Although these professionals were often found in the ruling circle during the single-party period, they were relatively few in number and always subordinate to the official group. Members of the free professions in alliance with private businessmen, two groups strengthened by the industrialization

9. For a full discussion of the role of private industry in Turkey see Robert W. Kerwin, "Private Enterprise in Turkish Industrial Development," *Middle East Journal,* 5 (Winter 1951), 21–38.

process, became the counter-elite which presided over the downfall of the bureaucrats.

Possibilities for Change

All these developments — organizational competition, the changing demand for skills, and the creation of new social groups — placed tremendous pressures upon the authority structure erected by Atatürk. This structure was predicated upon the loose but nevertheless authoritarian single-party rule by the official classes. In the past these classes had been more or less conceded their right to rule. However, the officials' prestige had been heavily eroded over the period of single-party rule; the hardship conditions fostered by the Second World War were particularly unpopular. Dissatisfaction and unrest were rife; the pressures for change were great.

In these circumstances the authority structure might well have become more authoritarian or more repressive. Private industry might have been chosen as a scapegoat for the financial woes of the country. An abrupt turn to nationalization would not have been out of character; the government had operated the textile mills quite profitably during the war. Powerful figures within the government advocated a hard line toward the strong political opposition which had developed both inside and outside of the People's Party.

On the other hand, there was also precedent for opening up the political system when it came under heavy pressure for change. Atatürk had tried twice — in 1924 and in 1930 — to move toward a more democratic system. Although both times the democratic experiments had been prematurely terminated, this alternative was available to President Ismet Inönü, who had come to power at Atatürk's death in 1938.

In 1946 Inönü chose to move toward a more democratic system by allowing the formation of the Democratic Party from dissidents within the RPP. Inönü has frequently been depicted as Atatürk's unimaginative lieutenant who took over the leadership of the Turkish Republic by default. This picture is incorrect. Although the most revolutionary changes did take place under Atatürk's firm direction, Inönü guided his countrymen into the unknowns of competitive party politics. Even Atatürk himself might have been unable to accomplish this transition so smoothly. There was strong opposition from within the RPP, and from

1946 on Inönü had to deal with the many members of the People's Party who wanted to rig elections in their favor.

Inönü, and undoubtedly most members of the bureaucratic elite, had not expected to be voted out of power when the political system opened up to party competition. The idea of democracy existed simultaneously with the elite's feeling that the Republican People's Party and a powerful administration provided the best way to develop the country. It was assumed that the country would recognize the long years of service rendered by the Republican People's Party. While opposition parties were expected to receive some support, certainly Inönü and the RPP would remain at the helm. But after twenty-seven years, the Turks were ready for a change. All those with grievances against the People's Party delighted in the opportunity to register their complaints. As one observer has noted, "after so long a period, even a party of angels would probably have been swept out of office." [10]

Inönü took what appeared to be a relatively small step, legitimizing political opposition. Four years later, in 1950, his party went down to defeat by the Democratic Party, which received 54 percent of the vote. Just as Atatürk's goals of industrialization and modernization had unexpected repercussions for the Republic's authority structure, Inönü's step toward democratization had profound implications. The official elite which had been elevated to power by Atatürk was forced to undergo major political, social, and economic adjustments; political competition had major effects upon the Kemalist authority structure.

Economic Growth and Political Competition

Under the leadership of Adnan Menderes, the Democratic Party set out to change the country. The austere etatism of the Republican People's Party was abandoned; economic development at both the national and local level was emphasized. The clearest statement of the Democratic Party's intent was contained in the program submitted to the Grand National Assembly on May 29, 1950:

> The aim and essence of our economic policies is to reduce to the minimum the interference of the State and to restrict the state sector in the economic field, and, by inspiring confidence, to en-

10. Bernard Lewis, *The Emergence of Modern Turkey* (London, Oxford University Press, 1961), p. 311.

courage the development of private enterprise to the utmost. Only those enterprises which due to their nature and operation cannot in any way be undertaken by private enterprise will be left for the state to operate. Such activities will consist only of those that have the character of a public utility or which can be considered basic industries. We intend to transfer all other existing state enterprises to private enterprise. We have decided to abolish those enterprises which seem unnecessary and to link to more certain principles the administration and control of the state economic enterprises and organizations in order to lighten their burden on the economy of the country.[11]

Although the Democrats made few significant structural changes favoring private business,[12] a very important psychological change took place. Private business correctly believed that its activities had taken on a new legitimacy in the eyes of the government. Furthermore, the "unjust" actions of etatist-minded bureaucrats could now be appealed under more favorable circumstances.

These subtle changes did affect the expansion of the private sector. Thus, the share of private to total manufacturing production increased from 58 percent in 1950 to 65 percent in 1954. Not only did existing private businessmen expand their operations, but many new industries were founded during this period. The number of new joint stock and limited companies increased from only three in 1950 to 56 in 1954, while their total capital grew from TL 1.4 million to TL 167.2 million.[13] Data from six cities on the pre-1960 period indicate that approximately 60 percent of their larger private industries were founded between 1946 and 1960, 18 percent between 1940 and 1945, 16 percent between 1923 and 1939, and 2 percent before 1923.[14]

11. Kerwin, "Private Enterprise," p. 25.
12. The Democrats did, however, follow the World Bank Mission's recommendation to found an Industrial Development Bank.
13. Alec P. Alexander, "Turkey," in A. Pepelasis, L. Mears, and I. Adelman, eds., *Economic Development: Analysis and Case Studies* (New York, Harper, 1961), p. 493. Alexander obtained his data from the International Cooperation Administration (now the Agency for International Development) and the Ministry of Economy and Commerce, both of which are located in Ankara.
14. These data are taken from a survey reported in Arif Payaslïoğlu, *Türkiyede Özel Sanayi Alanïndaki Müteşebbisler ve Teşebbüsler* [Enterprises and entrepreneurs in the field of Turkish private industry] (Ankara Political Science Faculty–Financial Institute, 1961), p. 36. Only industries employing fifty or

Although private enterprise prospered under a multiparty system, and although the Democrats pledged themselves to the private sector, etatism was not dead. In fact, between 1951 and 1960 eleven new state economic enterprises were founded — more than were started in any previous ten-year period. Although there was originally an attempt to sell one or two state factories, plans to transfer nonbasic state economic enterprises to the private sector were soon abandoned. Although public investment as a percentage of total investment fell (from 43 percent in 1950 to 38 percent in 1952) during the early years of Menderes' rule, this trend was reversed in the following years. The Democratic Party found building factories in the provinces an effective way of reinforcing its support in rural areas. As Menderes committed more and more funds to development projects, public utilities, and transportation, public investment as a percentage of total investment rose to a high of 62 percent in 1959.[15] Menderes took pride in achieving this extremely high rate of state investment without any centralized planning or coordination, but these policies led to a disastrously high rate of inflation.

This inflation helped fuel dissatisfaction with the Democratic regime. The government handled growing opposition by becoming increasingly repressive. The late 1950's were marked by increased political conflict which set the scene for the military coup of 1960. As Ülman and Tachau have noted, in Turkey the military, civil service, and intelligentsia are closely related. These groups "were adversely affected by the economic policies pursued after 1950. [The coup] was an attempt to stem the tide of rising power of newly emerging socio-economic groups." [16]

Between 1960 and 1965 Turkey experienced military rule and coali-

---

more people and located in Turkey's six largest cities were included here. More recently, Poroy has noted the phenomenal increase in industrial establishments in Istanbul and seven other cities between 1960 and 1964. In Istanbul, the number of industrial establishments with 10 or more workers grew from 3,579 in 1960 to 6,364 in 1964. Ibrahim Poroy, "Economic Development Planning in Turkey: The First Five Years, 1962–1967," paper presented at the Second Annual Meeting of the Middle East Studies Association, Austin, Texas, November 1968, p. 20.

15. Gultan Kazgan, "Structural Changes in Turkish National Income: 1950–1960," in Taufiq M. Khan, *Middle Eastern Studies in Income and Wealth* (New Haven, International Association for Research in Income and Wealth, 1965), p. 154.

16. A. Haluk Ülman and Frank Tachau, "Turkish Politics: the Attempt to Reconcile Rapid Modernization with Democracy," *Middle East Journal,* 19 (Spring 1965), 162.

44

tion government dominated by Inönü's Republican People's Party. Despite the uncertain political situation, economic opportunities in the private sector grew substantially during this period.[17] In 1965 the Justice Party, successor to the banned Democratic Party, attained power. A coalition government, dominated but not controlled by the Justice Party, was formed in February 1965 to act as a caretaker regime until the general elections.[18] In the election of October 1965 the Justice Party under the leadership of Süleyman Demirel obtained an absolute majority of 240 out of the 450 possible seats in Parliament. Between 1965 and 1969 the Justice Party governed in a relatively moderate fashion, keeping control over the most militant elements within the party.[19] Although the Justice Party retained a commitment to private enterprise, the State Planning Organization established by the military regime was continued, though with less influence. In the 1965–1969 period more temperate economic and political policies were followed, but inflation remained a problem. In the 1969 elections the Justice Party received 47 percent of the popular vote and, aided by a change in the electoral laws, 256 seats in the National Assembly.[20]

Political competition had several untoward consequences for the position of the administrative elite, particularly the once eminent bureaucrats in the Ministry of Interior. Peasants could use their votes and the threat of political repercussions to curtail to some degree the power of the provincial authorities. Moreover, the necessity of choosing candidates with popular appeal forced all parties (including the Republi-

17. Poroy, "Economic Development Planning."

18. The Justice Party received 10 of 22 ministerial portfolios in the coalition government. Four portfolios apiece went to the New Turkey, Republican Peasants', and National parties.

19. This control broke down significantly in February 1970 when 41 right-wing Justice Party members voted against the government's budget proposals. Dissidents subsequently formed a new party, taking the name of the Democratic Party. In March 1971 the military, upset by urban disorder and economic difficulties, intervened and forced the resignation of the Demirel government. A new, neutral cabinet supported by a three-party coalition was formed.

20. As Tachau has noted: "In 1965, a 'national remainder' system was in effect, which worked in favor of smaller parties by allowing them to pool certain votes gained in various provinces and assigning some seats on the basis of this national pool. The 1969 election law, on the other hand, dropped this provision, thus enhancing the fortunes of the larger parties at the expense of the minor parties" (Frank Tachau, with the assistance of Mary Jo Good, "The Anatomy of Political and Social Change: Turkish Parties and Parliaments, 1960–1970," *Comparative Politics,* forthcoming).

can People's Party) to recognize that bureaucrats did not make attractive candidates. The direct political power which bureaucrats had long enjoyed dwindled rapidly.

Peasants and the Vote

The Democrats owed their overwhelming victory to the Turkish peasants. For the first time in Turkish history a political power was directly obligated to the masses. By and large, the peasantry has remained loyal to the Democratic Party and its successor, the Justice Party, while these parties have been sensitive to the desires and grievances of the peasants.

This change in emphasis from control over the people to responsiveness to the people has drastically affected Turkish administrative practices. A case study of one Turkish district, Erdemli, has described this process in some detail. Until the multiparty period, the provincial and district governors ruled supreme over the rural areas. The villagers vividly remembered the days when it was common practice for a government official to make the village headman stand at attention during their business encounters. This process changed in the 1950's as the Democrats built their organization throughout the rural areas. It occasionally happened, and was generally feared, that a district governor who antagonized the local politicians would risk transfer to a less desirable area.[21]

The extent of these political pressures upon district governors is suggested in a 1956 survey of district administrators.[22] The officials were asked: "Do you come across political interference which can be considered harmful to the conduct of public affairs?" The distribution of answers was as follows: 14 percent replied "often," 38 percent "sometimes," and 40 percent said "seldom"; only 8 percent left the answer blank. In the same survey the district governors were asked about the people who acted as intermediaries in bringing citizens' requests to them. Almost two-thirds of the district governors (65 percent) listed "members of political parties" as intermediaries.[23]

21. Joseph Szyliowicz, *Political Change in Rural Turkey–Erdemli* (The Hague, Mouton, 1966), pp. 132–134.
22. This survey is described in Appendix A.
23. The introduction of district-level administration appears linked to increased local conflict; with size of the town held constant, 49 percent of those living in towns which were district administrative centers and only 28 percent

46

More recent data suggest that, in a competitive system, local party strength and public interaction with the administration are associated. A 1965 comparison of governors in districts where the Justice Party had a clear electoral majority with their counterparts in more competitive districts showed some differences between the two groups of administrators. The governors tended to report more interaction with their clients when the Justice Party had an electoral majority. Dividing the districts with Justice Party majorities into those where the vote was relatively concentrated and those where it was more dispersed did not change these findings. A Justice Party majority meant that more public demands were made upon the bureaucrats.

A typical response to a 1956 question about the advantages or disadvantages of employing local personnel in district administrative posts shows the bureaucrat's negative reaction to such pressure:

> We have thirty-three native born officials. It is harmful, because there is no such thing left as secrecy. Especially in this age of democracy, those who are relatives of political heads oppose everything, and push things so far as to be rude and discourteous.

Another district governor complained that "there is little possibility to get ahead now without political pull." [24] Such complaints were not absent in 1965. One district governor working in central Anatolia noted the difficulties caused by employees who are members of the local political establishment and have contacts in the government.

As we have seen, the district governor is an administrator with extensive responsibilities not only for local development but also for understanding and working toward the development goals of the Turkish nation. These two responsibilities may conflict. Villagers in a depressed district may be apathetic or opposed to the development strate-

---

of those living in towns which were not district centers reported some or much local conflict. Since district administration brings certain new services and presents the possibilities for others, such conflict is not surprising. It does not, however, make the district governor's job any easier. These data were taken from an analysis of the 1963 Turkish population survey. This study is described in J. Mayone Stycos, "The Potential Role of Turkish Village Opinion Leaders in a Program of Family Planning," *Public Opinion Quarterly*, 29 (Spring 1965), 120–130.

24. These quotes are taken directly from the answers to the 1956 survey of district and provincial administrators.

gies of the national government, particularly if additional work or higher taxes are involved. During the single-party period the district governor overcame local opposition in the traditional manner. According to the Village Law, villagers were subject to a headtax and obligated to provide a certain amount of labor (*imece*) each year. Zealous officials could arbitrarily use these measures to implement a proposed project. In fact, much of the economic development which occurred during the single-party period was achieved by authoritarian means. Secular schools, frequently unwanted or even opposed by villagers, were built by the use of compulsory labor; road construction was accomplished in part with forced labor via the medium of a road "tax"; and certain farm produce was collected forcibly. The district governor, as an agent of the central government, was responsible for implementing these national development policies.

The advent of multiparty politics changed conditions substantially. The district governor can play an important innovating role in the rural environment, but his powers of coercion have been severely limited. By virtue of his education and training the district governor can sometimes aid and prompt the populace into carrying out development projects for the good of the community, but he has been under real pressure to convince the villagers that his projects are worthwhile. The district governors have had to deal with villagers and local politicians interested in the distribution of the fruits of development. Villagers desire roads and improved sources of drinking water, credit facilities, and crop subsidies. Above all, they do not want to be heavily taxed or to have to contribute great labor in order to obtain these goals. The district governors have to help increase resources without alienating the citizenry.

From a more general viewpoint, debureaucratization — the tendency to relax hierarchical authority — results from an administrator's dependence upon his subordinates or clients. This dependence causes administrators to refrain from using authoritarian measures, increasing reliance on more personal, nonbureaucratic means of accomplishing tasks.[25] The ruralizing election of 1950 has caused debureaucratization of the district governor's job, but the administrator's relations with both subordinates and clients have been strained. The friction resulting from the bureaucrat's increased dependence upon the citizens was only

25. Peter M. Blau and W. Richard Scott, *Formal Organizations* (San Francisco, Chandler, 1962), p. 232.

one result of the ruralizing election. The political changes within Turkey have raised more general issues of development versus distribution.

The problems of economic change in modernizing areas have been conceptualized in terms of whether a country must choose between more rapid economic development and more equitable distribution of the fruits of such development.[26] In a modernizing democratic polity, demands are likely to be so strong as to compel efforts at a more equitable distribution, regardless of the effects upon long-term economic growth. From another point of view, however, the distribution which tends to accompany democratic politics is not necessarily detrimental to economic development. Thus, in the Turkish case, where peasants' "distribution" demands revolve around roads, adequate water supplies, land, credit facilities, and equipment, agricultural productivity stands to benefit from the satisfaction of these demands.

Development and distribution are not necessarily contradictory, but the concepts refer to important issues. In his efforts to handle such problems, the district governor is constantly on the firing line. The administrator most at home with these pressures may be very different from the type of person who performed well under a more authoritarian administrative structure. The new skills required by the district governors are interpersonal; they must be able to relate successfully to people of widely varying backgrounds. Such skills may have been less vital under the single-party regime.

Bureaucrats Face the Electorate

During the single-party period bureaucrats were heavily represented in the uppermost ranks of political power. Popularity or public appeal was not a relevant criterion for receiving a nomination. Atatürk relied heavily upon the bureaucrats in his drive for social reform and industrialization. Moreover, his party, the Republican People's Party, was

26. See, for example, Joseph La Palombara, "Distribution and Development," and Max F. Millikan, "Equity versus Productivity in Economic Development," in Myron Weiner, ed., *Modernization* (New York, Basic Books, 1966), pp. 218–232 and 307–320, as well as Joseph La Palombara, "An Overview of Bureaucracy and Political Development," in J. La Palombara, ed., *Bureaucracy and Political Development* (Princeton, N.J., Princeton University Press, 1963), pp. 3–33.

essentially dominated by the official classes (both bureaucrats and military men). The People's Party continued to recruit members of this traditional elite to political office long after Turkey's expanding economy had produced new groups desiring representation. The party which proved to be such a successful competitor to the RPP, the Democratic Party (DP), drew its support from the new elite groups (professionals and businessmen), originally almost to the exclusion of the bureaucrats and military men. Since the advent of the multiparty system, all parties have come to realize that Turkish voters are not particularly likely to vote for individuals with a bureaucratic background.

The bureaucrats' loss of political power in Republican Turkey is noticeable at all levels. The decline of the representation of the official class in the Grand National Assembly is particularly striking. The waning influence of the Turkish administrative elite and of the official class in general can be traced by comparing Table 3-1 with Table 2-4. Even in Assembly VII, the last of the single-party period, bureaucrats retained almost one-fifth of the seats. Although bureaucrats have not been excluded from political office during the multiparty period, they have been consistently outranked by all other occupational groups save the military. The free professions, private business, and agriculture have been the groups most strongly represented during the multiparty period.[27]

Not only did bureaucratic representation decline at the uppermost level of Turkish political life, but bureaucrats have also lost ground at the lower levels. A 1964 survey of Turkish mayorality candidates seeking office in provincial centers and larger towns reported that the younger the candidate, the less likely he was to have listed public service (civil service, military, or education) as his occupation. Table 3-2 demonstrates the extent to which professional people and those who work in commerce and industry have replaced the civil servant in political office. Furthermore, while three-fourths of those candidates over 40 had at one time worked in governmental service, less than half (48

27. Although it is true that bureaucrats retained a respectable degree of representation at the highest levels of political power, this, too, has recently diminished. In the last assembly of the single-party period, 26 percent of the cabinet members were former bureaucrats. In the Ninth and Tenth Assemblies this had dropped to 17 and 18 percent respectively. In the Thirteenth Assembly (1965–1969) only two (out of 23) of the Cabinet members had a bureaucratic background. Data on the Ninth and Tenth Assemblies were furnished the authors by Frederick W. Frey.

50

Table 3-1: Percentage of Various Occupations in Parliament (1943–1969)[a]

	VII 1943– 1946	VIII 1946– 1950	IX 1950– 1954	X 1954– 1957	XII 1961– 1965	XIII 1965– 1969	XIV 1969–
Government	19	14	10	9	9	7	9
Military officials	14	11	6	4	7	9	5
	33	25	16	13	16	16	14
Professions	31	35	45	44	46	45	44
Business	9	15	19	19	20	16	18
Agriculture	7	9	10	10	7	7	6
Other	19	15	11	14	11	16	18
Total number of deputies	492	499	494	537	449	450	449

Source: Frederick W. Frey, *The Turkish Political Elite*, p. 181, covering 1943 through 1957. Material on Assemblies XII through XIV was obtained from Frank Tachau with the assistance of Mary Jo Good, "The Anatomy of Political and Social Change: Turkish Parties and Parliaments, 1960–1970," *Comparative Politics* (forthcoming). There are slight differences here with data reported by C. H. Dodd, *Politics and Government in Turkey* (Berkeley: University of California Press, 1969, p. 206). We have combined their trade and banking categories to obtain the above "business" category, and their education, religion, journalism, and other to obtain the above "other" category. Data on Assembly XI were not available.

[a] Differences between pre-1950 and post-1950 Assemblies in the representation of officials were significant at the .05 level by a double Mood test adjusted for autocorrelation. One-tailed *t* tests were used in this book.

percent) of the younger group had ever worked for the government.[28] At a slightly lower level of political prominence, the representation of civil servants has slipped even more sharply. One study of provincial executive committee members noted that only 6 percent of the 318 persons questioned worked in public service, 29 percent were profes-

28. Frank Tachau, "Local Politicians in Turkey," in *Regional Planning, Local Government and Community Development in Turkey* (Ankara, Sevinç Matbaasï, 1966), p. 132.

Table 3-2: Occupations of Turkish Mayorality Candidates (1964)

	Age of candidate[a]	
Occupation	Over 40 (%)	31–40 (%)
Public service	32	21
Free professions	18	44
Commerce and industry	32	31
Farming	5	0
Other and unknown	13	4
Number of respondents	103	48

Source: Frank Tachau, "Local Politicians in Turkey," from *Regional Planning, Local Government and Community Development in Turkey* (Ankara: Sevinç Matbaasi, 1966), p. 132.

[a] Differences were significant at the .05 level by a chi-square test. This test was applied throughout this book to contingency tables involving independent observations.

sionals, 48 percent worked in industry or commerce, 6 percent were artisans, and 7 percent were farmers.[29]

The inability of bureaucrats to attract widespread popular support affected even the Republican People's Party's attitude toward the administrative elite. Under the pressures of political competition the RPP was forced to reverse its former policy and to welcome the new elite groups into its ranks. This process has once again demonstrated the relative pragmatism of Turkish political parties. No ideology was developed which would force one party (presumably the RPP) to continue to be a spokesman for the official classes, while the other party excluded these classes from its ranks. In fact, by the second election of the multiparty period, a higher percentage of the Democratic Party's deputies were former bureaucrats than were those from the Republican People's Party (9 percent versus 6 percent). This trend has continued in more recent elections, with officials at least as likely to be represented in the Justice Party as in the People's Party.[30]

29. Frank Tachau, "Provincial Politics," paper presented at a conference on Democracy and Social Growth in Turkey, New York University, May 1965.
30. Tachau, "The Anatomy of Political and Social Change."

52

Accompanying these changes in the occupational backgrounds of individuals elected to Parliament were changes in such other social background indicators as place of birth. In the 1940's the urban, developed Marmara region was heavily overrepresented, with 33 percent of the deputies born in this region, but after the ruralizing election of 1950 this percentage dropped to 21 percent. Changes were relatively slight during the 1960's, but by 1969 the distribution of deputies' birthplaces was reasonably close to that of the general population.[31] A related indicator of localism, the proportion of deputies born in the province which they represent, showed major increases with the introduction of the multiparty system in 1946 and the Democratic victory in 1950, along with a gradual increase to a high of 73 percent in 1969.[32]

Data on previous parliamentary experience clearly show the extent to which there was a break in recruitment after the ruralizing election of 1950 and the military coup of 1961. In most Turkish assemblies, about 50 percent of the members had had previous parliamentary experience. But only 19 percent of the Ninth Assembly (1950–1954) and only 16 percent of the Twelfth Assembly (1961–1965) had such experience. The continuity of the membership changed significantly at these two points in time. At the top leadership level, Tachau has noted that "the Menderes regime was led essentially by members of former close allies of the urban elite." [33] But the Democratic Party leadership was not permitted by the military to take part in the politicking which led to the formation of the Justice Party.[34] Justice Party leadership came from Democratic Party members of the lower echelons who had closer ties with the rural masses. The "ruralizing" process was thus carried a step farther.

31. *Ibid.*
32. *Ibid.*
33. *Ibid.*
34. The Democratic Party leadership was either in prison or forbidden to engage in politics.

4

Organizational Competition

A change in its environment can have a major impact upon any organization. Such change may cause organizational development or decline, independent of any action taken by the organization itself. Rourke has noted more generally that "administrative power may thus be extremely volatile, shifting . . . with changing tides of public opinion." [1] Administrative agencies are dependent upon public support for their activities. As the public becomes concerned with a particular activity, a previously neglected organization may find itself blessed with plentiful funds and powerful backers.

Organizations compete with each other in an environment in which the demand for a given set of services is continually shifting. New organizations may be formed, or older organizations may expand, altering the supply of agencies which can fill a particular social need. But internal pressures are also important. An organization may decline or develop because of changes in its own operations while the supply and demand factors remain unchanged.

Although organizational adaptiveness may be linked to organizational age, the relationships are unclear. One author has suggested that the longer an organization has existed, the more likely it is to continue to exist.[2] On the other hand, older organizations which have existed in a static environment may be no more adaptable to environmental change than their younger counterparts.[3] Just as environmental change may cause the decline of an organization which fails to take certain measures, so may it promote the development of an organization. Certain organizations may compete more effectively in a changed environment.

In the Turkish case we have singled out two different types of environmental pressure important in determining the fate of many public organizations. These pressures were produced by the drive to industrialize the country and the shift to a competitive political system.

1. Francis E. Rourke, *Bureaucracy, Politics, and Public Policy* (Boston, Little, Brown, 1969), p. 14.

2. Samuel P. Huntington, *Political Order in Changing Societies* (New Haven, Yale University Press, 1968), p. 13.

3. *Ibid.*, p. 13.

54

The following sections will focus upon how various organizations have been affected by these pressures, upon the phenomenon of organizational competition, and upon the response of organizations to hostile environments.

Environmental Pressures and Organizational Susceptibility

As was suggested earlier, an organization may be better off, worse off, or simply not affected by a certain type of pressure operating in its environment. How the organization is affected depends mainly upon the nature of the pressure, but another factor, the degree of organizational autonomy, may also be important.

Industrialization, with its disproportionate rewards for those individuals possessing technical skills and those organizations performing productive functions, had a direct impact upon Turkey's central ministries. Chapter 3 described how the salaries of bureaucrats working in the Ministries of Interior, Finance, and Foreign Affairs fell behind salaries available in the newer ministries, in the state economic enterprises, and especially in the private sector. The prestige of central ministries has undoubtedly suffered from these developments.

However, industrialization has also served to enhance the power of the central ministries — especially the Ministry of Finance. Several of the state economic enterprises — the powerful Central Bank, the Government Retirement Fund, and the National Lottery — were made the direct responsibility of the Ministry of Finance. This ministry has not only continued to carry out its basic function of financial administration, but has also been responsible for setting the guidelines of general investment policy, for regulating state economic enterprises and foreign economic relations, and for overseeing the whole state personnel structure. Only with the establishment in 1960 of the State Planning Office and the State Personnel Office was the Ministry of Finance relieved of some of its burgeoning responsibilities.

Political developments, specifically the advent of competitive party politics, have had a generally negative impact on the power and prestige of all the central ministries, although the impact on specific ministries has varied. Turkish bureaucrats simply could not be as influential in a multiparty democracy as they were in a single-party, semi-authoritarian polity. The Ministry of Interior, having been excessively powerful in the one-party period, has suffered the most in a democratic setting.

On the other hand, democratic politics may have enhanced the position of the Ministry of Foreign Affairs. Since the first free election in 1950, with the exception of the relatively short period of military rule, Turkey has tried with some success to alter her international image to that of a progressive democratic country. Her diplomats have probably reaped benefits from the multiparty period which have had little relevance for most other bureaucrats. The diplomat has shared the international prestige won by democratic politicians, while other administrators have found their personal power and prestige curtailed by political pressures.

The Ministry of Foreign Affairs' relative insulation from the pressures of multiparty politics points up another basis for comparison: public organizations differ in their degree of dependence upon other groups in the environment. Some American data suggest that a high degree of autonomy may be a characteristic of foreign offices, whose constituencies tend to be outside rather than within their countries.[4]

The Ministry of Interior, the organization least insulated from the pressures of competitive politics, is still powerful, serving as it does a large number of people and exerting its influence throughout the country. Officials in the Ministry of Interior have wide-ranging opportunities to benefit the public under their jurisdiction. These bureaucrats make vital decisions about how most of the rural development funds will be spent, but political factors are important at every step in the decision-making process. In a competitive system, their responsibilities seem to bring the district and provincial administrators more headaches than benefits; for every request that is granted, several others must be denied.

While organizations vary in their insulation from internal political pressures, so do different roles within the same organization vary in this respect. Thus, the district governors occupy boundary roles — significantly more exposed to political pressures than their friends working in the central offices of the Ministry of Interior. Guetzkow has noted that individuals who operate at the boundaries of organizations are subject to considerable strain.[5] This distinctly understates the problems facing the Turkish district governors.

4. Rourke, *Bureaucracy*, p. 57.
5. Harold Guetzkow, "Relations Among Organizations," in Raymond V. Bowers, ed., *Studies on Behavior in Organizations* (Athens, Ga., University of Georgia Press, 1966), p. 20.

56

Organizational Competition

Much of modern Turkish politics seems to revolve around the relative standing of different organizations; as in other modern societies, organizational stratification is a primary focus of elite political activity.[6] Interorganizational conflict may affect the political environment, while political and economic developments can change the social setting in which public and private organizations compete. A familiarity with organizational competition aids in understanding both the political environment and the changes in the relative statuses of the organizations which employ Political Science Faculty graduates.

With modernization and the growing role played by organizations of various types, competition for the control of resources seems to be intensified. Such competition, as well as the increased amount of information available in modern societies, leads to an increase in the importance of the rankings of organizations relative to each other.[7] At the same time, when conditions are changing rapidly, there is likely to be widespread disagreement about the bases for social ranking. "Rapid structural change in societies introduced uncertainty and dissensus on the principles of ranking of organizations." [8] The political and economic changes within Turkey in the 1950's undoubtedly contributed to the uncertainties in the system of social stratification. In the view of many people, economic organizations of the public and private sector gained status at the expense of the traditional ministries.

Stinchcombe also notes that "innovating leaders who found new organizations . . . have weak commitment to traditional stratification norms," and that "the norms by which organizations obtain their relative ranks tend to be unclear during the early stages of modern-

6. Arthur L. Stinchcombe, "Social Stratification and Organizations," in James G. March, ed., *Handbook of Organizations* (Chicago, Rand McNally, 1965), p. 144. The importance of considering organizational stratification is also noted by Neil J. Smelser and Seymour M. Lipset, eds., in *Social Structure and Mobility in Economic Development* (Chicago, Aldine Press, 1966), p. 6.

7. Stinchcombe, "Social Stratification and Organizations," p. 173.

8. *Ibid.,* p. 169. Much of the discussion in the literature on social stratification has talked about the changes from a ranking system, based upon families, to one based upon "special-purpose organizations." In many countries, however, the ranking of different special-purpose organizations may be changing at a significant rate.

ization." [9] This point is particularly relevant to Turkey. The leadership of new organizations may feel ambivalent toward the more traditional organizations. Indeed, a lack of opportunities in these organizations may well have motivated the "innovating leaders" to leave and become involved in developing new institutions. The behavior of successful innovators may also flout conventional standards. In Turkey during the late 1950's "conspicuous consumption" on the part of newly rich businessmen caused considerable resentment among the older elite.

Stinchcombe has hypothesized that:

> . . . rapid growth of the importance of stratification among organizations, entailed by modernization, tends to produce anomie in the politically crucial elites of the society, for their membership in the elite and their status within it depends on the status of their organizations. Because the norms governing the rankings or organizations are unsettled, and because commitment to what norms there are is weakened by the meteoric careers of organizational leaders, the means of organizational competition tend to become unlimited.[10]

The virulence of interparty strife in Turkey has been an obvious sign of such lack of restraint in political competition as, of course, was the military coup in 1960. On the other hand, the openness of Parliament to new elite groups and Turkish pride in possessing a democratic system have helped restrain competition.

When faced with competition, an organization may successfully alter its performance in order to improve its position, or it may be unable to meet the challenge and consequently suffer decline. What are the factors which determine an organization's ability to adapt when challenged by a hostile environment? Hage has summarized a number of studies, deriving several relevant hypotheses:[11]

1) The higher the centralization, the lower the adaptiveness.
2) The higher the formalization, the lower the adaptiveness.
3) The higher the stratification, the lower the adaptiveness.
4) The lower the job satisfaction, the lower the adaptiveness.

9. *Ibid.,* p. 144.
10. *Ibid.,* p. 176.
11. This is only a subset of the hypotheses put forward by Jerald Hage in "An Axiomatic Theory of Organizations," *Administrative Science Quarterly,* 10 (December 1965), 300.

58

The organizations discussed here vary along the dimensions mentioned by Hage, but it is difficult to assign rankings. However, by several criteria the Ministry of Interior might be predicted to be less adaptive than most of the other organizations. Data presented in this chapter suggest that the Ministry of Interior has been both more centralized and more formalized than the other ministries. In a later chapter it will be seen that within Interior the levels of stratification appear higher, and the levels of satisfaction lower, than elsewhere.

The distinction between public and private organizations may be relevant here. A number of respondents worked in enterprises with some private capital or in completely private businesses. Private enterprises have the relatively simple goal of earning a profit; most private organizations will attempt to make fundamental changes if such changes are necessary for their survival. On the other hand, public organizations tend to be responsive to policies set by politicians, rather than to pressures from customers or competitors. Because few public organizations face the danger of going out of existence, they often display a certain insensitivity to their clients. Indeed, public organizations providing essential services which cannot be obtained elsewhere may be prone to "inefficiency, decay, and flabbiness." [12]

Although they may be less sensitive than private organizations, public organizations do react to the process of decline. Bureaucracies have a number of strategies which they can use. They may attempt to improve their relative position by orienting themselves toward a different set of activities; both objectives and outputs can be modified. There may be less concern for satisfying the interests of members and more concern for satisfying clients.[13]

Organizations traditionally concerned with regulatory functions can become involved in development activities, projects or programs to break new ground can be initiated, and so on. As changes in the organization's environment take place, new opportunities for expansion often materialize. Such diversification can help insulate the organization from sudden changes which might adversely affect one or more of its activities. However, an organization's efforts to expand its functions can put it in conflict with competing organizations with vested interests.

12. Albert O. Hirschman, *Exit, Voice, and Loyalty* (Cambridge, Mass., Harvard University Press, 1970), p. 57.
13. Anthony Downs, *Inside Bureaucracy* (Boston, Little, Brown, 1967), p. 264.

By increasing its control over external forces an organization can place itself in a favorable position relative to other organizations; in doing so, the organization seems inevitably to become involved in political activity. One important way to effect political change is by modifying existing external structures. The participation of organizations in attempts to overthrow the government is perhaps the most dramatic manifestation of such efforts. Other ways to affect external structures include attempts to prevent the formation of competing groups. In countries with a large public sector, political conflict over new ministries and economic enterprises can be intense. In addition to trying to modify external structures, organizations may attempt to increase their own resources and minimize those available to competing groups. In public sector organizations such conflict is likely to take the form of legislative disputes over budgets and pay scales. Finally, organizations are likely to undertake efforts to change public preferences, running public relations campaigns and the like.[14]

Control Over the Environment

For the Ministries of Interior and Finance, control over the environment has meant control over new organizations and state economic enterprises.[15] This strategy has been only partially successful. Law 3460, under which state economic enterprises are regulated, was explicitly designed to give these enterprises as much autonomy as possible, permitting them, for example, to determine their own salary scales independently of the central government administration. State enterprises were to be free from bureaucratic interference by the traditional ministries and accountable only to a political body, the General Assembly of State Economic Enterprises drawn largely from Parliament.[16]

The tensions which have existed between the old and the new have

14. Some of the above has been influenced by material presented in Daniel Katz and Robert L. Kahn, *The Social Psychology of Organizations* (New York, Wiley, 1966), pp. 67–92.

15. Note Downs' proposition that all officials tend to oppose changes which "cause a net reduction in the amount of resources under their own control" and "decrease the number, scope, or relative importance of the social functions entrusted to them" (Downs, *Inside Bureaucracy,* p. 274).

16. For a critical analysis of the problems facing the state economic enterprises see A. H. Hanson, *Public Enterprise and Economic Development* (London, Routledge & Kegan Paul, 1965), pp. 344–346, 384–386.

60

been reflected in constant political and legal jousting. As noted earlier, during the single-party period members of the Grand National Assembly were heavily recruited from the older traditional ministries. These deputies were sensitive to criticisms of the new organizations voiced by their former colleagues. The state enterprises were nominally attached to ministries, and central administrators were quick to find abuses in the independent salary policies. The government finally yielded to this criticism. In 1940 the scale of salaries in state economic enterprises was fixed by law, and some attempt was made to equalize pay scales in the two types of government organizations.[17] But efforts to get around legal restrictions have continued; the payments of bonuses and fringe benefits to employees in the new organizations have expanded over the past several decades. The traditional ministries have responded to this situation by trying to have various matters concerning personnel placed under centralized control. A State Personnel Office was formed in 1960; its main function was to draft legislation which would set up equivalent pay scales for the various ministries and state economic enterprises. Despite the introduction of such legislation in the early sixties, both the equity issue and the problem of overall salary levels have continued to plague the government.[18]

In order to escape the provisions of (the revised) Law 3460, several other forms of organization have been created. In the middle 1950's foes of central bureaucratic control managed to set up annexed budget organizations, "revolving fund" organizations, and mixed enterprises with private sector participation. The annexed budget organizations have special status because at least part of their incomes is derived from their activities. Such income is often very small — i.e., universities, which are annexed budget organizations, have a small income from their book sales. The revolving fund organizations — supposed to be commercial undertakings too small to be categorized as state economic enterprises — have specially audited accounts over

17. Osman Okyar, "The Concept of Etatism," in Jerry R. Hopper and Richard I. Levin, eds., *The Turkish Administrator: A Cultural Survey* (Ankara, US AID Public Administration Division, 1967), pp. 212–213.

18. Recruitment of top graduates to some of the ministries has proved difficult under these circumstances. One resource available to the central ministries has been the awarding of university scholarships to promising young men under a contractual agreement specifying a number of years of service upon the individual's graduation. The Ministry of the Interior has increasingly been forced to use this method to obtain recruits for positions in the provincial administrative system. In contemporary Turkey the need to rely upon this method represents weakness rather than strength.

which the Ministry of Finance has only indirect financial control. In practice, many of the annexed budget revolving fund organizations are public service agencies which are able to use their financial and administrative autonomy for the benefit of organization members. The mixed enterprises with private sector participation have been completely outside the jurisdiction of the central ministries.

As might be expected, the state economic enterprises have made concerted efforts to expand their jurisdiction and independence. In the face of opposition from the central ministries, these efforts have involved such tactics as noncooperation, adding staff, "and creating subordinate units to duplicate what can be done more cheaply elsewhere." [19] One analyst of the Turkish scene has noted that following World War II "government enterprise was growing and feeding on itself. Special groups of individuals were building 'kingdoms' in certain state industrial or mining activities." [20] Although such activities led to a reaction against state economic enterprises, they do indicate that those enterprises have in many ways protected their own interests more successfully than the more traditional ministries.[21]

The central ministries have also attempted to restrict private industry. In this regard they have generally been supported by the state economic enterprises, which have always feared competition. The opposition of the central ministries, however, is more complicated. Many traditional administrators espouse an etatist and often nationalistic ideology.[22] Part of this is a result of their success under an etatist system and their vested interest in the status quo. Such sentiments dictate against cooperation with private or foreign business. As Guetzkow has noted, "When the competition between organizations involves divergent belief systems, incompatibility is due to ideological contradictions as much as to objective scarcities." [23]

Moreover, by restricting the growth of private enterprise the Min-

19. Fred W. Riggs, *Administration in Developing Countries* (Boston, Houghton Mifflin, 1964), p. 311.

20. Robert W. Kerwin, "Private Enterprise in Turkish Industrial Development," *Middle East Journal,* 5 (Winter 1951), 23.

21. If Turkey joins the Common Market as a regular member, significant changes would be necessary in many of the state enterprises.

22. Downs, in *Inside Bureaucracy* pp. 278–279, has noted certain characteristics of the bureaus most likely to develop elaborate ideologies. Such bureaus tend to be old, large, recruit selectively, provide only indirect benefits to large numbers of persons, have functions overlapping the functions of other agencies, and so on.

23. Guetzkow, "Relations Among Organizations," p. 30.

62

istries of Interior and Finance can exercise a measure of control over job opportunities. The advantages accruing to the central ministries (and the state economic enterprises) by a restriction of alternative job opportunities are clear; the ministries' bargaining power with their own employees is considerably enhanced. The engineering profession provides an indirect example of this. Although engineers are in general a very highly paid group, their salaries have tended to vary according to the existing opportunities for job mobility between the public and private sector. A comparison of the job structures of civil versus mechanical engineering showed that in the early 1960's 26 percent of the civil engineers were employed in the private sector, while only 14 percent of the mechanical engineers were so employed. This implies that "in comparison with the civil engineer, the mechanical engineer has fewer opportunities to move from the public to the private sector and even if he does make the move, his prospects for making as much money are slim." [24]

The Ministry of Finance has been actively involved in trying to limit private enterprise, going so far as to challenge policies set forth by elected political authority. For example, in October 1966 the President of the business-oriented Union of Chambers in Turkey told a regional meeting of his organization that the Ministry of Finance was undermining a project to set up a Mineral Bank, despite the interest expressed by the Prime Minister and the Minister of Industry. The Union of Chambers, and apparently the Prime Minister's office, wished to have the bank established in the private sector, or at least with special privileges granted to the private sector. But the Ministry of Finance "first said that it wanted to make this Bank a public economic enterprise," and when this did not prove feasible, "wanted to handle the minerals through eight banks which were not interested." [25] In this instance the Ministry of Finance lined up against the private sector and its allies in the Justice Party government.

One result of such activities has been to discourage private enter-

24. Mary Roan Rocchio, "The Political Socialization of Engineers in Turkey," unpub. master's thesis, Massachusetts Institute of Technology, Cambridge, Mass., 1965, p. 31.

25. Quoted from an article which appeared in the *Yeni Gazete*. This translation was taken from *The Pulse,* October 11, 1966, p. 1. In similar fashion, the Ministry of Finance, allied with the Army and State Planning Office, fought a battle against the private sector and Justice Party policies over the proposed sale of shares of the planned oil pipeline to the private sector. This was described in *Akis* and translated in *The Pulse,* October 13, 1966, pp. 3-4.

prise in certain areas of the economy.[26] Some of the friction between state and private interests has been lessened by their economic and geographic separation. Thus Kerwin has noted that in Turkey, "private investors were found in industries where the state was absent, where private enterprise had existed prior to the advent of etatism, and in a few cases where demand was so great that both state and private investments were attracted." [27] While public enterprise has been particularly strong in Turkey's Anatolian interior, private enterprise has continued to dominate developments in Istanbul, Izmir, and Ankara.[28]

In addition to trying to maintain control at the national level, the traditional ministries have also fought to retain the benefits of centralization in provincial administration. One of the reasons for the power of provincial administrators has been their legal responsibility for all activities taking place in the area under their jurisdiction. Thus, agricultural extension agents, health officials, and all other representatives of various ministries working in the provinces have been directly responsible to the Ministry of Interior's provincial governor, as well as to their home ministry. But despite their formal position of authority, the representatives of the Ministry of Interior have been dependent on other ministries in at least one important way. In order to obtain funds for rural development, the provincial administrator must obtain support from outside the Ministry of Interior. There is a premium on the governor's maintaining satisfactory relations with the other ministries.[29]

26. As Riggs has stressed, "the state, if it wishes, can subsidize its own operations from tax revenues, and can impose confiscatory taxes and other handicaps on the private firm so as to drive it out of business" (Riggs, *Administration in Developing Countries*, p. 308).

27. Robert W. Kerwin, "Etatism in Turkey, 1933–1950," in Hugh Aitken, ed., *The State and Economic Growth* (New York, Social Science Research Council, 1959), p. 246.

28. Malcolm D. Rivkin, *Area Development for National Growth* (New York, Praeger, 1965), p. 82. As noted earlier, the private sector's growth rate has been very high, and the Second Five Year Plan was modified to take this into account.

29. For example, the governor of Muğla province (in the Aegean region) was particularly concerned with education. He advised the provincial legislative assembly on the drawing up of a five-year plan to cover both the repair of old buildings and new school construction. Since local funds were inadequate for completion of the yearly programs, the Ministry of Education was consulted, and the Muğla governor eventually received a substantial grant to cover this program. Similar successful applications were made to the Ministry of Public

The relatively new stress on economic development has helped justify the Ministry of Interior's attempts to expand. Every new factory and every additional agricultural extension agent adds to the inspection and personnel problems for which the district governor is responsible. The Ministry of Interior has emphasized the need for more "technical personnel" to provide the staff necessary to fulfill their legal responsibilities, but their efforts have been only moderately successful. In some ways the situation has been one of task overload for the Ministry of Interior's district and provincial administrators. More generally, Walton and Dutton have noted that such overload conditions can "intensify the problem of scarce resources . . . may increase tension, frustration, and aggression; and may decrease the time available for the social interactions" that aid in containing conflict.[30] As might be expected, the Ministry of Interior has been unwilling to reduce the overload by voluntarily contracting its functions; thus, it opposed the formation of the Ministry of Village Affairs in 1963, but could not prevent the establishment of this new ministry to coordinate village development.

The emphasis on development accompanying political modernization has increased the power of the functionally differentiated organizations and ministries. The provincial governor's technical subordinates look to their own ministries for support. Professional training tends to turn the specialist's orientation away from his superior in the provincial administration. As Fesler has stressed, "the familiar drive of specialists for autonomy" leads to the adoption of strategies to bypass the generalist — the provincial governor.[31] In Turkey, tech-

---

Works to supplement local funds available for highway construction and work on water supply systems. Grants-in-aid were not sought in other important areas of rural development such as agriculture. See Şerif Tüten, "The Role of Local Governments in Development," in Frederick T. Bent and Louise L. Shields, eds., *The Role of Local Government in National Development* (Ankara, CENTO, 1968), p. 63.

30. Richard E. Walton and John M. Dutton, "The Management of Interdepartmental Conflict: A Model and Review," *Administrative Science Quarterly*, 14 (March 1969), 73. Walton and Dutton go on to treat task overload slightly differently, concentrating on departmental relations within one organization.

31. James W. Fesler, "The Political Role of Field Administration," in Ferrel Heady and Sybil L. Stokes, eds., *Papers in Comparative Public Administration* (Ann Arbor, Institute of Public Administration, University of Michigan, 1962), pp. 134–135.

nical ministries have attempted to circumvent control by the Ministry of Interior by setting up regional offices outside the jurisdiction of provincial authorities. Over two-thirds of the 17 ministries have developed regional organizations, and most of these do not ordinarily participate in the normal system of provincial administration.[32] The Ministry of Interior has waged a continuous battle with the new ministries about control over these offices, countering with a proposal to establish regional directorates and standardize the regional offices of various ministries. Any such measure would benefit the power of the Ministry of Interior, since a regional administration — possibly with a regional governor — would be largely staffed by members of this ministry.

Internal Change

Organizations often try to improve their competitive position by modifying existing procedures. At first, such modifications are likely to be minor, since a radical change in internal structure represents a threat to entrenched interests within the organization. Organizations under pressure may try to exert more control over their resources and personnel and to tighten up their supervisory practices. Thus Udy has asserted: "The greater the degree of conflict with the social setting, the greater the amount of authority exercised at all levels." [33] There is likely to be more concern with rational behavior and efficient use of resources.

Organizations which interact frequently with difficult clients and unfriendly interest groups try to exert strict control over their own operations, while relatively autonomous organizations have a more relaxed atmosphere. Unfortunately, information is not available to permit systematic longitudinal comparisons of internal control structures within several organizations over time. A variety of data sources will be used here to discuss the different Turkish organizations. However, most of the comparisons have to be cross-sectional, from one point in time.

Authority within the Ministry of Interior has been particularly for-

32. C. H. Dodd, *Politics and Government in Turkey* (Berkeley, University of California Press, 1969), p. 260.
33. Stanley H. Udy, Jr., "The Comparative Analysis of Organizations," in March, ed., *Handbook of Organizations,* p. 692.

66

malized and centralized. Over four thousand laws pertain to the duties of provincial and district governors.[34] In addition to legal controls, administrative courts subordinate to a Council of State handle formal complaints against the administration. Provincial and district administration comes under the scrutiny of inspectors from the Ministries of Interior and Finance who check adherence to regulations and fiscal procedures.

Within the Ministry of Interior, the provincial governor is the most powerful figure in provincial administration. He is both the representative of the national government in the province and the head of the provincial government. The provincial governor has direct authority over the district governors (except for hiring and firing) and over all other officials, organizations, and activities which take place in his province. Additionally, the provincial governor's recommendations are critical in determining his subordinates' chances for advancement within the Ministry of Interior.[35] Finally, the provincial governor, because of his control over the allocation of resources, has a power not found at lower levels of the administrative structure.

The end of the single-party system led to increased political pressure upon the provincial and district administration. Provincial governors have tried to handle such pressures by supervising the district governor's activities more closely. Pressure and conflict at the local level have led to a shift in power upward from the district to the provincial governor.[36] When political party members frequently mediate between the citizen and the district governor, the provincial governor seeks to protect himself by monitoring the district governor's communications with the central offices of the Ministry of Interior. By acting as a filter for information passing to the ministry's Ankara offices, the provincial governor can make sure his own interests are protected.[37] At the

34. Turhan A. Şenel, *The Ministry of Interior and the Role of the Kaymakam in Turkey* (Ankara, Çeviri Yayınevi, 1965), p. 20.

35. Note Downs' statement that "if superiors are to have significant control over subordinate climbers (ambitious bureaucrats), they must have an important influence on the latter's chances for promotion" (*Inside Bureaucracy,* p. 267).

36. This is compatible with Downs' law that "unrestrained conflict shifts power upward" (*ibid.,* p. 262). See also Udy, "The Comparative Analysis," p. 692.

37. Under certain circumstances, political pressures may act to loosen the administrative control of the provincial governor. According to one account, political pressures upon the provincial governor disrupted his relations with his

same time, such a check on communications aids the provincial governor in monitoring the activities of the district governors under his jurisdiction.[38]

Comparative survey data on organizational control illustrate some interesting differences among organizations. The 1965 study indicates a correlation between the pressures upon an organization and the tightness of control within the organization. As is seen in Table 4-1, the district governors were most likely to indicate that no one was in a position of authority over them in their day-to-day work. Since all district governors have the same legal relationship with their superiors — the provincial governors — this item registers the degree to which provincial governors are able to supervise their sometimes distant subordinates, as well as subjective differences among the district administrators. The rather arbitrary nature of the provincial governor's authority can be seen. District governors were more than twice as likely to say their superiors did not consult about decisions which affected them as the reverse (29 percent versus 13 percent). When the provincial governor is present, administrative controls are strict.

The responses most unlike those of the district governors came from graduates in the Ministry of Foreign Affairs. These graduates were likely to be working directly under their superior, but the style of administrative control emphasizes consultation. Diplomats also re-

---

subordinates — particularly with the district governors. In this situation, the district governor felt he was left without support or guidance from his immediate superior. See Joseph Szyliowicz, *Political Change in Rural Turkey-Erdemli* (The Hague, Mouton, 1966), pp. 132–133.

38. It is assumed that political pressures were greater when individuals seek help from others in presenting their petitions and complaints to the district governor. Political party members were not the only intermediaries; influential citizens, legal representatives, and municipal officials constituted the next most active categories of intermediaries. Seventy-seven percent of the district governors who reported political party members as intermediaries had to clear their communications through the provincial governor's office; only 53 percent of their counterparts in other districts had to do so. Similar findings were obtained when another independent variable dealing with the percentage of individuals using intermediaries was used; all differences were significant at the .05 level. Independently collected data (concerning control of communications) from the provincial governor survey also provide a partial check on the validity of the district governors' reports. Even though only subjective reports from the district governor are available, this information is meaningfully correlated with data from the provincial governor survey. Thus, the administrators' responses seemed to reflect objective conditions in the district.

Table 4-1: Political Science Faculty Graduates' Relationships with their Superiors in Various Organizations (1965)[a]

| Supervision | Ministry of Interior | | Minis-try of Finance (%) | Minis-try of Foreign Affairs (%) | Other old organi-zations (%) | New, non-central organi-zations (%) |
	District gover-nors (%)	Central offices (%)				
No immediate superior in day-to-day work	58	32	43	18	34	46
Superior usually consults	13	38	30	65	34	38
Superior does not usually consult	29	29	27	18	31	17
Number of respondents	77	34	44	34	32	79

[a] Differences among organizations were significant at the .01 level.

ported a high rate of interaction with their superiors (85 percent mention daily contact) and felt at liberty to complain if they disagreed strongly with a decision affecting their work. Eighty-three percent of the graduates in the Ministry of Foreign Affairs mentioned feeling free to complain, compared to 55 percent of the respondents in the Ministry of Finance, and 35 percent of those in the central offices of the Ministry of Interior.

Within the new, noncentral organizations there were considerable differences in the percentages of respondents claiming no immediate superior in their day-to-day work. Only 21 percent of the graduates in the new ministerial organizations and 33 percent of their counterparts in the state manufacturing enterprises had no immediate superior. In contrast, 52 percent of those in banks and 62 percent of the respondents in the private sector reported having no superior. Generally consultative superior-subordinate relationships seemed to be a feature of most of the new, noncentral organizations.

Ministries also exert control by the periodic shifting of their personnel from one assignment to another. Occupants of boundary roles, individuals who have frequent contacts with groups in the organizational environment, are prevented from developing identification with these groups by frequent rotation.[39] Field administrators, such as district and provincial governors, typically occupy positions at the boundary of their ministries; permanent ties with local politicians are minimized by these rotation policies.[40] Shifts may also occur at the instigation of influential citizens, although the Ministry of Interior has denied such tactics.[41]

Although an effort has been made to standardize district governors' tenure for a period of two or three years (according to the severity of conditions within the district), irregular shifts are still frequent, particularly at the time of elections. The tenure of the district governor's superior, the provincial governor, remains at the discretion of the Min-

Table 4-2: Tenure of Provincial Governors by Period[a]

	Period					
	1920– 1923 (%)	1923– 1946 (%)	1946– 1950 (%)	1950– 1960 (%)	1960– 1962 (%)	1962– 1967 (%)
Average tenure of provincial governor (in years)	0.8	1.9	1.7	1.8	0.9	1.8

Source: 1967 yearbooks from 40 provinces were consulted; data on the governor's tenure were available from 32 provinces.

[a] The time periods used in Table 4-2 are adapted from Frederick W. Frey, *The Turkish Political Elite*. Differences among the time periods were significant at the .01 level by a Cochran Q test.

ister of Interior. Career histories of provincial governors surveyed in 1956 indicated that the appointments in different provinces varied broadly. Although at this time the average time served in any single province was approximately two years, one governor spent over six

39. Guetzkow, "Relations Among Organizations," p. 21.
40. Fesler, "The Political Role," pp. 134–135.
41. For a discussion of a widely publicized case involving one district governor, see Dodd, *Politics and Government,* pp. 63–64.

70

consecutive years in Eskişehir, and another stayed less than eleven months in Denizli.[42]

Table 4-2 suggests that during periods when provincial government may be particularly upset — for example, during the 1920–1923 War of Independence and the period after the military coup of 1960 — governors may be rotated or replaced with considerable frequency. In the aftermath of the 1960 coup, civilian governors were replaced by military men throughout Turkey. These tactics give the central government an additional measure of control. At the same time, such tactics suggest the pressures associated with even the highest position in the provincial administration.

42. These data were originally presented in Turhan Feyzioğlu, Arif Payas-lïoğlu, Albert Gorvine, and Mümtaz Soysal, *Kasa ve Vilâyet Idaresi Üzerinde Bir Araştırma* [An investigation concerning district and provincial administration] (Ankara, Ajans-Türk Matbaasï, 1957).

5

Organizational Stratification

Interorganizational conflict constitutes an important part of contemporary Turkish politics. The outcome of such conflict influences the pattern of organizational stratification within the Turkish occupational structure. In modern societies organizational prestige tends to be translated into personal prestige of the elite; thus the fate of the organization is important to the individuals concerned. In traditional societies the situation appears to be more ascriptive. The prestige of the elite may determine the prestige of the organization. Turkey seems to be passing from the stage where an elite individual's status tended to determine that of his organization to a situation where organizational prestige is important to personal prestige. Thus, in addition to looking at how the organization is evaluated by the population at large and by prospective members, both the status of individuals entering the organization and conditions within the organization affecting its attractiveness should be considered. Such an investigation of organizational status is particularly helpful in placing the data on individual ministries in perspective.

There are many possible reasons for the differential ranking of organizations. Three variables — power, wealth, and prestige — have been put forward as particularly critical. With these variables in mind, criteria have been developed to aid in the assignment of status to different organizations. Some of the criteria refer to objective factors which seem to be both determinants of an organization's status and indicators of this status. Other, more subjective factors are indicators of organizational status which only indirectly act to determine an organization's relative position.

Determinants of Status-Power

1. The influence of the various organizations in Turkish society. This has been measured by the attributional method — asking informed individuals to rank various organizations according to their political power.

Determinants of Status-Wealth

2. The salary levels in the various organizations. If the educational qualifications for managerial positions in different organizations are similar, the status of an organization will be particularly dependent upon the salaries which it pays.[1]

Determinants of Status-Prestige

3. The relative status of individuals entering into and departing from various organizations. Individuals from more privileged backgrounds will tend both to enter the more desirable organizations and to stay in these organizations. When different programs of study lead to different organizations, students with high-status backgrounds will be disproportionately represented in the more competitive programs.

4. The relative achievement of individuals entering into and departing from various organizations. Individuals with more distinguished academic records will tend both to enter the more desirable organizations and to stay in these organizations.

5. The educational levels within the various organizations. Organizations which employ relatively high percentages of people with a university education are likely to be of higher status than organizations with relatively few university-educated people.

Indicators of Status-Prestige

6. The evaluation of typical jobs in various organizations by different groups in the population. This is the most common way of determining occupational status and has been used in many settings.

7. The evaluation of different programs of study by students, when individual programs are known to lead to career paths in specific organizations. If the link between program of study and organization is close enough, the evaluation of the program can serve as an indicator of organizational status.

1. There is at least one condition which can modify this proposition. When particular ethnic groups are recruited disproportionately to certain organizations, while others are excluded, status distinctions may be complicated by ethnic factors. One group may have wealth while another monopolizes official positions. For an elaboration of this, see the discussion of "pariah entrepreneurship" in Fred W. Riggs, *Thailand: The Modernization of a Bureaucratic Polity* (Honolulu, Hawaii, East-West Center Press, 1966), pp. 249–254.

8. The changes in enrollments in different programs of study over time, when individual programs are known to feed into different organizations. Although there may be a time lag before the status changes are reflected in enrollments, these changes probably reflect students' and administrators' evaluations of both career paths and organizations. Changes in enrollment, rather than absolute levels, are important here since some particularly desirable programs of study may be purposely kept small.

Additional Indicators of Status

9. The job satisfaction expressed by individuals working in particular organizations. It is presumed that people in higher status organizations are more likely to be satisfied with their work situation than are their counterparts in lower status organizations. This represents an extension of Inkeles's cross-national work on the satisfaction associated with various jobs,[2] and is based on the idea that job satisfaction is a reflection of organizational status as well as job level.

10. Rates of transfer into and out of various organizations. If a pool of individuals of similar educational qualifications is considered over a period of several years, relatively fewer of these individuals may transfer out of a higher-status organization and relatively more of them transfer into that organization than will be true for a lower-status organization. This criterion is somewhat tentative because some high-status organizations have very few high-level openings. Thus, these organizations have a high turnover at the lower and middle levels.

Power — Attributional Rating

Ranking the various organizations according to their power presents several problems. Outside the Ministries of Interior, Finance, and Foreign Affairs, there is great diversity. Thus, the State Planning Organization has been generally considered more powerful than the Ministry of Tourism and Information although this may have changed by the late

2. Alex Inkeles, "Industrial Man: The Relation of Status to Experience, Perception, and Value," *American Journal of Sociology*, 66 (July 1960), 1–31. Inkeles has noted that: "Those standing at the top are, as a rule, more satisfied than those in the lower positions. Indeed, in every country the proportion who report job satisfaction decreases quite regularly as we descend the steps of the standard occupational hierarchy."

74

1960's. Moreover, particular organizations may be very influential with regard to one set of issues and much less so concerning others.

The "panel" variant of the "attribution" method, by which a group of well-informed individuals rate various positions or organizations, has been widely used for the purpose of ranking units according to their influence. Frey presents data on the importance of various ministers which are relevant to this discussion.[3] As seen in Table 5-1, his

Table 5-1: Judges' Ranking of Importance of Posts for Four Time Periods

Position	1920–1923	1923–1939	1939–1950	1950–1957
Minister of Interior	65[a]	79	78	69
Finance Minister	68	77	79	73
Foreign Minister	74	78	80	66
Minister of Economics and Trade (Commerce)	—[b]	—	59	58
Minister of Customs and Monopolies	—	56	57	49
Minister of State Enterprises	—	—	59	50

Source: Frederick W. Frey, *The Turkish Political Elite*, p. 226.

[a] Frey used a rating scale ranging from zero to one hundred. He notes that "judges gave a rank of one hundred to the office or offices considered most important and graded all other offices accordingly." A number of more specifically political offices were included in the rating, but are not shown here.

[b] A dash indicates that the post was not ranked (or did not exist) during that period.

data indicate that the Ministers of Interior, Finance, and Foreign Affairs were more influential than the others, but that the ministries suffered a drop in relative influence when the Democrats came to power in 1950. The Ministry of Finance is rated as more important than the other ministries during the 1950–1957 period. Unfortunately, more recent attributional rankings are not available.

3. "Importance" was defined in the following fashion: the respondents were instructed to imagine that the *same* individual occupied each of the posts and then to rate the posts according to the relative *influence* of each over the regular activities of the assembly, including the cabinet (Frederick W. Frey, *The Turkish Political Elite* [Cambridge, Mass., M.I.T. Press, 1965], p. 226).

Wealth-Salary Scales

The status of various Turkish organizations would seem to be partially dependent upon their salary levels. Political Science Faculty graduates enter a number of different types of organizations, but comparatively few of these graduates have been employed in some of the new organizations with relatively high salary levels. In 1963 there were only 28 graduates of the Political Science Faculty working in the State Planning Organization and only 12 Faculty graduates were in the Ministry of Reconstruction and Resettlement. As such figures imply, there are not enough survey respondents to permit extended comparisons among individual organizations other than the Ministries of Interior, Finance, and Foreign Affairs.

Because of this, summary categories are used for the remaining organizations employing Political Science Faculty graduates. Included in the category "other old organizations" are all ministries and general directorates founded before 1950 and listed by the State Institute of Statistics as a general or attached budgetary organization. In general these older organizations resemble the central ministries in performing regulative and service functions, rather than being engaged directly in production.

The category "new, noncentral organizations" contains such diverse organizations as the newer government organizations, banks and other state economic enterprises, and private sector organizations. The new ministries are organizations founded since 1950 whose functions reflect the more complex state of the Turkish economy and the increased interest in rural development. Despite their disagreements with each other, these organizations share certain features which are important for this study. Most critically, many of the incentives and advantages offered by work in these organizations are quite different from those provided by the Ministries of Interior and Finance. Moreover, these new, noncentral organizations tend to recruit from the same set of Political Science Faculty graduates, many of whom are employed in the Ministries of Interior and Finance.

Survey information on salaries emphasizes the opportunities outside the central ministries (Interior, Finance, and Foreign Affairs). Graduates working in the new, noncentral organizations reported considerably higher salaries than those in the central and older ministries; these salaries were particularly impressive considering the relative youth of many individuals working outside the central ministries. Twenty-one

76

percent of the respondents in the newer organizations ($n = 14$) and 69 percent of those in the private sector ($n = 16$) earned monthly salaries of over 2,000 lira (the highest category).[4] Seventy-two percent of the graduates employed by banks ($n = 25$) and 46 percent of those in other state enterprises ($n = 24$) attained this salary level. As Table 5-2 indicates, bonuses and overtime must be taken into consideration in order to get an appropriate picture of salaries in the banks and other state economic enterprises.[5] Only the older graduates working in the central office of the Ministry of Interior reported earnings close to those in the new, noncentral organizations: 32 percent of the respondents in the central office of the Ministry of Interior claimed monthly salaries of over 2,000 lira.

As noted above, it is difficult to estimate total income from formal salary schedules alone; semilegal procedures and extra benefits abound. Among the central ministries, the Ministry of Foreign Affairs has been the most successful in providing for its employees; cost-of-living allowances have been used in this ministry. A salary differential during assignments abroad enables the diplomat to acquire material assets (better clothes, a larger apartment, and possibly a car) which support a higher standard of living during his home tours.

Prestige-Differential Recruitment and Individual Status

Much of the differential recruitment to various organizations is based upon processes governing selection to different sections of the Political Science Faculty. Because of a stringent foreign language examination, the political section recruits predominantly from those with more privileged backgrounds. These students are much more likely to have had the benefits of better language instruction in private schools or metropolitan lycées. The financial section — the second choice of the majority of Political Science Faculty graduates — also recruits disproportionately from the more privileged students. By reason of their personal backgrounds, the individuals who enter the Ministries of For-

4. Sixty-two percent of the private sector managers responding to another survey reported earnings over 2,000 lira monthly. Arif Payaslîoğlu, *Türkiyede Özel Sanayi Alanîndaki Müteşebbisler ve Teşebbüsler* [Entrepreneurs and enterprises in the field of Turkish private industry] (Ankara, Political Science Faculty — Financial Institute, 1961), p. 56.

5. For example, the Highway Department obtained permission to pay an annual bonus of up to three times an individual's monthly salary as a reward for meritorious service.

Table 5-2: Salary Distribution in Various Organizations

	Percentage of employees earning[a]		
	800 TL or less	801–2000 TL	2001 TL or more
Ministry of Interior (715)[b]	68	28	4
Ministry of Finance (450)	68	30	1
Ministry of Foreign Affairs[c] (224)	28	62	11
Other old organizations (established before 1950)			
Ministry of Commerce (59)	44	48	8
Ankara University (45)	69	24	7
Council of State (34)	55	28	17
Ministry of Customs and Monopolies (27)	66	33	1
New, noncentral organizations (established since 1950)			
State Planning Organization (28)	36	50	13
State Institute of Statistics (22)	75	24	1
Ministry of Tourism and Information (19)	61	36	2
Office of Prime Minister (16)	55	36	9
Ministry of Industry (15)	59	33	8
Ministry of Reconstruction and Resettlement (12)	31	30	39
Department of Highways (9)	34	40	26
Banks and other State Economic Enterprises			
Agricultural Bank (92)	54	45	1
Central Bank (37)	41	53	6
Sümer Bank (22)	23	68	9
Land Credit Bank (21)	47	48	5

Source: *Devlet Personel Sayïmï, I, Genel ve Katma Bütçeli Kurumlar* [State Personnel Census, I, General and Attached Budget Organizations] (Ankara, Devlet İstatistik Enstitüsü, 1965), and *Devlet Personel Sayïmï, III, Kamur Iktisadï Teşebbüsleri* [State Personnel Census, III, State Economic Enterprises] (Ankara, Devlet Istatistik Enstitüsü, 1967). These sources are hereafter referred to as, respectively, the 1963 and 1965 State Personnel Census.

[a] No responses have been eliminated from the percentaging. Differences among organizations were significant at the .01 level.

[b] The number of Political Science Faculty graduates in each organization is indicated in parentheses after the name of the organization.

[c] The Ministry of Foreign Affairs' salary structure is considerably more inflated than these figures show since diplomats receive a substantial cost-of-living adjustment, depending on where they are stationed. Figures for the state economic enterprises do not include important supplementary payments (bonuses, overtime, etc.).

Table 5-3: Attendance Distribution at Political Science Faculty, by Social Background (1946–1955 Graduates)[a]

Section attended at Political Science Faculty	Position of father					
	More privileged backgrounds			Less privileged backgrounds		
	Official from Ankara, Istanbul, Izmir (%)	Businessman from Ankara, Istanbul, Izmir (%)	Professional man (%)	Official from other areas (%)	Businessman from other areas (%)	Farmer (%)
Administrative (into Interior)	21	28	40	53	52	65
Financial (into Finance and others)	49	61	45	42	43	30
Political (into Foreign Affairs)	29	11	15	4	2	5
No answer	1	0	0	1	4	0
Number of respondents	84	18	20	119	56	57

[a] Differences were significant at the .01 level.

eign Affairs and Finance lend prestige to the section which trains them and to the organization which they join. On the other hand, the more upwardly mobile students tend to enter the administrative section, although a number of them study in the financial section.[6] The close

6. Although, as the figures in Table 5-3 show, more than half of the graduates come from official backgrounds, one should not conclude that a closed and elitist cooptation of bureaucrats exists. It is simply true that Turkish university graduates in general tend to have fathers with official occupations, no matter what their own occupational aspirations might be. Thus a survey of 426 Ankara University students noted that 55 percent came from official backgrounds. Since only 62 percent of our sample had fathers who were officials, one cannot say that the "Civil Service School" recruits disproportionately from sons of civil servants. For the survey data on Ankara University students see Özer Ozankaya, *Üniversite Öğrencilerinin Siyasal Yönelimleri* [Political orientations of university students] (Ankara, Sevinç Matbaası, 1966), p. 21.

Table 5-4: Distribution of Graduates among Various Organizations by Social Background (1956)[a]

| | Position of father | | | | | |
| | More privileged backgrounds | | | Less privileged backgrounds | | |
Organization	Official from Ankara, Istanbul, Izmir (%)	Businessman from Ankara, Istanbul, Izmir (%)	Professional man (%)	Official from other areas (%)	Businessman from other areas (%)	Farmer (%)
Ministry of Interior	19	28	40	54	50	65
Ministry of Finance	27	56	25	33	41	21
Ministry of Foreign Affairs	25	11	20	4	2	5
Other old organizations	19	—	15	4	4	9
New, noncentral organizations	10	6	—	5	2	—
Number of respondents	84	18	20	119	56	57

[a] Differences were significant at the .01 level.

correspondence between attendance at the administrative section and entrance into the Ministry of Interior is reflected in the almost identical percentages to be found by comparing Tables 5-3 and 5-4. Graduates with less privileged backgrounds were more likely to enter the Ministry of Interior than any other organization. The interest shown by sons of farmers is especially noteworthy.[7]

The data on the graduates' place of work in 1956 indicate the relatively broad appeal of the Ministry of Finance, although the interest in

7. An effort was made to separate sons of small landholders (peasants) from sons of large landholders; a relatively high proportion of sons of farmers (about 30 percent in each case) did not give information about family landholding or income. The analysis which was performed showed no differences among sons of different types of farmers.

80

this ministry shown by those with business backgrounds was especially great. However, graduates from every social background tended to leave Interior and Finance over the 1956–1965 period. Sons of professionals seemed particularly eager to move out of the Ministries of Interior and Finance. Overall, the data show the power of the new, noncentral organizations in attracting graduates from both higher-status and lower-status backgrounds.

Prestige-Differential Recruitment and Individual Achievement

If certain organizations are more desirable than others, they should attract Faculty graduates with more substantial records of university

Table 5-5: Distribution of Graduates among Various Organizations According to Grades (1956–1965)

Organization	1946–1955 graduates in 1956[a]		1946–1955 graduates in 1965		1958–1961 graduates in 1965	
	Fair grades (%)	Good grades[b] (%)	Fair grades (%)	Good grades (%)	Fair grades (%)	Good grades (%)
Ministry of Interior	50	43	39	32	42	26
Ministry of Finance	23	38	19	27	5	11[c]
Ministry of Foreign Affairs	10	10	11	11	2	11
Other old organizations	9	8	11	10	9	16
New, noncentral organizations	9	1	20	20	42	37
Number of respondents	151	223	151	223	45	19

[a] Differences were significant at the .05 level for 1946–1955 graduates in 1956. When the two sets of 1965 data were combined, differences were significant at the .05 level.

[b] Included in the "good grades" category are respondents with good grades and those with very good grades.

[c] Owing to nonresponse bias there is an under-representation of 1958–1961 graduates in the Ministry of Finance.

Table 5-6: Distribution of Graduates among Various Organizations According to Social Background and Grades (1956)

	Position of father									
	More privileged backgrounds[a,b]				Less privileged backgrounds[b]					
	Official from Ankara, Istanbul, Izmir		Businessman from Ankara, Istanbul, Izmir		Official from other areas		Businessman from other areas		Farmer	
Organization	Fair grades (%)	Good grades (%)	Fair grades (%)	Good grades (%)	Fair grades (%)	Good grades (%)	Fair grades (%)	Good grades (%)	Fair grades (%)	Good grades (%)
Ministry of Interior	24	16	38	20	60	49	50	49	61	68
Ministry of Finance	19	32	38	70	22	40	32	49	18	25
Ministry of Foreign Affairs	24	32	13	10	4	4	5	—	11	—
Other old organizations	16	18	—	—	4	4	9	3	11	7
New, noncentral organizations	16	2	13	—	9	3	5	—	—	—
Number of respondents	37	44	8	10	45	73	22	33	28	28

[a] There were not enough sons of professional men with fair grades ($n = 4$) to include the professional category.
[b] Differences were significant at the .05 level for both those graduates from more, and those from less, privileged backgrounds.

achievement in disproportionate numbers. An analysis of the grades of respondents in various organizations lends some support to this proposition, but the relationships are not as strong as might be expected. As may be seen in Table 5-5, a higher percentage of Faculty graduates with fair grades — as compared with graduates with good grades — entered the Ministry of Interior. Respondents with good grades tended to enter the Ministry of Finance in disproportionate numbers; yet by 1965 many of these graduates had transferred to the new, noncentral organizations.

An analysis of recruitment to the various organizations which combines social background data and university grades produces additional information. Table 5-6 shows how individuals with the dual advantages of privileged backgrounds and good grades were likely to avoid the Ministry of Interior, as were sons of officials from other areas with good grades — a group which is likely to be well-informed about opportunities in the bureaucracy.

Prestige-Educational Level

Certain organizations may be considered of high status because they employ a relatively high percentage of university graduates. These organizations are generally more likely to carry out high-level staff functions than to use relatively unskilled personnel to implement decisions made elsewhere in the government hierarchy. As seen in Table 5-7, university-educated personnel made up a higher percentage of those employed in the Ministry of Foreign Affairs and the State Planning Organization than they did in the other organizations. The well-known "elite" nature of the two former organizations may be partially based on the high percentage of university graduates which they employ. On the other hand, university graduates made up a relatively low percentage of those employed in the Ministries of Interior and Finance. Because of the service nature of banks, only a relatively small percentage of their employees were university graduates.

Prestige-Evaluation of Jobs

The decline in the esteem granted a bureaucratic career has been mentioned at various points in this discussion. Information on occupational prestige both supports this hypothesis and aids in ranking Turkish ministerial organizations. First of all, a bureaucratic career is not

Table 5-7: Distribution of University-educated Personnel in
Various Organizations

Organization	Percentage of employees with some university education
Ministry of Interior	23
Ministry of Finance	26
Ministry of Foreign Affairs	67
Other old organizations	
Ministry of Commerce	55
Ankara University	36
Council of State	58
Ministry of Customs and Monopolies	9
New, noncentral organizations	
State Planning Organization	69
State Institute of Statistics	40
Ministry of Tourism and Information	44
Office of Prime Minister	42
Ministry of Industry	40
Ministry of Reconstruction and Resettlement	59
Department of Highways	52
Banks and other state economic enterprises	
Agricultural Bank	7
Central Bank	19
Sümer Bank	20
Land Credit Bank	19

Source: The 1963 and 1965 State Personnel Censuses.

highly respected by students in Turkey's regular lycées. These are the
students in the most elite public secondary schools who traditionally
would have looked forward to a career in the civil service as a great
opportunity. Student choices concerning which careers they wanted to
enter and which careers they considered most prestigious are presented
in Table 5-8. Since the coding scheme combines politicians and civil
servants in one category, the ranking of a bureaucratic career was probably lower than even the figures of Table 5-8 would indicate.

The comments of a group of private businessmen underscored the
decline in prestige of a bureaucratic career. Although they ranked their
own profession considerably higher than did lycée students, these

84

Table 5-8: Evaluations of Various Careers by Lycée Students (1959)[a]

	Vocation most respected (%)	Vocation expects to enter (%)
Government and politics	12	7
Military	10	7
Free professions	49	53
Education	13	7
Business and trade	2	3
Housewife	12	22
Number of respondents	1,043	1,043

Source: Data collected by Frederick W. Frey, George W. Angell, Jr., and Abdürrahman Ş. Sanay.

[a] Some of the preliminary results of this analysis are presented in Frederick W. Frey, "Education," in Robert E. Ward and Dankwart A. Rustow, eds., *Political Modernization in Japan and Turkey* (Princeton, Princeton University Press, 1964), pp. 224–229. The open-ended questions were: "For which vocations do you, personally, feel the greatest respect?" and "What vocation do you expect to enter when you have finished your schooling?" The coding categories are all quite broad. Most of them are obvious except perhaps for the most important one — free professions. This includes such occupations as doctor, lawyer, engineer, architect, chemist, physicist, dentist, nurse, journalist, and so on.

businessmen concurred with the students in downgrading the status of bureaucrats in contemporary Turkish society. From a list of five professions the businessmen were asked to rank each in terms of the level of prestige granted it in the community. Less than 10 percent of the businessmen considered an official career to be the most prestigious profession. They clearly ranked it fourth, just above worker. The businessmen were also asked if their evaluations of different careers had changed over the past several decades. More than half indicated that their opinions had changed and that in the past they would have evaluated the prestige of the various careers quite differently. Both present and past evaluations are presented in Table 5-9.

Data relevant to specific ministries are provided in a survey by Kazamias.[8] Lycée students were asked to rank eleven occupational cate-

8. Andreas Kazamias, *Education and the Quest for Modernity in Turkey* (Chicago, University of Chicago Press, 1966), pp. 242–243.

Table 5-9: Ranking of Five Occupations by Turkish Entrepreneurs (1958)

| Occupations | Present ranking[a] | | | | |
	I[b]	II	III	IV	V[c]
Industrialist	54%	30%	9%	4%	3%
Free professions	24	22	42	10	2
Commerce	15	38	30	15	2
Official	8	5	15	57	15
Worker	0	6	4	13	77

| | Past ranking[a] | | | | |
	I[b]	II	III	IV	V[c]
Official	63%	13%	13%	8%	3%
Free professions	13	56	21	10	0
Commerce	13	25	38	23	1
Industrialist	11	60	27	54	3
Worker	0		1	6	93

Source: Arif Payaslïoğlu, *Türkiyede Özel Sanayi Alanındaki Müteşebbisler ev Teşebbüsler* [Entrepreneurs and enterprises in the field of Turkish private industry] (Ankara, Political Science Faculty — Financial Institute, 1961), p. 31.

[a] One hundred twenty-seven respondents ranked present occupations, while 71 respondents gave past rankings.
[b] Highest.   [c] Lowest.

gories in terms of the prestige and respect accorded the occupations by the Turkish people. The students ranked the free professions highest in public esteem (chosen by 43 percent).[9] A career as diplomat was ranked second highest, with 27 percent of the choices. The general category of "national government official" was far down the line. Such categories as "education," "businessman (big)," "military officer," and "religion" were ranked above "national government official."

9. The overwhelming endorsement of a career in the free professions seems to be another product of economic development during the Republican period. In fact, one author suggests that a career in the professions has replaced a bureaucratic career in terms of offering the most desirable life style in the contemporary Turkish economy. *Mediterranean Regional Project — Turkey* (Paris, Organization for Economic Cooperation and Development, 1965), p. 68.

86

Such a ranking scheme suffers from the fact that most of the free professions are of generally high standing, while the category of "national government official" covers a wide range of jobs. When students were asked to rank a list of specific governmental occupations in terms of prestige and respect, the positions of diplomat and deputy in the National Assembly were singled out most frequently; both positions received over 30 percent of the first-place choices. The job of provincial governor was selected by only 14 percent of the students and that of district governor by only 2 percent. These data help rank two of the central ministries. The prestige of the Ministry of Foreign Affairs, which carries out the diplomatic functions and provides most of the ambassadors, has been enhanced by the high esteem granted diplomats. On the other hand, the positions of provincial and district governor, which in the past attracted many aspirants to the Ministry of Interior, were no longer accorded high prestige by youth. The Ministry of Finance has no career slot as "visible" in Turkish society as that of the district governor or diplomat; thus, no occupation in the ministry was listed.

Evaluation of Different Programs of Study

As mentioned earlier, the association between enrollment in a given section of the Political Science Faculty and later entry into a particular organization was high enough to permit the use of data on the three programs of study (sections) to help evaluate the different ministries.[10] A survey of students entering the Faculty in 1961 gave a clear ranking of the programs of study.[11] Table 5-10 shows the political section to be the overwhelming first choice of all entering students. This is a definite endorsement of a career in the Ministry of Foreign Affairs, since graduates of the political section were very likely to take a job in this ministry.

The financial section was the obvious second choice. This program of study opens up the most varied career opportunities to students and probably indicates not only an endorsement of the Ministry of Finance

10. In the 1956 sample, 82 percent of the 1946–1955 graduates of the political section were in the Ministry of Foreign Affairs. Ninety-six percent of the graduates of the administrative section were in the Ministry of Interior, and 73 percent of the graduates of the financial section were in the Ministry of Finance.

11. Cemal Mïhçïoğlu, *Üniversiteye Giriş Sïnavlarïnïn Yeniden Düzenlenmesi* [An investigation of the new university entrance examinations] (Ankara, Sevinç Matbaasï, 1962), p. 62.

Table 5-10: Choice of Section at Political Science Faculty
by Entering Students (1961)[a]

Section chosen	First choice (%)	Second choice (%)	Third choice (%)
Administrative (into Interior)	6	14	75
Financial (into Finance and others)	16	68	13
Political (into Foreign Affairs)	77	15	8
No answer	2	2	4

Number of respondents = 217

Source: Cemal Mïhçïoğlu, *Üniversiteye Giriş Sïnavlarïnïn Yeniden Düzenlenmesi* [An investigation of the new university entrance examinations] (Ankara, Sevinç Matbaasï, 1962), p. 62.

[a] Differences were significant at the .01 level.

but also demonstrates interest in the newer ministries as well as in state economic enterprises, banks, and private sector. The little interest expressed in the administrative section was a definite vote against the Ministry of Interior. Section and ministry have always been very closely linked, and graduates of the administrative section are specifically prepared to staff the Ministry of Interior's provincial organization. Mïhçïoğlu mentions that after the first year, when students began to think about their professional future, more decided to enter the financial than the political section. However, there is little question that the political section (and thus the Ministry of Foreign Affairs) was still seen as most attractive.

This downgrading of the administrative section appears to be a fairly recent tendency; Mïhçïoğlu notes:

If the same questionnaire had been distributed twenty years ago, we think that the administrative section would have been chosen so frequently as to place it at the top of the list. Students no longer prefer this section because careers in the civil administration no longer offer the prestige and security which they once did. This is especially true since the era of multi-party politics, which has had the effect of making the administrative officer a puppet of the provincial party chiefs. The fact that district governors are paid little

88

and sent to hardship areas has also contributed to the diminishing prestige of administrative careers.[12]

Enrollments in Different Programs of Study

Because of the relationship between programs of study and later career opportunities, the relative enrollments in different sections at the Political Science Faculty can aid in evaluating the opportunities in the various types of organizations. Table 5-11 shows that enrollments

Table 5-11: Enrollments in Different Sections of Political Science Faculty over Time

Period[a]	Administra-tive (into Interior) (%)	Financial (into Finance and others) (%)	Political (into Foreign Affairs) (%)	Total number
1930–1935	44	40	15	203
1935–1940	36	55	10	356
1940–1945	28	61	12	414
1945–1950	43	47	10	537
1950–1955	47	46	8	623
1955–1960	26	65	8	777
1960–1965	26	58	16	953
1965–1967	20	65	15	483

Source: "Kaymakamlĭk Kursu" [Course for District Governors], *Amme Idaresi Bülteni* [Public Administration Bulletin], 15 (December 1967), 5.

[a] Differences in administrative section enrollments between pre-1955 and post-1955 were not significant by the Mood test.

in the different sections have fluctuated markedly since 1930. Since 1955, however, the enrollment in the financial section seems to have been on an uptrend, while the enrollment in the administrative section has decreased. Moreover, a new section — economic management and accounting — has recently been added to train students for the state economic enterprises and private sector. Enrollment in the political section has been kept low deliberately; as mentioned earlier, this sec-

12. Mĭhçĭoğlu, *Üniversiteye Giriş*, p. 63.

tion feeds into a relatively small number of positions in the Ministry of Foreign Affairs.

Job Satisfaction

Although job satisfaction is measured by several indicators on the different surveys, it seems clearest to present the data on job satisfaction reported by the 241 panel respondents in 1956 and 1965. As seen in Table 5-12, there were consistent differences in reported job satisfaction among the Ministries of Interior, Finance, and Foreign Affairs. The Political Science Faculty graduates in the Ministry of Interior were least likely to be satisfied; those in the Ministry of Finance were intermediate, while the Ministry of Foreign Affairs reported the highest level of satisfaction. Finally, graduates outside the central ministries appeared well-satisfied with their work; a breakdown of job satisfaction within the category of new, noncentral organizations will be presented in a later chapter.

Table 5-12: Job Satisfaction in Various Organizations (1956 and 1965)

Organization	Percentage satisfied	
	1956	1965
Ministry of Interior	32% (115)[a]	47% (89)[a]
Ministry of Finance	55% (66)	61% (41)
Ministry of Foreign Affairs	89% (27)	90% (30)
Other old organizations	68% (22)	70% (27)
New, noncentral organizations	91% (11)	87% (54)

Number of panel respondents = 241

[a] The numbers in parentheses indicate the number of panel respondents (1946–1955 Faculty graduates) located in each type of organization at the time of the two surveys.

Transfer Rates

Organizations can also be ranked according to the ease with which they have attracted and retained trained personnel. Table 5-4 has shown how Political Science Faculty graduates have tended to leave the Ministries of Interior and Finance over the nine-year period between 1956 and 1965. These overall changes can be more closely analyzed in terms of the number of respondents transferring into and out of the different ministries between 1956 and 1965.

Table 5-13 clearly shows that, compared with the Ministry of For-

Table 5-13: Graduates' Transfer Rates for Various Organizations (1956–1965)[a]

Organization	Transfer into		Transfer from		Net loss or gain		Graduates remaining in same or similar organization
	No.	(%)[b]	No.	(%)	No.	(%)	
Ministry of Interior	4	(3)	45	(35)	−41	(−32)	129
Ministry of Finance	10	(13)	40	(51)	−30	(−38)	79
Ministry of Foreign Affairs	6	(17)	1	(3)	+5	(+14)	36
Other old organizations	19	(95)	13	(65)	+6	(+30)	20
New, noncentral organizations	63	(450)	3	(21)	+60	(+429)	14

[a] Transfers between organizations in a given category (i.e., between organizations within the "other old" or the "new, noncentral" categories) were not counted here.

[b] These percentages were calculated using the number of 1946–1955 graduates in the given organization category over the 1956–1965 period as a base; the total number of respondents was 380. Information on two of the 1956 respondents was not available. Differences were significant at the .01 level.

eign Affairs, the 1946–1955 graduates of the Political Science Faculty were more likely to leave, and less likely to enter, the Ministries of Interior and Finance. Here again the data reinforce the high standing of the Ministry of Foreign Affairs. Although a higher percentage of respondents departed from the Ministry of Finance than from the Ministry of Interior, this trend is counterbalanced by the graduates transferring into the Ministry of Finance. Even though it is a net loser of personnel, the Ministry of Finance appears to possess the resources to pull some people away from other jobs to work in this ministry.

The criteria discussed above can be summarized in tabular form. As is seen from Table 5-14, the Ministry of Foreign Affairs was clearly of higher status than the two other central ministries. Although fewer data are available, the favorable position of the new, noncentral organizations was also reflected in the table. The convergence of the various criteria for organizational status was particularly impressive. Independent studies using different methods produced generally similar results.

These data on organizational stratification are relevant for a discussion of both organization theory and elite theory. In previous chapters the incumbents of formal positions in the Cabinet and in the Parliament have been described. Following the example of Frey and many other elite theorists, particular positions have been used as the criteria for membership in the political elite. In the brief treatment here, we have not dealt with changes in patterns of stratification among these political positions. Organization theory sensitizes one to changing patterns of stratification — both among political and among administrative elites. It seems likely, for example, that members of Parliament have been considerably more influential during the multiparty period than during the period of Atatürk's singleparty rule.

A comparison of elite theory and organization theory helps call attention to the differing ways in which recruitment has been treated here. In the discussion of political elites, changing patterns of recruitment to Parliamentary positions were treated as partial measures of the influence of those available for recruitment — Political Science Faculty graduates and bureaucrats in general. In the discussion of organizational stratification, changing recruitment patterns were used to help evaluate the organizations into which individuals were recruited. Although there are dangers in this use of recruitment data to study both changes in group influence and changes in organizational status, it seems justified. Cabinet and Parliamentary positions — and the individuals holding these offices — are of continuing significance in most party systems. These organizations — the Cabinet and the Parliament — are at such a high level in the stratification system that entry into them is of general importance in ranking those being recruited. On the

Table 5-14: Summary of Status of Different Organizations

Organization	Salary levels	Status of individual	Educational achievement	Edu-cational level	Evaluation of jobs	Evaluation of programs of study	Enrollment in program of study	Job satis-faction	Rates of transfer
Ministry of Interior	very low	very low	low	low	low	low	low	low	low
Ministry of Finance	low	low	high	low		high	high	low	low
Ministry of Foreign Affairs	high	very high		high	high	very high		very high	high
Other old organizations	high	high		high				high	high
New, noncentral organizations	very high	high				high	high	very high	very high

other hand, a number of indicators — not just those based on recruitment — reflect upon the patterns of organizational stratification described in this chapter.

From a developmental perspective, organizational stratification was markedly affected by the ruralizing election of 1950. Independent information on such changes over time was available from both the judges' and entrepreneurs' attributional rankings, from enrollments in the different sections, and from the author of the study of Political Science Faculty students. The Ministry of Interior with its high levels of interaction with the rural population was particularly hurt by this election. The new, noncentral organizations were aided by the stress on economic growth which accompanied the opening up of the one-party system. The system of organizational stratification which emerged in the 1950's and 1960's has had numerous implications for the behavior of individual administrators.[13]

13. Since we have used data on individual bureaucrats to help rank organizations, there are dangers of being tautological here. Fortunately, a number of other indicators described in this chapter led to the same ranking of organizations.

6
Individual Mobility

The factors treated in the previous chapters — organizational stratification, economic development, and political pressures — seem to have significantly affected Turkish administrative behavior. In this chapter and the next, changing patterns of organizational behavior will be discussed. The relationships between mobility, job satisfaction, and other variables will be explored and the reasons for this satisfaction — or the lack thereof — analyzed. We will look at both the process of job selection and the determinants of job satisfaction in order to study "the conditions affecting the valence of a job to a person." [1]

Such a discussion is relevant for organization theory in several respects. As was seen in Chapter 5, the levels of turnover and satisfaction provide a basis for comparing various ministries and organizations. Moreover, a substantial amount of research has been done on the relationships between these attitudinal and behavioral measures. The availability of extensive data from American organizations aids in interpreting the survey information from elite Turkish administrators. In addition, Turkish material can serve as a check on the cross-cultural validity of propositions derived from an American organizational context. Finally, the material from different Turkish ministries under various societal pressures helps isolate the effects of different organizational variables; such intrasocietal diversity leads to caution in generalizing about intersocietal differences.

Previous studies have generally considered both the internal composition and the particular opinions of elite groups without focusing upon change and mobility. We suggest that data on elite job satisfaction and other related variables are important for an understanding of both political stability and Turkish society. Since the beginning of the multiparty period, Turkish administrators have been subjected to political pressures quite different from those previously encountered. Research on the reactions of groups which have suffered a decline in power is lacking, but these Turkish findings seem most relevant. In a politicized environment, job dissatisfaction may be directly related to dissatisfaction with the system as a whole.

Data from the years 1956 and 1965 permit a linking of the politi-

1. Victor H. Vroom, *Work and Motivation* (New York, Wiley, 1964), p. 277.

cally relevant information with the lower-level hypotheses derived from organization theory. Modernization causes changes in the occupational reward structure which are related to job mobility and attitude change. The effects of political and social developments upon job satisfaction and mobility in various organizations can be considered. Identifying the characteristics of those individuals who have altered their career patterns in response to new opportunities is also important; mobile individuals may be both self-selected *and* "carried along on societal tides." [2] Several of these interrelationships will be discussed here; macro-level changes, in conjunction with organizational variables and individual characteristics, will be considered as determinants of attitudes and behaviors.

Conditions in 1956 and 1965

The 1956 data were collected near the midpoint of the Democratic Party's ten-year rule. By this time the patterns of local political influence on bureaucratic decisions had been clearly established. But, at the national level, the Democratic Party had not yet been involved in the excesses which paved the way for the military coup of 1960. Both the private sector and the state economic enterprises had expanded significantly under the Democratic Party, but inflation and balance-of-payments difficulties had detracted from overall performance. The inflation particularly hurt the official class — bureaucrats and military men on fixed salaries. In overall perspective, the 1956 survey data were gathered at a time when the bureaucracy was undoubtedly reacting to its loss of influence, but before the extremely agitated conditions which existed at the end of the decade.

Conditions in 1965 differed significantly from those prevailing in 1956. Several factors appear to have acted to diminish bureaucrat-politician conflict between 1956 and 1965. The politicians' experience with military intervention might have been expected to lessen local interference in administrative matters. The psychological shock associated with the end of bureaucratic dominance would seem to have passed by 1965. Bureaucrats may have been more used to the ways of local leadership in 1965 than in 1956.

As noted earlier, the popular successor to the Democratic Party — the Justice Party — pursued a relatively moderate course. In early

2. Arnold S. Feldman and Christopher Hurn, "The Experience of Modernization," *Sociometry,* 29 (December 1966), 378–395.

96

1965 the Justice Party formed a coalition government with several minor parties and then came into power on its own after the 1965 elections. According to one account, the conduct of Justice Party leader Suleyman Demirel suggested "flexibility and willingness to compromise rather than insisting on a whole loaf, a quality which cannot fail to impress those outside the party, much as it may irritate militant partisans within." [3]

The effects of political — as opposed to economic factors — are difficult to specify, since both political and economic conditions improved between 1956 and 1965. The 1956 survey and the data from 1965, collected in the months immediately preceding and following the election, help provide a picture of change over the nine-year period under study. In similar fashion, the historical material on social and political conditions in Turkey in 1956 and 1965 facilitates interpretation of empirical data from these two years.

Turning now to our survey analysis, the longitudinal comparisons utilize three types of information: 1) panel data: information from the same individuals at different stages in their life cycle; 2) age level data: information taken at different times from different people at the same stage in their life cycle; and 3) cross-sectional data: information on individuals at different stages in their life cycles, but experiencing similar societal events. Ninety-seven of the 241 graduates of the Political Science Faculty who responded to both the 1956 and 1965 surveys were from the classes of 1949–1952. For the age level analysis the 1956 responses of this group (Group A') can be compared with the 1965 responses of 69 graduates (Group B) from the classes of 1958–1961. Both groups of graduates, the classes of 1949–1952 and of 1958–1961, have had four to seven years in the working world, but at different points in time. The cross-sectional comparison will be made between the 1965 responses of the 1949–1952 graduates (Group A") and those of the 1958–1961 graduates.

The data in Table 6-1 can be approached in terms of both history (changes taking place within Turkish society) and maturation (changes associated with an individual's life cycle). Considered in isolation, the job satisfaction findings suggest the importance of societal changes. Thus, the two sets of 1965 data on job satisfaction (Groups A" and B) are quite similar, but there are substantial differences between the

3. A. Haluk Ülman and Frank Tachau, "Turkish Politics: the Attempt to Reconcile Rapid Modernization with Democracy," *Middle East Journal,* 19 (Spring 1965), 168.

Table 6-1: Organizational Attitudes and Mobility; Panel, Age Level, and Cross-Sectional Comparisons

	Group A' 1949–1952 grads in 1956 (%)	Group A" 1949–1952 grads in 1965 (%)	Group B 1958–1961 grads in 1965 (%)	Panel comparison (A' and A") (%)	Age Level comparison (A' and B) (%)	Cross-sectional comparison (A" and B) (%)
Percentage of respondents mentioning:						
Satisfied with job	40	60	61	+20[c]	+21[c]	+ 1
Recommend Political Science Faculty[a]	47	63	62	+16[c]	+15[c]	− 1
Work in central ministry or other old organization	96	79	60	−17[c]	−36[c]	−19[c]
Changed ministry or organization since graduation[b]	11	17	26	(6)	15[c]	(9)
Number of respondents	97	97	69			

[a] The item on recommending the Political Science Faculty was included because of its correlation with job satisfaction; this item seemed to provide another measure of such satisfaction. In the past, attendance at this faculty was associated with work in the public bureaucracy.

[b] The time periods used are unequal for any comparison involving Group A", since these 1949–1952 graduates surveyed in 1965 had been out of school on an average of 9 years more than other groups.

[c] Indicates that the difference between groups was significant at the .05 level or better by the appropriate test of significance. McNemar's test for correlated proportions was used for the panel comparisons.

1965 (Groups A" and B) and the 1956 data (Group A'). In 1965 the older graduates (Group A") reported levels of job satisfaction that were distinctly different from the 1956 levels expressed by the same individuals (Group A') and generally similar to the 1965 answers of a group of younger respondents (Group B). Both the job satisfaction item and the item on recommending the faculty show a greater similarity between the cross-sectional measurement taken in 1965 (Groups A'' and B) than between the other comparisons.

But age is important in another context. The data on place of work show a clear trend away from the old organizations; this trend is manifested differently in different age groups. Over the 1956–1965 period, about 15 percent of the panel study respondents from the classes of 1949–1952 left this type of government employment. On the other hand, the 1965 data still show substantial differences between older and younger graduates; 79 percent of the older graduates, as compared with 60 percent of the younger group, worked inside an old organization in 1965.

These findings on job satisfaction and interorganizational mobility are closely linked. Material presented in previous chapters has stressed the higher levels of job satisfaction found outside the Ministries of Interior and Finance. Age, place of work, and rank interact here. Although fewer of the older graduates than of the younger work outside the central ministries, this is partially balanced by the higher positions held by the older graduates. As we shall see later in this chapter, promotion in the Ministry of Interior (although not in the Ministry of Finance) is associated with increased job satisfaction.

Additional information from the 1956 survey indicates that relatively few Political Science Faculty graduates (17 out of a total of 380) were working outside the more established ministries at that time. This is partly a function of the respondents' age; in the past, graduates tended to move only after spending some time in the established ministries. Although the sample may slightly underestimate the percentage of Faculty graduates outside these ministries, in 1956 new opportunities for the graduates were not as widely diffused as in 1965. Armaoğlu and Birkhead note that organizations outside the central government did not yet consider persons who had training in political sciences necessary. In 1956 they could not "absorb even a small percentage of people with such an education." [4] These opportunities seem to have increased gradually through the fifties and sixties with the creation of new ministries and enterprises. The relatively high rate of Turkish eco-

4. Fahir Armaoğlu and Guthrie Birkhead, *Graduates of the Faculty of Political Science, 1946–1955* (Ankara, Public Administration Institute for Turkey and the Middle East, 1957), p. 46.

nomic growth has undoubtedly aided this process. Differences between the older and younger graduates may be due to the fact that the older administrators have become established in ministerial jobs and find it more difficult to switch to jobs in the state economic enterprises and private sector than do the younger respondents. The younger respondents have not become habituated to their jobs; they were more likely to have changed organizations at least once than were their older counterparts. Working outside the central ministries may also increase the visibility of other alternatives. Having once taken a job in a new, noncentral organization the graduate was very likely to move again.

Table 6-2 provides more specific data on place of work. A higher percentage of older graduates than of the younger were employed in the Ministries of Interior, Foreign Affairs, and Finance. Changes in the structure of the Turkish bureaucracy appear related to differences in the percentage of individuals choosing governmental organizations outside the three central ministries (Interior, Finance, and Foreign Af-

Table 6-2: Place of Work for 1956 and 1965 Respondents[a]

Place of work	Group A' 1949–1952 graduates in 1956 (%)	Group A'' 1949–1952 graduates in 1965 (%)	Group B 1958–1961 graduates in 1965 (%)
Ministry of Interior			
District governor	45	27	35
Other work	8	12	1
Ministry of Finance	21	12	6
Ministry of Foreign Affairs	14	13	6
Other old organizations	7	14	12
New government organizations	0	3	6
Banks and other state economic enterprises	4	14	28
Private sector	0	4	6
Number of respondents	97	97	69

[a] Differences between groups were significant at the .05 level for the panel, age level, and cross-sectional comparisons.

100

fairs). Between 1956 and 1965 a number of new ministries, institutes, and other governmental organizations with attractive salary structures were founded. A significant number of individuals left the central ministries between 1956 and 1965; in 1965 both the older and the younger respondents were more likely to be working outside the central ministries than were the 1946–1952 graduates surveyed in 1956. A preference for the new, noncentral organizations was particularly marked among the 1958–1961 graduates, and the relationship held up when corrections for nonresponse bias were made.

The differential holding power of various ministries is also of interest. Between 1956 and 1965 there was essentially no decline in the percentage of respondents remaining in the Ministry of Foreign Affairs. Proportionally, the Ministry of Finance and the Ministry of Interior experienced roughly similar losses over the nine-year period. The percentage of 1956 respondents in the Ministry of Finance declined from 31 to 23 percent, while the percentage in the Ministry of Interior also dropped markedly (from 46 to 35 percent).[5]

These data on job mobility become more understandable when linked with information on outside opportunities and job satisfaction. As noted earlier, the demand for individuals with financial training was particularly strong. The same factors that contributed to the stature of the Ministry of Finance — an expanding economy, focus on planned development, and increased appreciation for technical skills — also contributed to a situation in which the Ministry of Finance had to compete with all other governmental organizations and with the private sector for people with appropriate training. Table 6-3 demonstrates the 1965 distribution of the 1946–1955 graduates in our study. Graduates of the financial section of the Political Science Faculty were distributed throughout the economy, with only about half of them found in the Ministry of Finance. The contrast with graduates of the other two sections is clear: 73 percent of the administrative section graduates in our sample worked in the Ministry of the Interior (either as district governors or in the central offices) and 85 percent of the political section graduates worked in the Ministry of Foreign Affairs.

5. These figures are based on the sample of 380 1946–1955 graduates (which includes both 1965 respondents and nonrespondents); the changes shown in Table 6-2 are roughly equivalent to the changes observed over the entire sample. Because of nonresponse bias in 1965, the Ministry of Finance is somewhat under-represented in the panel data using the 1965 respondents. A similar problem existed for the 1958–1961 graduates studied in 1965. Of the 126 graduates sent questionnaires, 13 percent were in the Ministry of Finance.

Table 6-3: Distribution of 1946–1955 Graduates of Different Sections of Political Science Faculty[a]

| | Section Attended | | |
1965 place of work	Adminis-tration (%)	Finance (%)	Political (%)
Ministry of Interior	73	3	0
Ministry of Finance	3	51	0
Ministry of Foreign Affairs	1	5	85
Other old organizations	9	11	10
New government organizations	4	5	0
Banks and other state economic enterprises	6	20	0
Private sector	5	6	5
Number of respondents	176	161	39

[a] Differences were significant at the .05 level.

Not only did graduates of the financial section seem to have more employment options, but respondents in various organizations recognized the importance of training in economics and finance. Graduates were asked: "Which of your courses should be added to the curriculum and which courses should be emphasized?" and "If you were planning a six months' training course for administrators, what specific topics do you think it would be most valuable to include?" In Table 6-4 responses dealing with economics and finance are contrasted with those mentioning legal training.

The Turkish administrative elite seems to have responded to the new demands made by the shift from a regulative to a production-oriented system. Graduates in all organizations felt the need for an understanding of economics to deal with the new demands of development. Corresponding with this adjustment was the comparatively low value placed upon legal training. The only group still emphasizing the importance of law was found in the Ministry of Interior. The need was real for these graduates, since almost all of them had worked in the provincial administrative system. In such posts Ministry of Interior officials

Table 6-4: Course Orientations of Political Science Faculty Graduates in Various Organizations[a]

	Minis-try of Interior (%)	Minis-try of Finance (%)	Minis-try of Foreign Affairs (%)	Other old organi-zations (%)	New, noncentral organi-zations (%)
Economics Courses					
Two or more	32	53	50	53	54
One	39	36	35	35	35
Not mentioned	30	11	15	12	10
Law Courses					
Two or more	35	9	18	29	25
One	47	33	41	53	30
Not mentioned	18	58	41	18	44
Number of respondents	114	45	34	34	79

[a] The differences between the course orientations of graduates in various organizations were significant at the .05 level.

draw constantly upon their knowledge of the legal structure and, according to one study, should have even more legal training.[6]

Elite Mobility

One approach to elite mobility is provided by the literature on innovation.[7] By identifying the "innovators" as those individuals joining the new, noncentral organizations relatively early in their careers, both the 1946–1955 and 1958–1961 graduates can be considered from a similar perspective. Innovators are typically characterized as venturesome, as able to absorb the loss of an unprofitable innovation, and as possessing specialized or technical knowledge. A majority of innovators

6. Robert V. Presthus with Sevda Erem, *Statistical Analysis in Comparative Administration: The Turkish Consel d'Etat* (Ithaca, Cornell University Press, 1958), pp. 40–41.

7. Much of this literature is summarized in Everett M. Rogers, *Diffusion of Innovations* (New York, Free Press, 1962).

may come from formerly high-status groups which have suffered a loss of status from social or political changes. This formulation seems relevant to the 1946–1955 graduates employed in the new, noncentral organizations at the time of the 1956 survey, and to the 1958–1961 graduates working in such organizations in 1965.

Although there are substantial differences between 1956 and 1965 in the percentage of respondents classified as innovators (5 percent in 1956 and 40 percent in 1965), at both time periods the innovators tended to be sons of officials who had graduated from the financial section. Since the official group had suffered a status loss, the findings were clearly in line with the theory. The sons of officials were not more likely than others in their group to attend the financial section, but rather seemed particularly likely to seek work in the new, noncentral organizations. The data suggest that these graduates — given their less-than-outstanding grades and their family-derived knowledge of opportunities in the bureaucracy — realized that their career opportunities would be better outside of the traditional occupational channels. Perhaps these sons of officials were particularly sensitive to the loss of status which the bureaucracy had suffered. In 1956 the innovators were predominantly respondents with only fair grades, but by 1965 grades did not seem to be an important variable.

These individuals who joined the new, noncentral organizations shortly after graduation possessed characteristics setting them off from other respondents in the sample. The older graduates who moved to new, noncentral organizations during the 1956–1965 period seemed more generally representative of the sample; our further analysis deals with this mobility, focusing upon the respondents leaving the Ministries of Interior and Finance.

The differing demand for graduates of the three sections is clearly one factor underlying rates of mobility out of various ministries. Another factor is the level of job satisfaction. Table 6-5 shows that a number of dissatisfied individuals had left the Ministries of Interior and Finance for more agreeable work elsewhere. Job satisfaction in the Ministry of Interior was considerably less than in the other organizations in which Political Science Faculty graduates are likely to work. Although students of American organizations have postulated that much of the enhanced satisfaction of job-changers is due to the psychological phenomenon of short-term dissonance reduction after a difficult choice, this reaction did not seem prevalent among the Turkish respondents.[8] These administrators appear to have responded to objective differences in working conditions; satisfaction remained high regardless of how long a respondent had worked in a new, noncentral organization.[9]

Some of the reasons for the holding power and high job satisfaction observed in the Ministry of Foreign Affairs have been presented earlier. The comparatively small size, overseas cost-of-living allowances, and easy relationship between superior and subordinate contribute to high levels of job satisfaction reported by graduates working in the Ministry of Foreign Affairs. Chapter 5 stressed the prestige of the Ministry of Foreign Affairs and the high percentage of university graduates ("high status individuals") working there. Several propositions from March and Simon are relevant to this ministry:[10]

1. The greater the number of high status occupations and/or individuals in the organization, the stronger the identification of individual participants with it.

2. Individual participants who belong to an organization that has greater prestige than those to which other individuals of the same education and experience normally belong will identify more strongly with the organization than will others.

The continued popularity of the Ministry of Foreign Affairs lends

8. Victor H. Vroom and Edward L. Deci, "The Stability of Post-Decision Dissonance: A Follow-up Study of the Job Attitudes of Business School Graduates," unpublished paper, Graduate School of Industrial Administration, Carnegie-Mellon University, 1969. For a general evaluation of dissonance theory, see Robert B. Zajonc, "Cognitive Theories in Social Psychology," in Gardner Lindzey and Elliot Aronson, eds., *The Handbook of Social Psychology* (Reading, Mass., Addison-Wesley, 1968), I, 320–411.

9. Further analysis was performed using the respondent's number of reasons for satisfaction or dissatisfaction as a tentative index of the intensity of his feelings. The changes were in close accord with those reported in Table 6-5; the most dramatic changes occurred among respondents leaving the Ministry of Interior. Generally similar findings were obtained for the item on recommending the Political Science Faculty. Graduates who left the Ministries of Interior and Finance to work in new organizations, state economic enterprises, and so forth, were the most likely to change their evaluation of the Faculty. Of these graduates, in 1956 only 50 percent of those who were to leave the Ministry of Interior and 38 percent of their counterparts in the Ministry of Finance recommended the Political Science Faculty. By 1965, 75 percent of the respondents who left the Ministry of Interior for the new, noncentral organizations and 81 percent of those who left the Ministry of Finance recommended the Faculty. Such multiple indicator findings are discussed more extensively in Appendix C.

10. James G. March and Herbert A. Simon with the collaboration of Harold Guetzkow, *Organizations* (New York, Wiley, 1958), p. 75.

Table 6-5: Job Satisfaction and Job Change (1956 and 1965)

Position in		Satisfied with position		Number of respond- ents[a]
1956	1965	1956 (%)	1965 (%)	
STAYING				
Assistant district governor[b]	District governor	25	30	20
District governor	District governor	40	43	35
Ministry of Finance	Ministry of Finance	61	61	38
Ministry of Foreign Affairs	Ministry of Foreign Affairs	92	89	26
New, noncentral organizations	New, noncentral organizations	90	100	10
MAJOR PROMOTION[c]				
District governor	Higher-level in Interior	37	63	27
MOVING				
Assistant district governor and district governor	Other old organizations	20	80	10
Assistant district governor and district governor	New, noncentral organizations	19	81	16
Ministry of Finance	New, noncentral organizations	53	86	21

[a] The 241 individuals who responded to both the 1956 and the 1965 surveys provide the data for Table 6-5. There were 38 respondents whose 1956 jobs or 1956–1965 job changes did not fit into the pattern.

[b] Within the Ministry of Interior, the promotion from assistant district governor to district governor is essentially automatic. The more successful district governors are promoted, after a number of years, to higher level positions in the ministry.

[c] The differences between 1956 and 1965 satisfaction were significant at better than the .05 level for the Major Promotion group in Interior and for the groups leaving Finance and Interior (data for respondents moving into the other old organizations and the new organizations were pooled). These findings are discussed further in Appendix C.

support to another proposition. Downs has noted that "an organization can maintain high-quality personnel even if it does not experience relatively rapid growth in size, so long as it experiences such growth in the incentives it offers its members.[11] Between 1939 and 1960, the Ministry of Finance grew from 9,800 employees to 15,800, a 61 percent increase, while the Ministry of Interior expanded from 5,800 to 8,800, an increase of 52 percent, and the Ministry of Foreign Affairs added fewer than 200 employees (from 600 to under 800), an increase of about 30 percent. Despite this slow growth, the quality of personnel and job satisfaction within the Ministry of Foreign Affairs has remained very high. The benefits associated with foreign service — particularly the cost-of-living differential — have grown in order to permit diplomats to enjoy an appropriate standard of living.

On the other hand, organizational growth generally brings many benefits. March and Simon have suggested that "the faster the growth of the organization, the stronger the identification of individual participants with it." [12] The organizations started after 1950 have grown considerably since their founding. The largest of the new organizations characteristically employing Political Science Faculty graduates was the Ministry of Tourism and Information, with 1,015 employees (as of 1963), while the smallest, with 153 employees, was the State Planning Organization.

There were some differences in job satisfaction among the various types of organizations. Ninety-three percent of the graduates in the new ministerial organizations reported being satisfied with their jobs, as did 94 percent of the respondents in the private sector. Within the state sector there were considerable differences between graduates working in banks and those in other state economic enterprises. Eighty-eight percent of those in banks said they were satisfied, as compared with only 67 percent of the respondents in the other enterprises. The causes of this variation are not completely clear, but the respondents in the state enterprises were markedly less likely than their counterparts to mention "little political interference" as a reason for job satisfaction. Over 55 percent of the graduates in each of the other categories (new organizations, banks, and private sector) mentioned "little political interference," but only 25 percent of the respondents in the other state enterprises noted this reason for job satisfaction.

11. Anthony Downs, *Inside Bureaucracy* (Boston, Little, Brown, 1967), p. 264.
12. March and Simon, *Organizations,* p. 75.

Ministries of Interior and Finance

The data on job satisfaction and social background permit a comparison of occupational mobility between the Ministries of Interior and Finance. In the Ministry of Finance, dissatisfaction in 1956 was followed by promotion in the 1956–1965 period, while in the Ministry of Interior such dissatisfaction was particularly associated with leaving the Ministry. In the Ministry of Interior promotion led to increased job satisfaction, while this did not seem to be true in the Ministry of Finance.[13] The reasons for this are not clear; although respondents in the Ministry of Interior checked significantly more reasons for dissatisfaction than did those in the Ministry of Finance, holding job level constant eliminated many of these differences.

Some of the differences in rates of leaving the Ministries of Interior and Finance can be discussed in terms of three basic variables mentioned by March and Simon: the level of satisfaction with the organization, the visibility of acceptable alternatives, and the availability of these alternatives.[14] The respondents with financial training seem more likely to have had numerous contacts with individuals in the new enterprises and the state economic enterprises than were graduates in the Ministry of Interior. Many of the graduates in the Ministry of Finance combined work in Ankara with frequent inspection visits to the provinces; the nature of their work gave them wide contacts with other organizations which might be interested in their training. On the other hand, because of the demand for their skills, graduates in the Ministry of Finance are more visible than are their classmates in the Ministry of Interior. March and Simon's "level of satisfaction with the existing alternative" has already been dealt with; respondents in the Ministry of Interior were more likely to be dissatisfied than those in the Ministry of Finance.

The promotional possibilities within Interior are difficult to compare with those in Finance. Within the Ministry of Finance, graduates generally work as specialists. Many accountants (*hesap uzmanı*) and financial inspectors (*maliye müfettiş*) are at roughly the same level as

13. Only 5 out of the 13 panel study respondents (38 percent) in high-level positions in the Ministry of Finance in 1965 reported being satisfied with their jobs.

14. March and Simon, *Organizations,* pp. 107–108. They mention a fourth variable — the propensity to search for alternatives. Unfortunately we have no data relating to this.

108

Table 6-6: Job Satisfaction and Career Patterns in the Ministries of Interior and Finance (1956–1965)[a]

	Position by 1965				
	Re-mained in similar position (%)	Pro-moted to higher position (%)	Moved to other old ministry[b] (%)	Moved to non-central organi-zation (%)	Number of respond-ents
1956 District governors:[c]					
Satisfied	53	33	13	3	40
Dissatisfied	42	24	18	17	84
1956 respondents in low-level positions in Finance:[c]					
Satisfied	58	10	6	27	52
Dissatisfied	32	26	20	23	31

[a] This table utilizes both the 1965 respondents and the 1965 nonrespondents who occupied the relevant positions in 1956.

[b] In this category are included the two remaining central ministries (other than the one in which the respondent worked) and other ministries founded before 1950.

[c] Differences were significant at the .05 level for the respondents in both the Ministries of Interior and Finance.

district governors. Promotions within Finance tend to occur in steps within one's specialty. Of the 313 slots for inspectors and accountants, 237 were ranked as low and only 76 as high. Within the Ministry of Interior there were a number of higher-ranking positions to which district governors might aspire. In 1957 Gorvine and Payaslïoğlu mentioned 344 positions into which the 493 district governors could be directly promoted; these figures were roughly applicable for 1965.[15]

15. Albert Gorvine and Arif Payaslïoğlu, "The Administrative Career Service in Turkish Provincial Government," *International Review of Administrative Sciences,* 23 (1957), 472. The positions to which the district governors could be promoted were: assistant provincial governor — 81; member of board of

The information presented above is relevant to two theoretical constructs. As might be predicted from the March and Simon framework, rates of turnover in the Ministries of Interior and Finance were roughly similar. On the one hand, the effects of the greater visibility of outside alternatives for graduates in the Ministry of Finance and, on the other, the effects of the higher levels of dissatisfaction in the Ministry of Interior seem to cancel each other out. The data on satisfaction also aid ranking ministries according to Hage's predictors of organizational adaptability — job satisfaction and organizational stratification. The Ministry of Interior fares poorly with respect to both these variables. If stratification refers to "the disparity in rewards between the top and bottom status levels," [16] the major discontinuity between the district governor's levels of satisfaction and those found in higher positions in Interior is important. No such discontinuity is present in the other organizations; this finding suggests a higher degree of stratification — and lower adaptability — in Interior.

The panel study data provide another perspective on job changes. Although social background variables were fairly good predictors of the movement of Political Science Faculty graduates out of certain positions in the Ministries of Interior and Finance, these variables seem to have operated somewhat differently in the two ministries. As Table 6-7 indicates, individuals from privileged backgrounds were generally more likely to leave their jobs as district governors than were those with other backgrounds. On the other hand, there appeared to be no regular relationship between social background and the probability of a district governor's promotion. Those from less privileged backgrounds were about as likely to move to responsible positions in the Ministry of Interior as were their more favored counterparts.

The data from the Ministry of Finance show a different pattern. Respondents from privileged backgrounds may have been promoted more rapidly than the less privileged graduates. When sons of officials from metropolitan backgrounds were considered separately, the differences were especially striking. Thirty-three percent of the respondents in the Ministry of Finance who were both sons of officials and from metropol-

---

inspection — 80; provincial governor — 66; provincial security chief — 66; section chief in central organization — 25; head of general directorate — 12; member of the central organization of security — 10; member of the board of research — 4.

16. Jerald Hage, "An Axiomatic Theory of Organizations," *Administrative Science Quarterly*, 10 (December 1965), 289–320.

110

itan backgrounds ($n = 15$) were promoted; only 14 percent of the respondents who were sons of officials and lived outside the metropolitan
areas ($n = 28$) were promoted from relatively low-level to relatively
high-level positions in the same nine-year period. Again, no such differences were found in the Ministry of Interior.

Table 6-7: Social Background and Career Patterns in the Ministries
of Interior and Finance (1956–1965)[a]

	Position by 1965				
	Re-mained in similar position (%)	Pro-moted to higher position (%)	Moved to other old ministry[b] (%)	Moved to non-central organi-zation (%)	Number of respond-ents
1956 District governors:[c]					
Privileged	28	20	24	28	25
Less privileged	50	28	14	8	100
1956 respondents in low-level positions in Finance:					
Privileged	46	25	13	17	24
Less privileged	52	11	11	27	56

[a] This table utilizes both the 1965 respondents and the 1965 nonrespondents
who occupied the relevant positions in 1956. Similar patterns were noted
among respondents to the 1956 district governor survey.

[b] In this category are included the two remaining central ministries (other
than the one in which the respondent worked) and other ministries founded
before 1950.

[c] Differences were significant at the .05 level for respondents in the Ministry
of Interior, but not in the Ministry of Finance.

From a more general perspective, movement appears easier for the
graduates from the more privileged groups. In the Ministry of Interior,
where working conditions were most difficult, these administrators
were more likely to leave. In the situation where conditions were more

satisfactory — the Ministry of Finance — the more privileged individuals may have been more likely to be promoted.

Relationships among Variables

A more systematic analysis of the relationships among variables produced some surprising findings. The predictors of career mobility varied both over time in one ministry (Interior) and between ministries (Interior and Finance). Here we are dealing with relationships which are presumed to be more important for theory-building than percentage comparisons among marginal frequencies, yet regularities are hard to isolate.[17] Such findings illustrate the organizational diversity found within the governmental structure of one political system. In the face of this within-system variation, the difficulties associated with cross-national studies should be obvious.

At the time of the 1956 survey, the respondents in the Ministry of Interior were all in the relatively undesirable positions of district governor or assistant governor. Few of the respondents' classmates had been promoted out of the district administrator category. The relationships between either rank in Interior or year of graduation, on the one hand, and 1956 job satisfaction on the other were comparatively small. The main relationships were between social background, job satisfaction, and 1965 place of work. Graduates from more privileged backgrounds were more likely to be dissatisfied with their work and to leave the Ministry of Interior over the 1956–1965 period. Dissatisfied graduates were also more likely to leave during this nine-year period, but the magnitude of the coefficients in Table 6-8 suggests that social background affected career mobility independent of its effects upon job satisfaction.[18]

The data on 1965 rank in the Ministry of Interior are less clearcut. The main predictors of 1965 rank are two intercorrelated variables — the respondent's year of graduation and his rank nine years earlier. Compared to these variables, the coefficients reported for social background and 1956 job satisfaction are relatively small. However, given

17. For a discussion of theory-building in comparative studies, see Adam Przeworski and Henry Teune, *The Logic of Comparative Social Inquiry* (New York, Wiley, 1970).

18. The absolute value of the association between social background and 1965 job (staying in the Ministry of Interior or leaving) is higher than the association between job satisfaction and 1965 job.

112

Table 6-8: Predictors of Career Mobility — Ministry of Interior[a]

	Social background (high; low)	1956 job satisfaction (satisfied; dissatisfied)	1956 rank in Interior (district governor; low)	Faculty grades (good; fair)	Year of faculty graduation (1946–50; 1951–55)
1965 job (Interior; moved)	−.19[b]	.11	−.01	−.07	.07
1965 rank in Interior (high; district governor)	.07	.08	.13	.06	.22[b]
Social background		−.18[b]	.01	.03	.04
1956 job satisfaction			−.12	.00	.01
1956 rank in Interior				−.01	.54[b]
Faculty grades					−.12

[a] The values of the product-moment correlations are shown here. All variables are dichotomized. Data from 160 respondents in the Ministry of Interior in 1956 form the basis for this table. Correlation coefficients are calculated from these respondents, except for the coefficients relating 1965 rank in Interior with various factors. These runs were made utilizing 113 respondents remaining in the Ministry of Interior in 1965. Gamma values were about twice those of the product-moment correlations.

[b] This relationship was significant at the .05 level.

the structural constraints of an administrative system in which seniority is critical and formal demotion unlikely, these latter associations are the more interesting and form the basis for our earlier discussion.

Further analysis of the panel data from the Ministry of Interior permits a comparison of actual mobility and the expressed desire to leave. Several points emerge from the data presented in Table 6-9. Respondents from more privileged backgrounds tended to leave the Ministry of Interior between 1956 and 1965; those who remained in Interior in

1965 appeared more committed to this ministry than their counterparts from less privileged backgrounds. Job satisfaction was a predictor both of actual leaving and of the expressed desire to leave. As noted earlier, the effects of rank on mobility varied according to the overall career stages of our pool of respondents. Early in the administrator's career, his rank was not correlated with staying or leaving. But when bureaucrats were promoted out of district governors' jobs into high-level positions in the Ministry of Interior, they were reluctant to leave. More generally, these data illustrate how both selective leaving and career patterns may alter the relationships among variables studied at two different times in a single organization. Such differences would not be picked up on a single cross-sectional study.

Data from the Ministry of Finance exhibit a somewhat different pattern from the Interior data. Although 1956 job satisfaction is correlated with the respondent's 1965 job (staying in the Ministry of Finance or leaving), social background alone is not an important predictor of staying or leaving. Among the graduates in the Ministry of Finance, the older, more high-ranking graduates were more likely to leave than were their younger counterparts; this was true despite the marked positive association between rank and job satisfaction which existed in 1956. Such a loss of the higher-ranking administrators suggests the pull effect provided by outside opportunities.

The predictors of 1965 rank within Finance were different from the predictors of staying or of leaving. The strongest correlation was between 1965 rank and social background; a disproportionate number of graduates from more privileged backgrounds were likely to be promoted to high-level positions in the 1956–1965 period. The relationships between 1965 rank and the other variables were substantially weaker. Problems of nonresponse bias did not permit further analysis of the panel data from the Ministry of Finance.

The correlation matrices generated for the Ministries of Interior and Finance differ significantly. The signs of the coefficients are similar for only 10 of the 20 entries in the two matrices. Moreover, there are marked differences in the magnitudes of the coefficients whose signs do agree. Since roughly similar respondents are involved in each ministry (i.e., all are Political Science Faculty graduates) and since the differences between ministries hold controlling for the social background of the respondents, differential recruitment cannot be responsible for the variation between organizations. We need to treat the findings in terms of concepts which operate at the organizational level, for such factors

114

Table 6-9: Mobility and Nonmobility in the Ministry of Interior (1956 and 1965)[a]

	Social back-ground (high; low)	Job satis-faction (satis-fied; dis-satisfied)	Rank in Interior (rel. high; rel. low)	Faculty grades (good; fair)	Year of Faculty gradu-ation (1946–50; 1951–55)
Mobility and non-mobility of panel respondents in Interior in 1956 (stayed; moved between 1956 and 1965)	−.24[b]	.16 (1956 satis-faction)	−.02 (1956 rank)	.01	.10
Attitude toward moving expressed by panel respondents in Interior in 1965 (wanted to stay; wanted to move)	.23[b]	.16 (1965 satis-faction)	.23[b] (1965 rank)	−.06	.11

[a] The values of the product-moment correlations are shown here. All variables are dichotomized. The first row of coefficients in this table corresponds to that of Table 6-8, except that only panel respondents ($n = 106$) are used here. The second row of coefficients was generated using 78 panel respondents remaining in the Ministry of Interior in 1965. For 1956 rank the sample was divided between district governors and lower-level positions; in 1965 the sample was split between higher-level positions and district governors. The table relates the respondents' mobility or nonmobility in the 1956–1965 period and his desire to move in 1965 to the appropriate variables at each time period.

[b] This relationship was significant at the .05 level.

seem critical to the relationships among the individual-level variables.

To state the problem another way, the differences between the Ministries of Interior and Finance might be summarized in more general terms:

Table 6-10: Predictors of Career Mobility — Ministry of Finance[a]

	Social background (high; low)	1956 job satisfaction (satisfied; dissatisfied)	1956 rank in Finance (high; low)	Faculty grades (good; fair)	Year of faculty graduation (1946–50; 1951–55)
1965 job (Finance; moved)	.06	.18[b]	−.09	−.01	−.10
1965 rank in Finance (high; low)	.21[b]	−.06	.16	−.03	−.10
Social background		−.18[b]	.01	.10	−.06
1956 job satisfaction			.45[b]	.17[b]	.12
1956 rank in Finance				.15	.24[b]
Faculty grades					.10

[a] The values of all variables are dichotomized. Data from 108 respondents in the Ministry of Finance in 1956 form the basis for this table. Correlation coefficients are calculated from these respondents, except for the coefficients relating 1965 rank in Finance with various factors. These runs were made utilizing 68 respondents remaining in the Ministry of Finance in 1965.

[b] This relationship was significant at the .05 level.

1. Predictors of turnover will vary from organization to organization. Although job satisfaction was a good predictor of staying or leaving both ministries, the role of social background, ministerial rank, and year of graduation differed between the Ministries of Interior and Finance.

2. Predictors of career success will vary from organization to organization. As would be expected, 1956 rank was correlated with 1965 rank within both ministries; but this finding was trivial. Social background appeared to play a greater role in the Ministry of Finance than in the Ministry of Interior, while the role of seniority clearly differed in the two organizations. Job satisfaction was not consistently related to career success.

116

But just noting the presence of variation is not enough; an attempt must be made to explain such variation.

Organizational Status and Career Mobility

The perspective provided by organization theory is broadened by considering a development-related paradox. In the organization performing the more professional and technical work (the Ministry of Finance), the patterns of promotion seem more ascriptive than in the more traditionally bureaucratic organization (the Ministry of Interior). Organizations may clearly differ with respect to several factors which might be expected to make up a single "modernization" dimension. But from a theory-building standpoint, the possibly significant differences between the Ministries of Interior and Finance cannot be systematically explored with the comparative case study data available here. Instead, we can only advance some reasons for the interorganizational variation, building upon the material presented in the earlier chapters. Here we suggest that differences in organizational status underlie many of the differences in career mobility between the Ministries of Interior and Finance. Stratification theory and organization theory must be combined in order to interpret the findings.

Reference to different system-level pressures upon the Ministries of Interior and Finance can contribute to an understanding of our findings. The consequences of the ruralizing election of 1950 have made the district governor's role a particularly difficult one, while economic growth and the demand for technical skills have made a career in the Ministry of Finance less attractive now than it was in 1956. Individuals in the Ministry of Finance may suffer from relative deprivation when they compare themselves with their counterparts from the financial section of the Political Science Faculty who are making much more money elsewhere. Relative deprivation — the fact that individuals compare their own experiences with their past, with their expectations, and with the jobs held by their acquaintances — is related to several other social comparison processes.[19] Vroom, for example, has noted that feelings of inequity or injustice arise "as a response to perceived discrepancies between the ratios of rewards to such 'inputs' or 'invest-

19. One study has noted that "the greater the obstacles the person has overcome in order to obtain the organization's rewards the greater the commitment." See Oscar Grusky, "Career Mobility and Organizational Commitment," *Administrative Science Quarterly*, 10 (March 1966), 488–503.

ments' on the part of individuals." [20] From a slightly different perspective, graduates working as district governors and in the Ministry of Finance may be especially subject to "role strain," finding it difficult to fulfill all their role demands.[21]

Concepts such as "feelings of inequity" and "role strain" are rather difficult to operationalize. If feelings of inequity can arise for a number of reasons, it is probably hard to specify when these feelings are present to such a degree as to affect other variables. A more useful concept may be that of "status incongruence." Status incongruence occurs when two conditions are present: some status factors of an individual rank much higher than others and these differences are inconsistent with the normative expectations of the environment in which the given individual moves. We presume that the expectations of the Political Science Faculty graduate and of his family and friends (a significant part of his "environment") are that he will occupy an important respected position in Turkish society. But the status of the Ministry of Interior in particular has been affected by social changes; Faculty graduates in this ministry and in Finance may be subject to status incongruence. Protracted job dissatisfaction may be an indicator of this incongruence; status incongruence may be responsible for the fact that several hypotheses from American organizational research are not verified by these data.[22]

This set of findings from the Turkish data relates to seniority, promotion, and job satisfaction. A number of American studies have found that 1) length of time in an organization is positively associated with job satisfaction;[23] and 2) rank in an organization is positively associated with job satisfaction.[24]

The Turkish data are somewhat complicated. For district governors

20. Victor H. Vroom, "Industrial Social Psychology," in Lindzey and Aronson, eds., Handbook of Social Psychology, V, 205.

21. William J. Goode, "A Theory of Role Strain," American Sociological Review, 25 (August 1960), 483–496.

22. Andrzej Malewski, "The Degree of Status Incongruence and Its Effects," in Reinhard Bendix and Seymour Martin Lipset, eds., Class, Status, and Power (New York, Free Press, 1966), pp. 303–308.

23. This proposition was suggested by the discussion in Richard M. Cyert and Kenneth R. MacCrimmon, "Organizations," in Lindzey and Aronson, eds., Handbook of Social Psychology, I, 573. See also March and Simon, Organizations, p. 74; March and Simon hypothesize that "apart from self-selection the length of time (in an organization) itself results in increased identification."

24. Vroom, Work and Motivation, pp. 130–132.

118

and assistant district governors within the Ministry of Interior, neither seniority nor rank was associated with job satisfaction. Promotion out of the district governor's job was what was critical. On the other hand, within the Ministry of Finance, rank (but not year of graduation) was significantly correlated with job satisfaction in 1956, but by 1965 there was essentially no relationship between rank and seniority on the one hand and job satisfaction on the other.

Status incongruence and organizational stratification can help explain other kinds of data. Differential status incongruence may be responsible for the fact that, in both the Ministries of Interior and Finance, respondents from privileged backgrounds were more likely to be dissatisfied than were their less privileged counterparts. But, depending upon the organization, such dissatisfaction may manifest itself in a number of ways. The data indicate that in a less desirable organization (the Ministry of Interior), the efforts of relatively privileged individuals may be directed toward moving into another organization. On the other hand, in a higher-status organization (the Ministry of Finance) the efforts of such individuals may be directed toward being promoted within the organization. Such a formulation suggests why the predictors of turnover and career success vary both between the two ministries studied here and within each ministry. In the higher-status organization the resources of the graduates from privileged backgrounds (perhaps including influence and connections) were used for promotion; in the lower-status organization these resources appear to have been used to escape.

Data on job turnover can also be summarized and integrated with organization theory findings from American research. The scope of a number of findings can be increased by reference to the Turkish material; the basic model forwarded by March and Simon is used here.

1) The rate of turnover is a function of the desire to move (low job satisfaction). This was true for both the Ministries of Interior and Finance; the respondent's job satisfaction was associated with remaining within his organization.[25]

25. Peter M. Blau, "Organizations: Theories of Organizations," in David L. Sills, ed., *International Encyclopedia of the Social Sciences,* (New York, Macmillan and Free Press, 1968), XI, 302–303, and March and Simon, *Organizations,* pp. 100–108. March and Simon mention an additional factor — the propensity to search for alternatives. They suggest that "the greater the habituation to a particular job or organization, the less the propensity to search for alternative work opportunities." Unfortunately, we have no data relating to this

2) The rate of turnover is a function of the perceived availability of outside alternatives (the perceived ease of moving). This perceived availability of outside alternatives is a function of the visibility of the alternatives and the actual availability of acceptable alternatives. Some propositions are directly relevant to visibility:

a. The larger the number of organizations visible to the participant, the greater the number of extraorganizational alternatives. Here we have assumed that, due to the nature of their work, Political Science Faculty graduates in the Ministry of Finance find more organizations visible to them than do their counterparts in the Ministry of Interior. No direct data were available. Other propositions concern the actual availability of alternatives:

b. Changes in technology may raise the number of extraorganizational alternatives available to some workers and lower the number available to others. Both the Turkish data on organizational choice and that on preferred field of university training have suggested how technical changes have increased the number of alternatives available to graduates with economics training.

c. The higher the level of economic activity, the greater the number of extraorganizational alternatives. This proposition seemed to be true, but there were several ·complicating factors. Lags between the starting of an activity and a demand for trained individuals may cause lags in the number of available alternatives. Political instability associated with particular kinds of activity may act to limit the extraorganizational alternatives which an individual will consider.

Finally, March and Simon advance several propositions linking an individual's characteristics to his perceived availability. We lack such perceptual data, but do have information on actual movement. The hypotheses are reworded to relate to such mobility, rather than to perceived availability:

d. The older the individual, the less likely he is to move. The younger graduates of the Political Science Faculty, those from

propensity to search for alternatives. Most of the propositions listed are summarized from March and Simon, but these are just a subset of their propositions.

the classes of 1958–1961, did tend to move more than their older counterparts. Among the graduates from the classes of 1946 to 1955, there were no strong relationships between date of graduation (a measure of approximate age) and turnover.

e. The higher an individual's rank, the less likely he is to move.[26] The data here are rather complex. Reflecting the findings on satisfaction, district governors seemed about as apt to leave the Ministry of Interior as were the assistant district governors. On the other hand, even in relatively undesirable organizations like the Ministry of Interior, positions of sufficient rank (above that of district governor) can be quite attractive. Considering the market for their skills, individuals occupying such positions may have few incentives to leave. But when high-ranking individuals are in particular demand outside the organization, higher interorganizational mobility is likely to result. Achievement of high rank in such technical organizations as the Ministry of Finance may provide visibility and validate ability in the eyes of potential employers. Perhaps because of this, there was little relationship between rank and propensity to leave the Ministry of Finance.

f. Members of low status groups will be less likely to move than will be members of high status groups. As discussed earlier, movement out of the Ministry of Interior was greater for individuals from more privileged backgrounds, but few differences were noted for the Ministry of Finance.

26. This hypothesis was suggested by Vroom, *Work and Motivation*, p. 130.

7

Satisfaction and Dissatisfaction

In the previous chapter, job satisfaction, job position, and turnover in various ministries were discussed. This chapter will expand upon these themes by concentrating upon the reasons for satisfaction and dissatisfaction. In the organizational competition for influence and resources, the respondents' subjective evaluation of jobs helps provide a partial measure of organizational success. This analysis will suggest the weak points and strong points of the organizations treated in this study, and show how individual reactions have changed over time.

The longitudinal data are treated here in several different ways. As mentioned earlier, the Turkish data are particularly valuable because cross-cultural information helps test theoretical notions derived from research on American organizations. Moreover, most data from other studies in the developing areas were not collected over time. Other investigators have not been able to study individual job mobility and the effects of such mobility upon attitudes. Another point concerns the micro-macro distinction. Although some material on managers and organizations in developing societies has been available in the past, these data have been treated solely from the perspective of organization theory. A fundamental premise of this discussion is that these organizational changes have a special relevance to politics in a modernizing society. Elite reactions to organizational growth and decline have important implications for the Turkish political system.

Job Rewards and Job Complaints

Individuals can be satisfied or dissatisfied with their jobs for many reasons. As Katz and Kahn have noted: "Rewards are not only monetary; they also include prestige and status, gratifications from interesting work, identifications with group products, and satisfactions from decision-making." [1] Individuals have needs for esteem, autonomy, and a sense of self-actualization; dissatisfaction with one's job might result from a lack of any of these.

1. Daniel Katz and Robert L. Kahn, *The Social Psychology of Organizations* (New York, Wiley, 1966), p. 42. See also Victor H. Vroom, *Work and Motivation* (New York, Wiley, 1964), p. 132.

In dealing with job satisfaction and individual need, a number of questions arise. Three of these will be discussed here:

1. Which reasons for job satisfaction or dissatisfaction seem to be most salient for the individual?

2. What is the relationship between the reasons the individual gives for being satisfied with his work and his reasons for being dissatisfied?

3. How are attitudes toward one's work affected by change in job position and organization?

After a respondent had signified job satisfaction or dissatisfaction, he was asked to check one or more reasons for expressing this attitude. The wording of the reasons for satisfaction and dissatisfaction varied according to context. Thus, "little political interference" (as a reason for satisfaction) and "too much political interference" (as a reason for dissatisfaction) can be subsumed under "political factors." Combining the respondents liking their jobs for a particular reason with those disliking their work for the same reason produces a measure of saliency for each reason.

The work of Haire, Ghiselli, and Porter on managerial job satisfaction provides some of the analytical categories. These categories are derived from Maslow's work on the hierarchy of need satisfaction.[2] According to Maslow, a particular class of needs will tend to be most salient at a given point in time for a given individual. As a class of needs at a lower level in the hierarchy (such as the need for security) becomes satisfied, Maslow predicts that higher-level needs will become stronger. Following its satisfaction, the strength of a given need decreases.

Table 7-1 shows that pay, political factors, self-realization, and autonomy all seem to be salient reasons for job satisfaction or dissatisfaction. Job prestige and security are clearly less salient. Such findings are interesting from a comparative perspective. Haire, Ghiselli, and Porter's study of 14 countries found self-actualization, autonomy, and security to be important for private sector managers.[3] Items dealing

2. See Mason Haire, Edwin E. Ghiselli, and Lyman W. Porter, *Managerial Thinking: An International Study* (New York, Wiley, 1966) and Douglas T. Hall and Khail E. Nougaim, "An Examination of Maslow's Need Hierarchy in an Organizational Setting," *Organizational Behavior and Human Performance,* 3 (February 1968), 12–35. See also A. H. Maslow, *Motivation and Personality* (New York, Harper, 1954).

3. Since the items on the Haire, Ghiselli, and Porter study were worded differently from the questions included in this research, the comparisons must be made with caution.

with pay and political factors were not used, while prestige was ranked low in importance. The importance of pay and political interference in the Turkish context point up problems of working within any theoretical scheme. Can reasons for satisfaction be equated with needs? Should pay be included in the "security" category and political factors classified under "autonomy"?

Table 7-1: Reasons for Job Satisfaction and Dissatisfaction among Graduates of Political Science Faculty

Reasons mentioned[a]	Group A' 1949–1952 graduates in 1956 (%)	Group A" 1949–1952 graduates in 1965 (%)	Group B 1958–1961 graduates in 1965 (%)
Pay	70	50	42
Political factors	57	50	36
Self-realization			
Opportunity to increase knowledge	57	59	51
Job interest	46	32	29
Autonomy			
Authority	60	52	52
Responsibility	37	39	42
Prestige	34	32	29
Security	42	24	21
Other reasons			
Promotional opportunities	30	21	29
Geographical location	32	27	14
Number of respondents	97	97	69

[a] For panel comparisons, differences of about 10 percent were usually significant at better than the .05 level. For age level and cross-sectional comparisons, differences of about 12 percent were usually significant at better than the .05 level.

Although our data do not permit systematic inter-national comparisons, the comparisons over time provide some perspective. The Turkish data from 1965 suggest a decline in the saliency of pay, political factors, and security. These items were mentioned less frequently by both older and younger 1965 respondents. As would be expected from the discussion in the previous chapter, we suggest that these overall changes are a result of several factors — systemic changes, individual reactions to these changes, and normal promotions. The possibility that some of this change is due to measurement error is treated in Appendix C. A preliminary approach to these data is based on distinguishing the reasons for job satisfaction from those for dissatisfaction.

The relationship between job satisfaction and job dissatisfaction has been the subject of considerable theorizing. One formulation predicts that reasons for job satisfaction are negatively correlated with those for job dissatisfaction: respondents mention different factors, depending upon whether they are satisfied or dissatisfied. Herzberg's two-factor theory of job satisfaction is responsible for this proposition: "The 'motivator' variables lead to high job satisfaction but do not in their absence contribute to job dissatisfaction; the 'hygiene' variables contribute in their absence to job dissatisfaction but not in their presence to job satisfaction." [4] Variables classified as motivators include the opportunities for recognition and achievement, the responsibility of the job, the interest of the work, and the possibilities for promotion. The factors of hygiene include supervision, interpersonal relations, physical working conditions, salary, the policies and administrative practices of the organization, benefits, and job security. Although this theory has been called into question by several studies, it still provides a framework for organizing the data on liking or disliking one's job.

As stressed earlier, the overall levels of job satisfaction vary among the groups studied. Only 40 percent of the 1949–1952 graduates surveyed in 1956 were satisfied with their jobs; by 1965, 60 percent of graduates reported being satisfied. By way of comparison, 61 percent of the 1958–1961 graduates surveyed in 1965 were satisfied with their work. These differences are particularly important since a satisfied individual was permitted to mention only positive reasons; only reasons for dissatisfaction were counted for graduates dissatisfied with their work. As the shift in overall job satisfaction implies, fewer reasons for dissatisfaction were given in 1965 than in 1956. This change was less marked with respect to the reasons for job satisfaction; the increased satisfaction reported in 1965 may have been more dependent

4. Robert Quinn and Robert L. Kahn, "Organizational Psychology," *Annual Review of Psychology,* 18 (1967), p. 456. See also Frederick Herzberg, Bernard Mausner, and Barbara B. Snyderman, *The Motivation to Work* (New York, Wiley, 1959).

Table 7-2: Comparison of Reasons for Job Satisfaction and Dissatisfaction in 1956 and 1965

	Reasons for satisfaction[a]			Reasons for dissatisfaction[a]		
Reasons mentioned[b]	Group A' 1949–1952 graduates in 1956 (%)	Group A'' 1949–1952 graduates in 1965 (%)	Group B 1958–1961 graduates in 1965 (%)	Group A' 1949–1952 graduates in 1956 (%)	Group A'' 1949–1952 graduates in 1965 (%)	Group B 1958–1961 graduates in 1965 (%)
Pay	21	27	26	49	23	16
Political factors	19	36	26	38	14	10
Self-realization Opportunity to increase knowledge	32	42	38	25	17	13
Job interest	28	26	22	18	6	7
Autonomy Authority	28	30	30	32	22	22
Responsibility	24	23	30	13	13	12
Prestige	20	25	20	14	7	9
Security	9	17	9	33	7	12
Other reasons Promotional opportunities	10	12	20	20	9	9
Geographical location	9	16	7	23	11	7
Number of respondents	97	97	69	97	97	69

[a] Individuals could give more than one reason for satisfaction or dissatisfaction. The wording of reasons for satisfaction and dissatisfaction varied as was appropriate in the context. For example, "little political interference" (as a reason for satisfaction) and "too much political interference" (as a reason for dissatisfaction) were listed under "political factors."

[b] For panel comparisons, differences of about 10 percent were usually significant at the .05 level. For age level and cross-sectional comparisons, differences of about 12 percent were usually significant at the .05 level.

126

upon fewer negative factors than upon more positive reasons. Table 7-2 presents the reasons for job satisfaction and dissatisfaction mentioned by the various types of respondents.[5]

The data in Table 7-2 provide a test of the Herzberg two-factor theory of job satisfaction in a non-American environment. The findings are not definitive, but the Herzberg theory is not generally supported. The substantial negative correlations between the reasons for job satisfaction ("motivator" variables) and the reasons for job dissatisfaction ("hygiene" variables) which Herzberg would predict are not found. The three correlations range from .114 for the 1949–1952 graduates surveyed in 1956 to .524 for the 1958–1961 graduates questioned in 1965. Other correlations were calculated for panel respondents who remained in the same ministries in the 1956–1965 period. In no case were the results in line with the Herzberg two-factor theory.

Further analysis indicates that somewhat different reasons for job dissatisfaction were mentioned in 1965 than in 1956. The correlations among the various reasons for dissatisfactions are markedly lower for the 1956–1965 panel (A' and A") and age level (A' and B) comparisons than is the correlation for the cross-sectional (A" and B) comparison.[6] The rank order correlations among reasons for dissatisfaction are .45 (panel comparison), .32 (age level comparison), and .63 (cross-sectional comparison). The corresponding correlations for reasons for satisfaction are .52, .75, and .64 respectively.

Tables 7-1 and 7-2 also suggest that when organizations are under severe strain (as in 1956), the most salient factors may be different from those stressed in more settled times (as in 1965).[7] Among re-

5. It should be noted that the 1949–1952 graduates included in the panel study were not completely representative of the larger group of 241 1946–1955 graduates who responded to both questionnaires. Of the larger group, 52 percent were satisfied in 1956 and 68 percent in 1965. Trends with regard to the reasons for satisfaction or dissatisfaction were, however, similar.

6. Thus, although the absolute percentage of those complaining about their level of responsibility remained constant among the panel respondents between 1956 and 1965, the relative position of this item changed markedly over the nine-year period. Among the 1949–1952 graduates surveyed in 1956, an unsatisfactory level of responsibility was the least frequently selected reason for dissatisfaction. This complaint had moved to fifth among the ten reasons for dissatisfaction listed by these same graduates in 1965.

7. The Ministry of Foreign Affairs was relatively insulated from the changes over the 1956–1965 decade, but there were some attitudinal developments. Graduates who stayed in this ministry were much less likely in 1965 than in 1956 to mention job interest as a reason for satisfaction. The percentage select-

spondents remaining in the Ministries of Interior and Finance over the 1956–1965 period, the only substantial differences (10 percentage points or more) in the reasons for job satisfaction involved a rise in the percentage of respondents mentioning a lack of political interference. Pay and political interference were more salient in 1956, contributing disproportionately to the dissatisfaction prevalent at that time.

The data can be discussed from a slightly different perspective. Reasons for satisfaction and dissatisfaction can be defined as "salient over time" if an individual checks a particular reason in both 1956 and 1965. As long as the same reason is mentioned at both points in time the response is counted, regardless of whether the individual's job satisfaction remained the same or changed.

This approach shifts the focus of the analysis toward the individual. Are reasons important to a given bureaucrat in 1956 also important to him in 1965? Maslow's ideas about the changing saliency of various needs might suggest a negative correlation between the reasons given by an administrator in 1956 and those given by him in 1965; the data do not support such a prediction.

The results showed that an individual's probability of checking a given reason for satisfaction or dissatisfaction in 1965 were largely independent of his choice in 1956. Although each of the reasons — political factors, opportunity to increase knowledge, and authority — was salient over time to between 32 and 40 percent of the respondents, these joint probabilities could have been calculated from the marginal probabilities in 1956 and 1965. Such findings held up for individuals with different career patterns.

The Turkish findings are also at variance with American data suggesting that, as managers advance, their need for security decreases.[8] The Turkish material indicates that differences between 1965 and 1956, differences either in working conditions or in the job market, were responsible for the lower saliency of job security in 1965. Both the older panel respondents and the younger graduates were less con-

ing job interest drops from 77 percent to 39 percent over the nine-year period. Respondents in Foreign Affairs were also less likely to mention prestige, promotional opportunities, and geographical location in 1965 than in 1956. Given the high levels of overall satisfaction in this ministry, these changes do not seem critical. They do indicate, however, that such factors as responsibility and authority commensurate with the job, little political interference, and opportunities to increase knowledge were comparatively more important determinants of job satisfaction in the Ministry of Foreign Affairs in 1965 than in 1956.

8. Hall and Nougaim, "Maslow's Need Hierarchy," p. 12.

128

cerned about job security in 1965 than in 1956. An individual's perception of the demand for his skills — rather than his age or his organizational rank — is probably what is important here.

Socialization versus Recruitment — Job-Related Attitudes

The time-series data also permit a discussion of the relative importance of socialization in a role versus recruitment to a role. According to Katz and Kahn, "the role might shape the attitudes and perceptions of the individual [socialization], or the individual might be selected for his psychological goodness-of-fit to the role requirements [recruitment]." [9] Perhaps the most interesting comparisons are among the panel respondents who in the 1956–1965 period remained district governors, were promoted out of the district governor's job, or left the Ministry of Interior.

The data in Table 7-3 "argue strongly for a causal relationship between the office an individual occupies in an organization and his expressed attitudes on job-relevant matters." [10] Although the 1956 district governors who were later promoted were somewhat more concerned about job security and professional advancement than their less successful colleagues, other differences were slight. But by 1965 there were substantial differences in the job-related attitudes of these two groups.

Selective leaving (and recruitment to new organizations) can also be an important factor. The data presented in Table 7-3 indicate that the 1956 respondents who later left the Ministry of Interior were particularly concerned about their job security. Other factors, such as pay and political interference, were quite important, but responses to the job security item most clearly separated those who moved out of Interior from those who stayed. The reasons for such marked concern are not completely clear; as Table 7-4 shows, the job security item did not distinguish leavers from stayers within the Ministry of Finance. Indeed, there were few attitudinal differences between those who remained in the Ministry of Finance and those who left in the 1956–1965 period.

Differences between the Ministries of Interior and Finance, in 1956 and in 1965 may partially explain the data in Tables 7-3 and 7-4. The 1956 situation in the Ministry of Interior was inherently more stress-

9. Katz and Kahn, *Social Psychology of Organizations,* p. 189.
10. *Ibid.,* p. 189.

Table 7-3: Ministry of Interior — Dissatisfaction and
Mobility (1956–1965)

	Remained in job[a]		Given major promotion[b]		Moved to new job[c]	
	District governor 1956 (%)	District governor 1965 (%)	District governor 1956 (%)	Ministry of Interior 1965 (%)	Asst. dist. gov. and dist. gov. 1956 (%)	New, non-central organization 1965 (%)
Dissatisfied with job	57	54	59	37	81	19
Reasons for dissatisfaction:						
Pay	46	34	52	15	69	0
Political Factors	49	34	48	22	69	0
Lack of self-realization						
No chance to increase knowledge	20	20	15	15	44	13
Lack of job interest	9	0	7	4	19	0
Little autonomy						
Little authority	23	40	26	15	38	13
Little responsibility	11	23	22	7	19	0
Low prestige	9	3	4	4	0	13
Lack of security	17	17	37	11	69	13
Other reasons:						
Few promotional opportunities	9	9	22	7	31	0
Poor geographical location	20	20	19	4	50	0
Number of respondents	35		27		16	

[a] For respondents who remained in their jobs as district governors, the differences between 1956 and 1965 were significant at the .05 level for the reasons concerning authority.

[b] For respondents who were given a major promotion, the differences between 1956 and 1965 were significant at the .05 level for reasons concerning pay, political factors, and job security.

[c] For respondents who moved to a new job, the differences between 1956 and 1965 were significant at the .05 level for all reasons except job interest responsibility, and prestige.

Table 7-4: Ministry of Finance — Dissatisfaction and Mobility (1956–1965)

	Remained in job[a]		Moved to new job[b]	
	Ministry of Finance 1956 (%)	Ministry of Finance 1965 (%)	Ministry of Finance 1956 (%)	New, non-central organization 1965 (%)
Dissatisfied with job	40	37	48	14
Reasons for dissatisfaction:				
Pay	34	24	38	5
Political factors	8	3	5	0
Lack of self-realization				
No chance to increase knowledge	21	5	19	10
Lack of job interest	19	9	29	10
Little autonomy				
Little authority	29	5	33	5
Little responsibility	3	8	0	5
Low prestige	16	8	38	5
Lack of security	13	5	14	5
Other reasons:				
Few promotional opportunities	21	8	24	10
Poor geographical location	3	3	5	5
Number of respondents	38		21	

[a] For respondents who remained in their jobs, the differences between 1956 and 1965 were significant at the .05 level for the reason concerning authority.

[b] For respondents who moved to a new job, the differences between 1956 and 1965 were significant at the .05 level for reasons concerning pay, authority, and prestige.

ful than that prevailing in the Ministry of Finance. In 1956 district governors were subject to social and political pressures with which respondents in the Ministry of Finance did not have to deal. The Ministry of Interior — and particularly its district-level representatives — bore the brunt of the changes resulting from the ruralizing election. Because of these pressures, those who were to leave the Ministry of

Interior seem much more upset than their counterparts who left the Ministry of Finance in the 1956–1965 period. In a sense, those who left Interior were "pushed" out; those who left Finance were "pulled" away from their positions.

In 1956 the potential "leavers" in Interior may have been particularly concerned about political pressures leading to job transfers. At this time job possibilities for graduates of the administrative section were still quite restricted. The 1956 respondents who felt especially insecure may have wanted to leave but have been unable to. Additional data on job mobility accord with this interpretation. Much of the mobility out of the Ministries of Interior and Finance appears to have taken place after 1960. The political turbulence characteristic of the late fifties may well have made people hesitate to switch jobs.

Regardless of ministry, job security seemed less important in 1965 than in 1956. A lack of job security, the third most frequently mentioned reason for dissatisfaction in 1956, became the next-to-least mentioned reason in 1965. Job opportunities for Political Science Faculty graduates have improved since 1960, while inflation has lessened the advantages of holding a government job up to retirement age. More theoretically, the rewards earned through seniority in the system have declined, while the opportunities in organizations stressing such individual rewards as better pay have increased.[11]

Political Interference and Autonomy

Political interference in the workings of the bureaucracy seems to have declined markedly over the nine-year period. The 1956 complaints in this regard at least partially represent reactions to the opening of the political system and the consequent loss of power by the old urban elite. The year of the survey appears to have been particularly critical. A more detailed analysis of the Ministry of Interior emphasized the decline in reported political interference while pointing up other areas of subjective change. The district governors were about as satisfied in 1965 as in 1956, but some of the reasons for satisfaction had changed. Governors in 1965 tended to be more concerned about their authority and responsibilities, but less upset about political interference.

The data not only suggest that political pressures upon the district

11. *Ibid.*, p. 341.

governor may have been less in 1965 but also that the district governor had learned to get less upset about political pressures by 1965. These governors play important "boundary roles," mediating between the administration and the village leadership. The "ruralizing election" altered both the district governor's role and the roles of the peasants and politicians with whom he interacted. The "forced role innovation" which followed the 1950 election led to new administrator–client relationships and considerable debureaucratization. By 1965 these role changes may have become to some degree institutionalized;[12] the governor no longer had sole responsibility for and authority over many important developments in his district. These new conditions of authority had partially replaced overt political interference as a source of discontent.

The change in subjective political interference may also reflect some "organizational learning" by the representatives of the Ministry of Interior.[13] Although district governors in an area with a Justice Party majority reported more political pressures than did bureaucrats in more competitive districts, by 1965 the governors had partially adjusted to the new situation. Governors in districts dominated by the Justice Party were no more likely to report job dissatisfaction, to favor government "for the people" (as opposed to the "by the people"), or to feel that politicians hinder development than were their counterparts in areas lacking a Justice Party majority.

In contrast, graduates promoted out of jobs as district governors reported considerably higher satisfaction in 1965 (63 percent satisfied in 1965 as compared with 37 percent in 1956). Better pay (the mention of this item went from 4 to 30 percent), more job security, a preferred location, and better learning opportunities were all more frequently noted in 1965 than in 1956. But perhaps most important was

12. "Forced role innovation" is treated by S. N. Eisenstadt in *Essays on Comparative Institutions* (New York, Wiley, 1965), pp. 38–40. Stinchcombe has noted that the degree of dependence of superiors on inferiors is influenced by such factors as: the capacity of inferiors to organize in opposition to superiors and the degree of institutionalized dependence of superiors on inferiors, especially by devices of free competitive electors — Arthur L. Stinchcombe, "Social Structure and Organizations," in James G. March, ed., *Handbook of Organizations* (Chicago, Rand McNally, 1965), p. 182.

13. James G. March, "Some Recent Substantive and Methodological Developments in the Theory of Organizational Decision-Making," in Austin Ranney, ed., *Essays on the Behavioral Study of Politics* (Urbana, University of Illinois Press, 1962), pp. 198–199.

Table 7-5: Political Factors' Contribution to Job Satisfaction in the Ministry of Interior[a] (1956–1965)

Attitude of respondents	Panel respondents remaining in job		1946–1955 graduates				1958–1961 graduates
			Panel respondents remaining in job		Panel respondents given major promotion		
	Asst. district governor 1956 (%)	District governor 1965 (%)	District governor 1956 (%)	District governor 1965 (%)	District governor 1956 (%)	Ministry of Interior 1965 (%)	District governor 1965 (%)
Satisfied with job Little political interference	25 5	30 5	40 6	43 3	37 7	63 48	42 8
Dissatisfied with job Too much political interference[b]	70 60	70 40	57 49	54 34	59 48	37 22	50 29
Number of respondents	20	20	35	35	27	27	24

[a] The percentage total for satisfied and dissatisfied individuals often does not reach 100 percent because of "no answers." The data from the Ministry of Interior are organized in terms of the typical career pattern in this ministry: Political Science Faculty graduates first work in low-level positions in the Ministry of Interior; they then become district governors. The more successful district governors are promoted, after a number of years, to higher-level positions in the ministry.

[b] Differences in complaints about too much political interference between 1956 and 1965 were significant at the .05 level if data on assistant district governors and district governors remaining in their jobs were aggregated. Differences for respondents given a major promotion were also significant at the .05 level.

134

the bureaucrats' insulation from certain types of political pressures. The percentage of these successful respondents mentioning "little political interference" as a reason for satisfaction soared from 7 to 48 percent over the nine-year period.

Although both district governors and those in high-level positions in the Ministry of Interior reported considerable contact with politicians (45 percent of both groups mention weekly contact with politicians), they may have been in touch with very different types of politicians.[14] Individuals in high-level posts tend to spend their time in the metropolitan areas or in provincial centers, coming into contact with higher-level political leaders generally having at least a lycée education. On the other hand, the district governors deal with less-educated small-town politicians and village headmen whose maneuvering may be especially grating. Status is important here. An individual or group with lower status (the local leadership) is exerting substantial influence over an individual (the district governor) of higher status. Research in American organizations has emphasized that such an arrangement tends to cause role dissatisfaction and conflict.[15]

Pay

From a more general perspective, the relationship between job satisfaction and pay is significant. Despite differences in standards of living, pay remains important for managers in other countries.[16] There is some evidence that Turkish administrators in different types of organizations have made economic progress. The cost-of-living index went from 79 to 164 over the 1956–1965 period, but Table 7-6 suggests that salaries were up more than that.[17] Despite this, relative deprivation may have been severe; satisfaction stemming from the receipt of wages is dependent not on the absolute amount of these wages, but on the relationship between that amount and some standard of comparison

14. A discussion of the social backgrounds of Turkish mayors is provided in Ruşen Keleş and Cevat Geray, *Türk Belediye Başkanları* [Turkish mayors] (Ankara, Ayyıldız Matbaası, 1964).

15. Richard E. Walton and John M. Dutton, "The Management of Interdepartmental Conflict: A Model and Review," *Administrative Science Quarterly*, 14 (March 1969), 76.

16. Lyman W. Porter and Edward E. Lawler, III, *Managerial Attitudes and Performance* (Homewood, Ill., Irwin, 1968), p. 60.

17. Z. Y. Hershlag, *Turkey: The Challenge of Growth* (Leiden, E. J. Brill, 1968), p. 334.

Table 7-6: Salaries in the Ministry of Interior and New, Noncentral Organizations (1956–1965)

	Older graduates (Classes of 1946–1955)			Younger graduates (Classes of 1958–1961)	
	Remained in Ministry of Interior (1956–1965) (%)	Ministry of Interior (1956) New, noncentral organizations (1965) (%)	Remained in new, noncentral organizations (1956–1965)[a] (%)	Ministry of Interior (1965) (%)	New, noncentral organizations (1965)[a] (%)
1956 Monthly Salaries[b]:					
300 T.L. or less	23	13	0		
301–400 T.L.	52	50	0		
More than 400 T.L.	24	37	100		
1965 Monthly Salaries[b]:					
1400 T.L. or less	28	38	0	92	35
1401–2000 T.L.	61	6	20	8	39
More than 2000 T.L.	11	56	80	0	27
Number of respondents	82	16	10	25	26

[a] Most of these graduates had the advantage of academic training in the financial section of the Political Science Faculty. This training is of some advantage in the competition for high-paying jobs in the new, noncentral organizations.

[b] Differences among groups were significant at the .05 level for each time period.

used by the individual.[18] This relative deprivation may be an especially important determinant of lower job satisfaction in the Ministries of Interior and Finance. Graduates in these ministries have social and business contacts with their classmates in higher-paying jobs outside

18. Vroom, *Work and Motivation*, p. 151.

the central ministries. As might be predicted, low pay was a particularly salient cause of dissatisfaction among graduates remaining in the Ministries of Interior and Finance.

Although the percentage of respondents mentioning low pay as a reason for dissatisfaction declined substantially between 1956 and 1965, the relative position of this item remained fairly constant. Low pay was the most frequently cited reason for dissatisfaction among the 1956–1965 panel respondents, and the item second most frequently mentioned by the 1958–1961 graduates. Moreover, in both 1956 and 1965 the reasons most frequently given for not recommending the Political Science Faculty concerned pay.

Opportunities for better pay are closely linked with the movement out of the Ministries of Interior and Finance into high-paying jobs in the new, noncentral organizations.[19] Among individuals who left the Ministry of Finance the percentage mentioning good pay as a reason for satisfaction rose from 43 percent (in 1956 in the ministry) to 67 percent (in 1965 outside the ministry).[20] Other factors related to the change in satisfaction which accompanied leaving the Ministry of Finance include more prestige (29 to 43 percent), more responsibility (33 to 57 percent), and a greater opportunity to learn (43 to 67 percent).

Stress, Satisfaction, and Mobility

The material presented in the last two chapters has given some perspective on the individual consequences of increased intergroup competition. As the new, noncentral organizations have profited in the post-1950 political environment, the traditional organizations' control over their environment has decreased. The reactions of administrators in various organizations — particularly in the Ministries of Interior and Finance — have been treated here. Several career alternatives have been available to bureaucrats in these ministries. An

19. Somewhat over 25 percent of the panel study respondents leaving the Ministries of Interior and Finance ($n = 36$) over the 1956–1965 period for work outside the central and older ministries made their move before 1960. The exact percentage is difficult to specify because of the possibilities for intermediate moves, but it is probably under 35 percent.

20. "Over 2,000 lira monthly" was the top salary category in our survey. Fifty-six percent of those leaving the Ministry of Finance reported a monthly salary of over 2,000 lira.

individual could stay in his organization and seek a promotion (successfully or unsuccessfully), or he could move to another organization. Much of the analysis has been concentrated upon this promotion–leaving dichotomy in an effort to explain the relationships between attitudinal factors and career patterns.

As has been previously noted, the Ministry of Interior can be distinguished from the Ministry of Finance according to several theoretically relevant criteria. During the 1950's the Ministry of Interior's relations with its clients were in a state of flux; this ministry was under considerable stress, and had experienced a significant loss of status. We cannot definitively show that one of these factors — rather than the others — was of critical importance. In a similar fashion, we do not know whether particular attitudes held by the assistant district governors and the district governors are due to their being in relatively low-level managerial jobs or due to their working in boundary roles; both types of positions seem to be difficult ones.

The data from two points in time help in generating appropriate propositions. If we assume that the Ministry of Interior was under significantly more stress in 1956 than in 1965, but that this ministry's status was similar in 1956 and in 1965, some hypotheses can be tentatively sorted out:

1) Client interference is likely to be perceived as particularly serious in organizations experiencing severe stress.

    a. Such interference may be especially difficult for individuals in low level managerial positions.

    b. Such interference may be especially difficult for individuals in boundary roles.

2) Attitudinal differences between those who leave an organization experiencing severe stress and those who stay are likely to be greater than differences between leavers and stayers in other organizations.

3) Individuals filling low-level managerial positions in organizations which have experienced a significant loss of status are particularly likely to be dissatisfied.

4) Individuals in boundary roles in organizations which have experienced a significant loss of status are particularly likely to be dissatisfied.

The organizational environment is clearly an important influence upon job satisfaction; it may change markedly from time to time. Public sector organizations must deal with problems of political interference substantially greater than those faced by organizations in the

138

private sector. In government organizations, concerns about political interference, pay, and security may vary more widely than do other attitudes. During unsettled times, these factors are likely to be particularly salient.

The differences between the data on political interference and those on pay are significant. Severe conflict between the bureaucrats and the new political groups, as indicated by the political interference data, seems to accompany a ruralizing election. In 1956 the power of the Ministry of Interior was being severely restricted, and the bureaucrats, no longer responsible for the modernization of their nation, were decidedly unhappy. By 1965 the perceived pressures had diminished substantially.

The information on pay is quite different. Whereas complaints about political interference were concentrated in the Ministry of Interior at one point in time, complaints about pay were more generally distributed across ministries and over a period of time. These findings, along with cross-national information on other bureaucracies, emphasize the public administrators' pervasive discontent with his economic condition.[21]

The data also have more general implications for organization theory. First of all, theoretical formulations which do not deal with political factors may be inappropriate for research on problems of public bureaucracies. Variations in levels of political interference in administrative matters are important in terms of both job satisfaction and system stability. From a disciplinary perspective, the organization theory literature has grown up rather independent of the writing on public administration, and any findings which help bring these two bodies of literature together are valuable.

Secondly, the material presented here has emphasized that individuals' job mobility occurs at the same time that opportunity structures — jobs and organizations — are also changing. Both individual and organizational adaptations have been occurring simultaneously, but individual adaptation seems to have taken place more rapidly. Such a judgment is hazardous, but new patterns of organizational choice appear more definite than changes in the internal operations of the ministries. More generally, an increased study of these change processes would seem valuable for organization theory. What are the

21. Leslie L. Roos, Jr. and Noralou P. Roos, "Bureaucracy in the Middle East: Some Cross-Cultural Relationships," *Journal of Comparative Administration,* 1 (November 1969), 281–300.

conditions under which various kinds of adaptation are likely to — or likely not to — take place?

At the macro-level, we might speculate about the political significance of the administrative attitudes studied here. Elite complaints about political interference and pay may have particularly destabilizing effects upon the political system. The parallels between the Turkish bureaucrats' complaints in 1956 and those attributed to the military in the pre-1960 period are certainly suggestive.

The following quotations from Harris emphasize the pressures of pay and political interference upon the military:

> The Democrats . . . allowed military pay to lag far behind the rapidly rising cost of living. From the emotionally charged recitals of complaints by officers at their straitened circumstances, it is clear that the Democratic Party permitted the status and prestige of the military profession to sink lower than it had at any time since the founding of the republic . . .

> . . . as the political crisis deepened, both the Democratic Party and the opposition would seek with increasing directness the support of the military establishment against the other. In the final analysis, it was these efforts to manipulate the armed forces as a political tool that destroyed the tradition of political neutrality so painstakingly erected over the years.[22]

In 1956 both administrators and officers felt the strains of a political system unable to cope with the results of a ruralizing election. Chapter 9 will deal with some of the bureaucrats' reactions to the military and politicians in 1965, while Chapter 8 explores the satisfaction and mobility data in greater detail.

22. George S. Harris, "The Causes of the 1960 Revolution in Turkey," paper presented at the Second Annual Meeting of the Middle East Studies Association, Austin, Texas, November 1968, pp. 8 and 25.

8

Futures, Causes, and Additivity

The previous chapters have discussed job satisfaction and mobility from several perspectives, but the analysis has in large part depended upon relatively straightforward tabulation of the questionnaire responses. More advanced methods for handling data from two points in time are available; these methods both help clarify the relationships among variables and permit us to approach some new questions. Questions made more amenable to analysis include:

1. Where are the Political Science Faculty graduates likely to be working in the future? Some simple Markov models will be used for the projection of the organizational mobility data up to 1974.

2. What are the causal relationships between job position and job satisfaction? A cross-lagged panel approach helps identify the linkages between these variables, but the data are difficult to work with.

3. What are the interrelationships among a number of variables? In this analysis an effort is made to handle several variables simultaneously. Special techniques based on the assumptions of statistical additivity are used for this purpose.

Futures

Much of our analysis has focused upon the movement of administrators from one position or organization to another. As Vroom and MacCrimmon have noted:[1]

> . . . the career development process can be represented as a stochastic process. A model of a stochastic process shows the likelihood of movement from one state (i.e., position or organization) of the system to any other state over some specified time period. The state occupied at some future period depends in a probabilistic manner on states previously occupied.

1. Victor H. Vroom and Kenneth R. MacCrimmon, "Toward a Stochastic Model of Managerial Careers," *Administrative Science Quarterly*, 13 (June 1968), 28. Stochastic models represent only one of several possible approaches to individual mobility. For a discussion of such approaches, see Harrison C. White, *Chains of Opportunity* (Cambridge, Mass., Harvard University Press, 1970).

The "state" can be any characteristic of an administrator (organizational level, job satisfaction, type of organization) defined so that a respondent occupies one, and only one, state at a given time.

In a zero-order Markov model, "the probability of movement from any given state to each of the possible states over some given time interval depends solely on the current state." [2] Assuming that the probabilities of an individual changing from one state to another (the "transition probabilities") will remain constant through time is computationally convenient. The use of relatively long time intervals tends to cancel out minor variations in mobility, making the assumption of constant transition probabilities more reasonable.

The organizational changes in our sample of older Political Science Faculty graduates (classes of 1946–1955) can be studied through the use of a Markov model. Thus, Table 8-1 illustrates one way to consider the job changes between 1956 and 1965. This table is percentaged horizontally using the decimal notation to aid in tracing changes among respondents found in a particular type of organization in 1956; the probabilities that a graduate in a given organization in 1956 stayed or moved in various ways by 1965 are presented in Table 8-1. For example, the second line of the table shows that 66 percent of the 1956 respondents in the Ministry of Finance remained in this ministry in 1965; to put it another way, an individual's probability of staying in the Finance Ministry over this nine-year period was 0.66.

By assuming constant transition probabilities, the data presented in Table 8-1 can be used to generate estimates of the distribution of the respondents in 1974. Thus, the probability of an individual leaving the Ministry of Interior over the 1965–1974 period to work in a new, noncentral organization is taken to remain the same as during the 1956–1965 interval. The validity of this assumption is probably dependent upon reasonable economic growth and a continued expansion of opportunities in the state economic enterprises and private sector. Highly unstable political conditions might well reduce the rate of transfer. The political environment during the late 1950's seemed more turbulent than that encountered in the late 1960's period, but the political

2. Vroom and MacCrimmon, "Toward a Stochastic Model . . . ," p. 28. These methods are discussed in some detail by T. W. Anderson, "Probability Models for Analyzing Time Changes in Attitudes," in Paul F. Lazarsfeld, ed., *Mathematical Thinking in the Social Sciences* (New York, Free Press, 1954), pp. 17–66.

Table 8-1: Organizational Mobility (1956–1965)

1956 Organization	1965 Organization					
	Minis-try of Interior	Minis-try of Finance	Minis-try of Foreign Affairs	Other old organ-izations	New, non-central organ-izations	Number of respond-ents
Ministry of Interior	0.74	0.03	0.01	0.09	0.13	174
Ministry of Finance	.01	.66	.03	.03	.27	119
Ministry of For-eign Affairs	.00	.03	.97	.00	.00	37
Other old organizations	.06	.06	.00	.61	.27	33
New, noncentral organizations	.06	.06	.00	.06	.83	17

NOTE: This table is based on information from the 380 respondents to the 1956 survey. The numbers in the table give the probability of a respondent in a particular organization in 1956 being in a given organization in 1965.

and economic events of 1971 probably acted to slow transfers among organizations.

By making this assumption of constant transition probabilities, the probability matrix for job changes in the 1956–1965 period can be squared to produce a table for estimated job changes over the eighteen-year period from 1956 to 1974. The results of this procedure are presented in Table 8-2.

These results can be summarized by showing the percentage of the 380 graduates employed in the different types of organizations in 1956, 1965, and estimated 1974. As is seen in Table 8-3, if this projection were to prove correct, the shift of Faculty graduates into the new, non-central organizations will have reached major proportions by 1974. Only the Ministry of Foreign Affairs will remain relatively unaffected. Almost one-quarter of the graduates in the Ministry of Interior in 1956 will be joined by about two-fifths of those in the Ministry of Finance and in the other, old ministries in moving to jobs in the new organizations, state economic enterprises, banks, and the private sector.

Table 8-2: Estimated Organizational Mobility (1956–1974)

1956 Organization	Estimated 1974 organization					Number of respondents
	Ministry of Interior	Ministry of Finance	Ministry of Foreign Affairs	Other old organizations	New, noncentral organizations	
Ministry of Interior	.56	.06	.02	.12	.23	174
Ministry of Finance	.03	.46	.06	.05	.41	119
Ministry of Foreign Affairs	.00	.04	.95	.00	.01	37
Other old organizations	.10	.10	.00	.39	.41	33
New, noncentral organizations	.10	.09	.00	.09	.72	17

NOTE: This table is derived from information from the 380 respondents to the 1956 survey. The numbers in the table give the estimated probability of a respondent in a particular organization in 1956 being in a given organization in 1974.

Table 8-3: Respondents Employed in Different Organizations (1956–1974)

	1956 (%)	1965 (%)	Estimated 1974 (%)
Ministry of Interior	46	35	28
Ministry of Finance	31	23	19
Ministry of Foreign Affairs	10	11	12
Other old organizations	9	10	11
New, noncentral organizations	5	20	30

NOTE: This table is derived from information from the 380 respondents to the 1956 survey.

There are several ways to extend this estimation technique. The 380 graduates can be broken into subgroups according to such variables as social background, university grades, and so forth. Estimates can then be made from the probability matrices generated for each subgroup. The probability matrices were analyzed in this manner from four social background groups: sons of officials from metropolitan areas, sons of officials from other areas, sons of businessmen, and sons of farmers. The estimates were generally in line with the findings summarized in Table 8-3: large losses from the Ministries of Interior and Finance were predicted over the 1965–1974 period. The projections for sons of businessmen showed especially large changes, even after correction for an insufficient number of respondents in some of the categories. We estimated that at least 36 percent of the sons of businessmen in the sample would be working in new, noncentral organizations by 1974.[3]

The information presented in Chapter 6 suggests several variables which might alter the mobility projections. Mobility can be considered in a more sophisticated fashion by incorporating information on job satisfaction and position in the ministerial hierarchy. Since satisfied individuals were less likely to change their organization than the dissatisfied ones, this technique makes it possible to incorporate changes in job satisfaction between 1956 and 1965 into the probability matrix. However, only within the Ministry of Interior is there a really significant change in job satisfaction between 1956 and 1965. This is due to the promotion of individuals from district governors' positions to jobs in the central offices of the Ministry of Interior. Moreover, there are fairly sizable differences (about 13 percent) in the frequency with which satisfied and dissatisfied graduates leave this ministry.

By squaring a 10 × 10 probability matrix which incorporates type of organization (5 categories) and job satisfaction (2 categories for each type of organization), a more refined estimate of the 1974 distribution of the 241 panel study respondents can be made.[4] This estimate, presented in Table 8-4, is strikingly close to that made from the

3. Additional analysis using the 1946–1955 graduates' grades and date of graduation showed few overall differences in propensity to leave the central ministries. Since the younger graduates (the classes of 1958–1961) showed such different career tendencies, it is unfortunate that panel data were not available for these respondents.

4. The 241 respondents — rather than the 380 respondents — were used in order to have measures of job satisfaction in both 1956 and 1965.

Table 8-4: Job Satisfaction and Dissatisfaction in Organizations
(1956–1974)

	1956 (%)	1965 (%)	Estimated 1974 (%)
Ministry of Interior			
Satisfied	16	19	17
Dissatisfied	32	19	14
Ministry of Finance			
Satisfied	15	11	7
Dissatisfied	13	6	4
Ministry of Foreign Affairs			
Satisfied	10	11	12
Dissatisfied	1	1	1
Other old organizations			
Satisfied	6	8	8
Dissatisfied	3	3	4
New, noncentral organizations			
Satisfied	4	19	29
Dissatisfied	0	3	4
Total percentage			
Satisfied	52	68	74
Dissatisfied	48	32	26

NOTE: This table is based on 236 graduates who answered both the 1956 and the 1965 surveys and for whom job satisfaction data were available. Due to nonresponse bias in the Ministry of Finance this table is not directly comparable with Table 8-3.

simple 5 × 5 matrix for the same 1956–1965 panel respondents. The percentage of graduates in the Ministry of Interior rises by only slightly more than 2 percent, while the percentage in the other types of organizations changes even less. In similar fashion, data on an individual's position within the Ministries of Interior and Finance were incorporated into a probability matrix without significantly altering the estimate. Finally, the matrix combining the data on organizational type with those on job satisfaction is of further interest in providing an estimate of future job satisfaction.[5] The percentage of satisfied panel

5. More complicated probability models are presented in Isadore Blumen, Marvin Kogan, and Philip J. McCarthy, "Probability Models for Mobility," in

respondents grew from 52 percent in 1956 to 68 percent in 1965, with the percentage of such respondents estimated to reach 74 percent by 1974.

As noted earlier, these estimates must be taken as informed speculation. They seem to be dependent upon the following assumptions:

1. Economic growth, probably at the per capita rate of about 4 percent per year. A lower growth rate would lower organizational mobility.
2. The formation of new organizations and the continued growth of comparatively young organizations.

Estimates are difficult, but several hundred new managerial positions annually are probably necessary to maintain the rates of mobility projected here. As White has stressed in a more theoretical connection, organizations are interrelated. New jobs and retirements may appear primarily in certain types of organizations, so that patterns of mobility in other organizations are dependent upon these former organizations.[6] Unfortunately, we do not know the precise linkages between economic development, organizational mobility, job satisfaction, salary scales, and so forth. Better quantitative data on the number of both qualified individuals and managerial vacancies would facilitate the study of mobility.

Other kinds of variables introduce additional complications. Political turbulence is likely to slow mobility, while stability would tend to facilitate it. Individual maturation may also play a role: as bureaucrats age, the security associated with work in the central ministries could well be of increasing importance. The collection of another set of data — preferably in 1974 — is clearly desirable. Such new information would permit testing of the simple model put forward here and facilitate the use of more sophisticated models.

Paul F. Lazarsfeld and Neil W. Henry, eds., *Readings in Mathematical Social Science* (Cambridge, Mass., M.I.T. Press, 1968), pp. 318–334, and Leo A. Goodman, "Statistical Methods for the Mover-Stayer Model," *Journal of the American Statistical Association,* 56 (December 1961), 841–868. These formulations depend on rather extensive time-series data and did not seem appropriate for use with the 1956–1965 information.

6. White, *Chains of Opportunity,* p. 19. Estimates dealing with the increase in the supply of managerial positions in the 1956–1965 period have been made in Appendix D.

Causes

The analysis of data from two points in time presents a number of problems. Within the last several years, the difficulties in drawing causal inferences from such data have been emphasized. Duncan, for example, has stated that "no set of 2W2V (two waves of data collection with two variables) will answer a question about direction of causal influence or relative importance of causes except on some set of definite assumptions." [7] Despite Duncan's cautions, we believe that the nature of the Turkish data permits making some limited causal statements; our assumptions will be spelled out and, whenever possible, be subjected to empirical test.

There are a number of general problems with panel analysis, including:

1. The possibility of significant measurement error. Duncan has noted that the panel design calls attention to the importance of measurement error, since it involves measuring the same characteristic(s) repeatedly, whereas remeasurement (test-retest) is one of the techniques commonly used to detect and estimate the extent of measurement error.[8] The assumptions of panel analysis and test-retest differ. The test-retest technique estimates reliability by assuming no change in true scores, while panel analysis focuses upon the possibilities for interpreting actual change in true scores.

2. The presence of causes common to the variables being studied. An observable third variable or latent factors common to both variables might be responsible for changes in the two variables.

3. Two-way causation and mutual influence of the variables.

4. The role of time. Causation might be simultaneous or lagged; different assumptions about the role of time may lead to different indications about the direction of effects.

Some of these problems are discussed in this chapter; Appendix C treats these issues in more detail.

7. Otis Dudley Duncan, "Some Linear Models for Two-Wave, Two-Variable Panel Analysis," *Psychological Bulletin,* 72 (1969), pp. 177–182. Some of the problems of panel analysis are also discussed in David A. Kenny, "Common Factor Model with Temporal Erosion for Panel Data," paper presented at Social Science Research Council Conference on Structural Equation Models, Madison, Wisc., November 12–16, 1970.

8. Otis Dudley Duncan, "Some Linear Models for Two-Wave, Two-Variable Panel Analysis, with One-Way Causation and Measurement Error," unpub. manuscript, University of Michigan, Ann Arbor, Michigan, 1970.

148

Regardless of problems in specifying causality, panel analysis permits approaching the relationships between job position and job satisfaction more systematically than was done in Chapter 6. For analyzing panel studies, Lazarsfeld has devised a method making use of a 16-fold table to "display frequencies for each of two dichotomous variables measured on two occasions." [9] This method allows the tracing of individual changes over time with considerable precision. Another technique compares correlation coefficients between the two variables measured on two occasions. This method of "cross-lagged panel correlation" involves a comparison of variables *A* and *B*, "measured for all individuals at time *t* and again at *t* + *k* (*k* = arbitrary remeasurement interval)." [10] Figure 8-1 shows the six correlations used for this comparison.

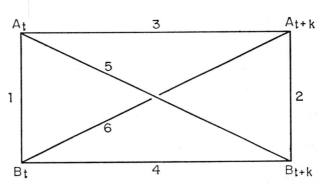

Figure 8-1. Six correlations among two variables measured twice.

This method assumes that the vertical correlations 1 and 2 will both be positive and of approximately the same magnitude. The horizontal correlations 3 and 4 reflect the consistency of each variable between the two time periods. The original formulation of cross-lagged panel analysis was that if variable *A* could be said to cause variable *B*, "then the 'effect' should correlate higher with a prior 'cause' than with a

9. Donald C. Pelz and Frank M. Andrews, "Detecting Causal Priorities in Panel Study Data," *American Sociological Review*, 29 (December 1964), 837. The method is described in Seymour M. Lipset, Paul F. Lazarsfeld, Allen H. Barton, and Juan Linz, "The Psychology of Voting: An Analysis of Political Behavior," in Gardner Lindzey, ed., *Handbook of Social Psychology* (Reading, Mass., Addison-Wesley, 1954), pp. 1124–1175.

10. Pelz and Andrews, "Detecting Casual Priorities . . . ," p. 837.

subsequent 'cause.' " [11] Correlation 5 $(A_t B_{t+k})$ should be larger than correlation 6 $(A_{t+k} B_t)$.

In a recent article, Rozelle and Campbell have suggested that, when lagged cross-sectional correlations are compared, at least four hypotheses are in competition.[12]

> Increases in A increase B, and decreases in A decrease B.
> Increases in A decrease B, and decreases in A increase B.
> Increases in B increase A, and decreases in B decrease A.
> Increases in B decrease A, and decreases in B increase A.

If there is a significant inequality between the cross-correlations $r_{A_1 B_2}$ and $r_{B_1 A_2}$, a separation can be made between two pairs of hypotheses. Where $r_{A_1 B_2} > r_{B_1 A_2}$,

the joint effect of A increases B and B decreases A	is greater than	the joint effect of B increases A and A decreases B

Some recent thinking on cross-lagged panel analysis has emphasized the difficulties in choosing between the two confounded hypotheses (i.e. A increases B and B decreases A) which have been jointly affirmed by the inequality between the cross-correlations.[13]

The number of rival hypotheses are limited to some degree by the nature of the Turkish data. Generally speaking, individuals did not move from being satisfied to being dissatisfied; moreover, administrators did not move from the new, noncentral organizations back into the Ministries of Interior or Finance. It is difficult to talk about increase and decrease with dichotomous data, but it is clear that the change is unidirectional. There is no "decrease" in either the job satisfaction or the organization variable. Because of this, the phrases in Rozelle and Campbell's competitive hypotheses which mention "decrease" might be eliminated. The alternative hypotheses become:

11. Donald T. Campbell and Julian C. Stanley, *Experimental and Quasi-Experimental Designs for Research* (Chicago, Rand McNally, 1967), pp. 67–69.

12. Richard M. Rozelle and Donald T. Campbell, "More Plausible Rival Hypotheses in the Cross-lagged Panel Correlation Technique," *Psychological Bulletin,* 71 (1969), p. 74.

13. I am grateful to David A. Kenny for his suggestions concerning this panel material. See also Kenneth I. Howard and Merton S. Krause, "Some Comments on 'Techniques for Estimating the Source and Direction of Influence in Panel Data,' " *Psychological Bulletin,* 74 (1970), pp. 219–224.

1. "Increases" in *A* "increase" *B*. Moving into the new, noncentral organizations (and out of the Ministries of Interior and Finance) leads to increased satisfaction.

2. "Increases" in *B* "increase" *A*. Increased satisfaction leads to moving into the new, noncentral organizations (and out of the Ministries of Interior and Finance). This hypothesis is somewhat implausible and assumes that changes in satisfaction operate in a "dynamic" way to cause mobility. The most plausible suggestion is that "static" job dissatisfaction leads to movement out of the Ministries of Interior and Finance.

An examination of the appropriate 16-fold tables indicates that movement out of Interior and Finance tended to *produce* job satisfaction, while working in the new, noncentral organizations tended to *preserve* this satisfaction. As is seen in Table 8-5, of the 13 dissatisfied respondents who left the Ministry of Interior for the new, noncentral organizations, ten reported being satisfied with their jobs in 1965. All

Table 8-5: Mobility and Attitude Change — Ministry of Interior and New, Noncentral Organizations (1956–1965)

1956	1965			
	Ministry of Interior (Satisfied)	Ministry of Interior (Dissatisfied)	New, noncentral organizations (Satisfied)	New, noncentral organizations (Dissatisfied)
Ministry of Interior: Satisfied	22	9	3	0
Ministry of Interior: Dissatisfied	19	34	10	3
New, noncentral organizations:[a] Satisfied	0	0	8	1

[a] Because there were no dissatisfied panel respondents in new, noncentral organizations in 1956, this table contains 12 — rather than 16 — cells. The actual number of respondents in each category is presented in this table; there are 109 respondents in this table.

three of the satisfied respondents who switched from the Ministry of Interior to the new, noncentral organizations remained satisfied in 1965; of the nine satisfied respondents in the new, noncentral organizations in 1956, only one became dissatisfied over the nine-year period.[14]

As is seen in Figure 8-2, the cross-lagged panel data for organizational mobility and job satisfaction are both clear and consistent. Although caution is called for in making causal interpretations from panel studies, the findings are unambiguous: the $r_{o_1 s_2}$ correlations are higher than the $r_{o_2 s_1}$ correlations, while the vertical (synchronous) correlations are of a similar magnitude at both time periods. Insofar as panel data from two points in time permit causal inference, the analysis indicates that mobility out of the Ministry of Interior into the new, noncentral organizations caused increased job satisfaction. Additional work with the Ministry of Finance data has raised some questions concerning mobility out of this ministry.[15]

Such causal formulations are often complicated by problems in treating time and lagged causation. The data from our sample are rather straightforward. For the 1956 respondents in the Ministry of Interior, where levels of dissatisfaction were quite high, there were no differences in job satisfaction between those leaving relatively early in the 1956–1965 period and those leaving comparatively late. On the other hand, a disproportionate number of 1956 respondents in the Ministry of Finance who left relatively early in the nine-year period were likely to be dissatisfied. There were no differences in 1965 satisfaction between those respondents who had been working in the new, noncentral organizations only a short time and those who had been employed in such organizations for a considerably longer time. These findings strongly suggest that the causal linkage between job satisfaction and organizational mobility is lagged. Job dissatisfaction might over time have led to a change in organizations, if openings were available. On the other hand, an individual's job satisfaction seems to have been rapidly affected by the organization in which he works.

14. See the discussion of this in A. H. Yee and N. L. Gage, "Techniques for Estimating the Source and Direction of Causal Influence in Panel Data," *Psychological Bulletin,* 70, 2 (1968), pp. 115–126.

15. In Appendix C these data are examined further in terms of standard scores based on the number of reasons for satisfaction or dissatisfaction; inferences for the Ministry of Interior are stronger than those for the Ministry of Finance. Various models incorporating measurement error are also explored.

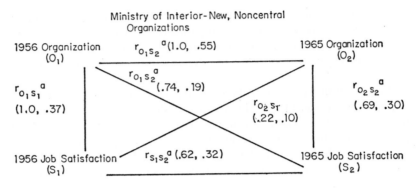

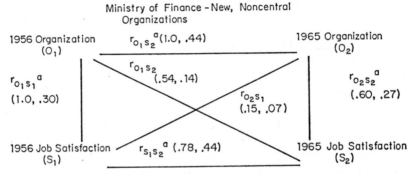

Figure 8-2. Organizational mobility and job satisfaction. The measures of association were (gamma, tau-b = phi). There were 109 respondents in the Ministry of Interior — New, Noncentral Organizations analysis and 68 respondents in the Ministry of Finance — New, Noncentral Organizations analysis. The tau-b, or phi measure, which also corresponds to the product-moment correlation for 2×2 tables, is probably the more appropriate for these data. Appendix C treats these data in greater detail.

[a] Relationships were significant at the .05 level.

Promotion and job satisfaction within the Ministries of Interior and Finance can be studied from a similar perspective, but some additional difficulties are posed. Data from the Ministry of Interior illustrate a general problem in research on hierarchical organizations; the movement of individuals from position to position greatly complicates analysis. Because of promotional patterns within Interior, cutting points could not be adjusted so as to have an adequate number of respondents in each category for both 1956 and 1965. Because of this, an

8-fold table can represent the respondents' positions and job satisfaction in 1956 and 1965. In 1956 all the respondents from the classes of 1946–1955 were either district governors or in lower-level positions within the Ministry of Interior. In 1965 some of the respondents had been promoted to higher-level positions, while none of these graduates remained in the positions below district governor. This situation is presented in Table 8-6.

Table 8-6: Position and Satisfaction within the Ministry of Interior (1956–1965)[a]

	1965			
	Low position		High position	
1956[b]	Satisfied with job	Dissatisfied with job	Satisfied with job	Dissatisfied with job
Low position: Satisfied with job	11	7	10	2
Low position: Dissatisfied with job	11	27	8	6

[a] In comparison with data in the previous sections, slightly fewer panel respondents are reported here. A few respondents have been eliminated (5 from this table) due to an absence of data on one of the four items. There are 82 respondents in this table. The table is 8-fold rather than 16-fold because there were no 1956 respondents in high positions in the Ministry of Interior.

[b] Included in low positions in 1956 were 61 district governors and 21 assistant district governors.

The cross-tabulations summarized in Chapter 6 have suggested that within the Ministry of Interior: 1) a change in job position (promotion) was associated with increased satisfaction; and 2) job satisfaction may tend to lead to a change in job position (promotion). This relationship was, however, not statistically significant. Because of the problem with cutting points, a complete cross-lagged panel analysis could not be carried out. The correlation between 1965 position and 1965 job satisfaction ($r_{p_2 s_2}$ = .55, .08 for gamma and phi measures) is considerably higher than that between 1965 position and 1956 satisfaction ($r_{p_2 s_1}$ = .29, .02). Although Campbell and Stanley caution

154

that "the many irrelevant sources of correlation occurring between data sets collected upon the same occasion tend to inflate the $r_{p_2 s_2}$ values," the relative magnitude of $r_{p_2 s_2}$ and $r_{p_2 s_1}$ are such that position appears to be a more important determinant of job satisfaction than vice-versa.[16] Such a finding is in line with the findings of Porter and Lawler, who note that the extrinsic rewards of a job (rewards administered by the organization — often linked to job position) are direct causes of job satisfaction.[17] On the other hand, job satisfaction feeds back only indirectly to affect the rewards administered by the organization.

The information from respondents staying within the Ministry of Finance presents a somewhat different picture. Six out of the eight individuals who moved from low to high positions during the nine-year period were dissatisfied in 1956. None of these individuals changed their minds about their work between 1956 and 1965; the satisfied respondents remained satisfied, and vice-versa. The promotion of the eight 1956 respondents without any corresponding change in job satisfaction led to identical correlations between 1956 position–1956 job satisfaction and 1965 position–1965 job satisfaction. Although these data should be taken as highly tentative, the somewhat puzzling relationship between promotion and job satisfaction suggests that early experience in the ministry may be an important determinant of later satisfaction, regardless of later experience. As mentioned earlier, relative deprivation may be a particular problem for this group which elected to stay in the Finance Ministry, while their cohorts moved to better jobs on the outside.

Additivity

Estimating the attitudes and behavior of particular types of individuals becomes difficult when very detailed types are specified. In the Turkish data, controlling simultaneously for ministry, rank, and social background leaves relatively few individuals in any given category. More generally, Mosteller has noted that "in every field of statistical activity where we have contingency tables involving many variables,

16. Campbell and Stanley, *Experimental and Quasi-Experimental Designs,* p. 69.
17. Lyman W. Porter and Edward E. Lawler, III, *Managerial Attitudes and Performance* (Homewood, Ill., Irwin, 1968), p. 165.

we find that our data thin out so that we cannot make cell-to-cell comparisons at as fine a level as we could desire." [18] Rather than making comparisons among cells containing an inadequate number of respondents, Mosteller has developed a method for generating cell estimates "from the margins by giving up the contributions of the higher-order effects." [19] Thus, having four variables and using the six two-dimensional margins, we can estimate the three- and four-dimensional tables. Within specified limits, this method preserves the frequencies at each level of each variable, as well as the two-dimensional associations presented in the six two-way marginal tables. Third- and fourth-order effects resulting from the interactions of sets of three or more variables are ignored.

Mosteller's estimation procedures were used to help examine the relationships among four variables important for the Ministries of Interior and Finance: 1956 rank, 1956 job satisfaction, social background, and 1956–1965 organizational mobility. Table 8-7 illustrates the four-dimensional interrelationships among variables for both the actual data and that estimated from the two-dimensional margins. The relatively close fit between actual and estimated data acts to increase our confidence in the reliability of the results, even though the numbers of respondents are small.

As Table 8-7 suggests, despite the fact that the bivariate correlations among 1956 rank, 1956 job satisfaction, and 1956–1965 organizational mobility do not attain statistical significance, some important relationships may be present. The results of percentaging the data for marginal categories with over fifteen respondents are shown in Table 8-8. The relationships are somewhat confused for the relatively few assistant governors; this may be a consequence of the rather small sample. The district governors' mobility was in line with the predictions; an interaction between dissatisfaction and a relatively privileged background is suggested by both the estimated and the actual data.

18. Frederick Mosteller, "Association and Estimation in Contingency Tables," *Journal of the American Statistical Association,* 63 (March 1968), 18. Mosteller presents an extensive discussion of his estimation procedures in this article.

19. *Ibid.,* p. 19. In this connection, Mosteller notes that "the size of chi-square for a given departure from a random distribution is approximately proportional to sample size, a cause for rejoicing when we want to detect differences, but an interfering variable when we want to compare departures from proportional distributions" (*ibid.,* p. 2).

Table 8-7: Estimated and Actual Data for Ministry of Interior: Analysis of Four Variables

Data estimated from two-dimensional margins (number of respondents)

1956 rank:	Dist. Gov. Satisfied		Dist. Gov. Dissatisfied		Asst. Dist. Gov. Satisfied		Asst. Dist. Gov. Dissatisfied	
1956 job satisfaction: Social background[a]	High	Low	High	Low	High	Low	High	Low
1965 Job — Interior	3	27	11	45	1	13	4	15
1965 Job — Left	1	7	10	17	1	3	3	5
		38		83		18		27

Actual data (number of respondents)

1956 rank:	Dist. Gov. Satisfied		Dist. Gov. Dissatisfied		Asst. Dist. Gov. Satisfied		Asst. Dist. Gov. Dissatisfied	
1956 job satisfaction: Social background	High	Low	High	Low	High	Low	High	Low
1965 Job — Interior	3	29	8	46	3	9	4	17
1965 Job — Left	0	6	13	16	0	7	2	3
		38		83		19		26

[a] The "high" and "low" social background categories correspond to the "more privileged" and "less privileged" categories used in previous chapters.

Table 8-8: Mobility of District Governors in the Ministry of Interior —
Estimated and Actual Data

| | Percent remaining in Interior in 1965 | |
	Estimated	Actual
District governors (1956):		
Satisfied in 1956, less privileged background	83 (35)[a]	79 (34)[a]
Dissatisfied in 1956, less privileged background	74 (62)	73 (62)
Dissatisfied in 1956, more privileged background	52 (21)	38 (21)
Assistant district governors (1956):		
Satisfied in 1956, less privileged background	81 (16)	56 (16)
Dissatisfied in 1956, less privileged background	75 (20)	85 (20)

[a] The number of respondents in each category is given in parentheses.

The data from the Ministry of Finance did not show the clear trends depicted for the Ministry of Interior. Job satisfaction seemed to influence the organizational mobility of low-ranking administrators from less privileged backgrounds, but other relationships are unclear. The

Table 8-9: Mobility of Personnel in the Ministry of Finance —
Estimated and Actual Data

| | Percent remaining in Finance in 1965 | |
	Estimated	Actual
High-ranking personnel in Ministry of Finance (1956):		
Satisfied in 1956, more privileged background	71 (14)[a]	65 (17)[a]
Satisfied in 1956, less privileged background	63 (38)	68 (34)
Low-ranking personnel in Ministry of Finance (1956):		
Satisfied in 1956, less privileged background	82 (17)	84 (22)
Dissatisfied in 1956, less privileged background	60 (15)	47 (15)

[a] The number of respondents in each category is given in parentheses.

158

estimated and actual data produced by the four-variable analysis are summarized in Table 8-9; the remaining categories contained an insufficient number of respondents for percentaging and comparison.

Finally, we should mention that these data reinforce the findings reported in previous chapters. The relationships among variables differ substantially between the Ministries of Interior and Finance. The relationships among rank, job satisfaction, social background, and organizational mobility are not in complete accord with the findings reported from American organizational research. On the other hand, within each ministry there are a number of regularities. Many of the factors seem roughly additive, permitting a fair degree of prediction from the two-dimensional margins.

Elites and Organizations over Time

Much of the literature on political development and elite theory has ignored advances in handling time-series and multi-variate data. This discussion has been directed toward applying some methods used in other social sciences to problems of political science and organization theory. Although the focus has been at the micro-level, upon data pertaining to individuals, the discussion is relevant to important political problems.

This approach represents an effort to extend our knowledge of the administrative elite's job satisfaction and organizational mobility. Improving the political scientist's ability to predict elite satisfaction and mobility is one possible result of the research initiated here. Environmental changes — macro-level political and economic events — are likely to influence this mobility, but the structural and attitudinal variables discussed in these chapters will probably continue to be important.

The analysis also helps spotlight those respondents who seemed eager to leave the more traditional ministries. Dissatisfied district governors from more privileged backgrounds were identified as especially prone to leave the Ministry of Interior. If outside opportunities had not been available, these individuals might have been particularly alienated; if, in the future, mobility were to be blocked, they might become disproportionately upset about their careers.

In summary, we have examined the relationships among a few variables for which panel data were available. Unfortunately, such longitudinal data do not exist for many attitudes immediately relevant to

Turkish social and political problems. However, the 1965 study did include a number of attitudinal questions concerning the bureaucrat's orientations toward other interest groups in Turkish society. These will be discussed in the following chapter.

9
Bureaucrats, Businessmen, and Politicians

Previous chapters have dealt with the effects of political and economic modernization upon the Turkish bureaucracy and with Turkish administrators' individual responses to new pressures and challenges. The separation between the organizational and the individual response is clearly important. The central ministries have tried to maintain their relatively powerful position in Turkish society, but a sizable number of Faculty graduates have left the Ministries of Interior and Finance for new opportunities elsewhere. In the light of these findings the attitudes of Political Science Faculty graduates toward various elite groups in Turkish society are difficult to predict. An individual's organizational position might influence him one way, while career possibilities pulled him another.

The development literature is not very helpful in generating hypotheses relevant to the administrators' opinions of businessmen and politicians. Several studies of individual countries have noted bureaucrat–politician conflict without specifying its organizational and attitudinal dimensions.[1] High levels of contact with businessmen and politicians might — or might not — be associated with negative attitudes toward these elite groups. One hypothesis is suggested by research on anticipatory socialization. Many of the attitudes of administrators planning to leave the Ministries of Interior and Finance might be expected to resemble the attitudes of their counterparts already in the new, non-central organizations.

Elite Groups: Contributions and Prestige

The attitudes of Political Science Faculty graduates showed little of the hostility toward politicians and businessmen suggested by comparative administration theorists and many commentators on the Turkish scene.[2] Nor was there a self-righteous conviction on the part

1. See, for example, Lucian W. Pye, *Politics, Personality, and Nation Building* (New Haven, Conn., Yale University Press, 1962).
2. Frederick W. Frey, *The Turkish Political Elite* (Cambridge, Mass., M.I.T. Press, 1965), pp. 391–393; Kemal Karpat, "Society, Economics, and Politics in Contemporary Turkey," *World Politics,* 17 (October 1964), 60–63; W. B. Sherwood, "The Rise of the Justice Party in Turkey," *World Politics,* 20 (October

of these graduates of the "Civil Service School" that the official class plays an indispensable role in Turkish development. In the 1965 survey, when graduates were asked, "In which of the following ways can a citizen best benefit his country?" their answers favored business and politics: 46 percent said by being a businessman, 20 percent said by holding a political office, 11 percent mentioned working in the government administration, 6 percent said by practicing one of the free professions, and only one person noted serving in the military. Fifteen percent of the graduates did not answer. Businessmen and politicians — the groups which most successfully challenged the traditional power and prestige of the Turkish official class — were the two groups seen as making the biggest contribution to the development of the Turkish state. Government administrators were ranked a poor third, and almost no one had a kind word to say for the military.

This low evaluation of the military should not be dismissed lightly. The military was responsible for the 1960 coup, which has frequently been interpreted as an effort to restore the influence of the official classes. After assuming power, the military pushed through a series of measures aiding the bureaucracy and the intelligentsia.[3] The National Unity Committee's creation of the State Planning Organization was an explicit attempt by the military to give bureaucrats more control over the private sector of the economy. Similarly, the major constitutional changes (proportional representation and the creation of a second chamber) were intended to strengthen the Republican People's Party — the party traditionally favored by the official classes.

However, the army's attempt to restore the influence of the official classes was ill-fated. The military men proved particularly inept in economic matters, coming under heavy pressure to return the country to civilian rule. The army ignored Atatürk's precept of nonintervention in civilian politics and, as a consequence, "their prestige and influence in Turkish society has suffered a grievous blow."[4] This low evaluation of the military seemed shared by civilian members of the official class. Bureaucrats had little sympathy for a return to military rule, even if in the short run their own power might have been enhanced.

1967), 56–59; Robert W. Kerwin, "Private Enterprise in Turkish Industrial Development," *Middle East Journal,* 5 (Winter 1951), 34.

3. Karpat, "Society, Economics, and Politics," p. 62.

4. Frank Tachau and A. Haluk Ülman, "Dilemmas of Turkish Politics," *The Turkish Yearbook of International Relations* (Ankara, Ankara Üniversitesi Basïmevi, 1964), p. 33.

Table 9-1: Respondents' Attitudes toward Potential Contribution and Prestige of Various Occupations

Attitude of respondent	Ministry of Interior		Ministry of Finance (%)	Ministry of Foreign Affairs (%)	Other old organizations (%)	New, noncentral organizations (%)
	District governors (%)	Central offices (%)				
Citizen can best benefit country by being:[a]						
Businessman	65[b]	69	40	27	31	60
Politician	19	8	34	35	38	24
Administrator	10	16	23	12	14	8
Professional	7	3	0	19	17	7
Soldier	0	2	0	0	0	0
Mentioned as prestigious occupation:[c]						
Businessman	9	18	7	13	24	20
Politician	5	0	11	4	7	9
Diplomat	10	14	7	0	14	14
Other administrative position	32	29	14	9	14	25
Professional:						
Doctor	37	25	30	22	31	19
Engineer	32	29	15	22	34	20
Judge[a]	36	29	7	0	21	17
Lawyer	3	4	0	0	0	7
Military[a]	17	14	4	4	0	9
Number of respondents	59	28	27	23	29	59

[a] Differences were significant at the .05 level for these questions.
[b] The percentages are based on a total sample *n* which excludes those who did not answer these questions.
[c] The item concerning prestigious occupations was open-ended and permitted multiple responses.

As is seen in Table 9-1 the graduates' somewhat surprising disparagement of the importance of the military's contribution was rivaled by their modesty in assessing the bureaucrat's role in national development. As discussed earlier, the Political Science Faculty graduates' low evaluation of the civil servant did not depend solely on questionnaire responses, but was reinforced by the respondents' mobility out of the central ministries.

The bureaucrat's modest estimation of his role can be compared with the Turkish soldier's justification of the army's role in the 1960 coup:

> The group which was in power after 1954 trampled on all the rights of the nation. It deceived the nation. It dragged the country into disaster in the economic and social fields . . . The pride of the Turkish Armed Forces, the only organized force in the country, was broken by every possible means. The uniform — the most basic inheritance of our history — was brought to a state where it shamed its wearer . . . The nation was ready, or more correctly, was forced to use "the right of revolt against oppression." The Turkish Armed Forces, which were its essence, its spirit and its greatest guarantee, used this right.[5]

This clearly expresses the feelings of at least some members of the armed forces. Although bureaucrats have resented their low salaries and were strongly opposed to the partisan intrusions in the civil service made during the Democratic regime,[6] their attitudes toward politicians and businessmen seem to have been tempered over time.

These attitudinal data may also represent an adjustment to the conditions produced by the original ruralizing election and the Justice Party's electoral strength. As we have seen, many members of the bureaucratic elite have changed their career patterns in response to the

5. "Interview with Major Orhan Erkanli," *Cumhuriyet*, July 20, 1960. This translation is taken from "Interviews with Members of Turkey's National Unity Committee" (New York, U.S. Joint Publications Research Service, 21 October, 1960), JPRS #6127, p. 23.

6. One measure taken by the Democrats to give them more power over bureaucrats was a law passed in 1954 which gave the government power to retire judges and professors compulsorily after twenty-five years' service. This was particularly potent against judges, since "one does not normally become a judge of the Court of Appeal in less than twenty-five years." See Bernard Lewis, "Democracy in Turkey," *Middle Eastern Affairs*, 10 (February 1959), 67.

political and economic developments which accompanied modernization. A relatively high respect for the roles of businessman and politician encourages psychological acceptance of the objective changes in the power of these two groups. The fact that bureaucrats did not rate their own positions more highly may represent both a loss of self-confidence and a change in the bureaucrats' former belief in their unique role in Turkish modernization. Such feelings also suggest that the administrator's moral commitment to his work and position was eroded by developments during the multi-party period. If the administrator's role is to be less significant, there is less reason for individuals to become highly committed to such positions.

Graduates of the Political Science Faculty were generous in their evaluation of the contribution which politicians and businessmen have made to Turkey's national development, but were less deferential in the prestige accorded these two groups. Only 7 percent indicated a political career was one of the vocations for which they felt most respect, and only 15 percent mentioned business. In contrast, 28 percent mentioned the medical profession and 26 percent cited an engineering career.[7] This low ranking is not surprising. A business career has never been very prestigious in Turkish society, and few people think of politicians as practicing a vocation. Finally, these data on prestige may be of less significance than the material on the contribution of different groups to Turkish development. Cross-national studies of occupational prestige have noted that the free professions are generally evaluated very highly while businessmen and, to a lesser degree, politicians are not. These Turkish findings may merely reflect this similarity of prestige rankings across countries. As was pointed out earlier, when the same question was asked of a group of Turkish lycée youths in 1959, only 2 percent of them mentioned a business career, and only 11 percent a political or administrative career in government service.

A breakdown by organization of these items dealing with contribution and prestige provides further information on attitudes toward various elite groups. Graduates in the Ministry of Interior and the

---

7. It has been postulated that this similarity is due to "the essential structural similarity shared by all nations of any degree of complexity." Robert W. Hodge, Donald J. Treiman, and Peter H. Rossi, "A Comparative Study of Occupational Prestige," in Reinhard Bendix and Seymour Martin Lipset, eds., *Class, Status, and Power* (New York, Free Press, 1966), p. 321.

noncentral organizations appeared generally supportive of the businessman. In this regard there were few differences among individuals in the new ministries, state economic enterprises, and the private sector. Respondents working in the Ministries of Finance and Foreign Affairs felt less positively toward the businessman, perhaps because of conflicts over issues such as development plans and tariff regulations.[8] Graduates in the Ministry of Foreign Affairs were more likely to note the potential contribution made by the politician, while those in the Ministry of Finance mentioned the politician and the administrator.

Graduates in the Ministry of Finance were most likely to mention the contribution of the administrator, and on another item reported the most favorable image of the civil servant.[9] Since both favorable and unfavorable images were reported — sometimes by the same individual — one appropriate measure is the percentage of favorable responses minus the percentage of unfavorable responses. The largest positive difference — 27 percent — was noted by graduates in the Ministry of Finance; the most hostility was shown by respondents in the new, noncentral organizations. More of these graduates held unfavorable views (38 percent) of the civil servant than gave favorable views (11 percent).

Politicians: Interaction and Friction

Questions exploring the bureaucrats' reactions to politicians were included in the survey. This relationship between bureaucrat and politician was a matter of particular concern, since a number of authors have stressed the political role of the administrator in developing countries. Pye, for example, has stated that "in many of the new countries administration would be far more effective if administrators were to

8. As will be discussed later, graduates working in the Ministry of Finance also showed a great deal of hostility toward politicians. Perhaps these respondents felt that an individual could benefit the country by *replacing* the current crop of politicians. It should also be noted that two different Turkish words were used for "politician" in the two questions. The term used in the questions presented in Table 9-1 was *siyasi bir mevki* which has some connotation of statesman. The term used in the question "do politicians help or hinder national development?" was *politikacïlar*. It has been suggested that this term has more of a connotation of local party organizers and activists.

9. The phrasing of the question was, "If you were to describe your general image of a Turkish civil servant, what sort of a person would that be?"

adopt more aggressive measures and seek to be more political and less legalistic." [10] The handling of political pressures is often seen as particularly important. Thus, Eisenstadt notes that "within the political sphere the equivalent of . . . self-sustained growth is the ability to absorb varieties and changing types of political demands and organization." [11]

One set of questions concerned the graduates' day-to-day interactions with peasants and with politicians and the friction which appears to accompany such interaction. An especially relevant item inquired about public demands upon administrators. Bureaucrats who thought the public makes *many* (rather than some or none) extra demands upon them (above and beyond what they do for the public in the ordinary course of their jobs) were generally those having frequent contact with peasants and with politicians. This question on demands provides a measure of pressure from the public — particularly the peasants — and its representatives.

Table 9-2 shows definite regularities across the questions on friction. Respondents working in the Ministry of Interior, both in the central offices and in the district administration, had frequent contact with peasants and their political representatives. Almost as a corollary of this, these bureaucrats expressed the most dissatisfaction both with political interference in their work and with the heavy pressures from public demands. In contrast, graduates working in the noncentral organizations and in the Ministries of Foreign Affairs and Finance reported relatively little contact with the politicized peasantry. These graduates also registered many fewer complaints about political interference and heavy public demands.

The district governor's work invites political pressure and the friction accompanying such pressure. Administrators in higher-level jobs in the Ministry of the Interior appear to have had more contact with local leadership than did their counterparts in other ministries, but less than did the district governors. Since personnel in the central offices of the Ministry of Interior dealt with matters of major interest to grassroots politicians and their constituencies (boundary disputes, changing the location of district seats, granting provincial budgetary

---

10. Lucian W. Pye, *Aspects of Political Development* (Boston, Little, Brown, 1966), p. 23.

11. S. N. Eisenstadt, "Bureaucracy and Political Development," in Joseph La Palombara, ed., *Bureaucracy and Political Development* (Princeton, N.J., Princeton University Press, 1963), p. 96.

Table 9-2: Interaction and Friction among Administrators,
Peasants, and Politicians[a]

| | Ministry of Interior | | Minis-try of Finance (%) | Minis try of Foreign Affairs (%) | Other old organ- izations (%) | New, non- central organ- izations (%) |
	District gover- nors (%)	Central offices (%)				
INTERACTION						
Frequent contact with:						
Both peasants and politicians	44	32	7	18	21	10
Peasants only	50	27	13	12	15	20
Politicians only	1	12	9	29	15	17
Daily contact with peasants	94	44	7	6	18	18
Daily contact with politicians	16	18	7	21	9	18
FRICTION						
Dissatisfied with job because of:						
Political interference	59	46	6	—[b]	13	0
Changed mind toward work because of:						
Political situation	20	24	4	0	21	11
Public makes many extra demands	74	47	9	24	21	23
Number of respondents	80	34	45	34	34	79

[a] Differences were significant at the .05 level for all variables.
[b] So few people in the Ministry of Foreign Affairs expressed any dissatisfaction with their jobs that this question was not applicable.

requests), these bureaucrats also were concerned about political interference and public demands.

The relationships between interaction and friction are substantial. Individuals reporting frequent contact with *both* peasants and politicians were the most likely to be dissatisfied because of political interference, to have changed their minds about their work, and to say that the public makes many extra demands. A comparison of the other respondents indicated that emphasis on contact only with peasants was more closely associated with friction than was the mention of contact only with politicians. Peasant demands seemed to produce more friction than did the demands of the politicians with whom respondents in the Ministry of Foreign Affairs and in the other, old organizations had relatively frequent contact.

These findings suggest other questions: Was friction with peasants and their political leadership likely to affect an individual's overall evaluation of politicians and other interest groups? Did organizational differences in the evaluation of politicians tend to correspond with differences in contact? Table 9-3 presents the percentage of respond-

Table 9-3: Attitudes of Administrators toward Politicians and Pressure Groups[a]

| Attitudes of Respondents | Ministry of Interior | | Ministry of Finance (%) | Ministry of Foreign Affairs (%) | Other old organizations (%) | New, non-central organizations (%) |
	District governors (%)	Central Offices (%)				
Politicians hinder national development	18	21	33	21	18	39
Index of negative feelings toward interest groups						
Medium	33	3	18	21	18	35
High	1	3	11	0	3	11
Political pull is important	33	44	47	29	47	39
Number of respondents	80	34	45	34	34	79

[a] Differences were significant at the .05 level for all variables.

ents saying that politicians "hinder" the national development of Turkey. Such a negative response would seem to indicate hostility toward politicians as a group. This question was part of a series asking, "Which of the following groups do you feel help, hinder, or are unimportant to the national development of Turkey?" In addition to politicians, respondents were asked to express their opinions about workers, peasants, village headmen, members of the free professions, professional and interest groups, administrators, and foreigners. Appendix C describes the index constructed to measure negative feelings toward interest groups. The data regarding politicians were presented separately, rather than being included in the index. Respondents were also given the following statement: "Some people think that 'political pull' (knowing the right person) plays an important part in whether the government will help a private citizen with some problem he has; other people don't think so. In your opinion, does political pull play an important part or not?" Those who emphasized the importance of political pull are included in Table 9-3.

A very different pattern is discernible from these data. The most negative attitudes toward politicians and other pressure groups were held by graduates working in the Ministry of Finance and in some of the new, noncentral organizations. Respondents in the new ministries and state economic enterprises were very critical of politicians; 43 percent in each group believed politicians hindered development. The graduates working in the private sector were less critical. Only 25 percent said politicians hindered development, and 40 percent (the highest percentage of any group) said they helped. Graduates in the Ministry of Foreign Affairs expressed much less animosity toward specific groups, while respondents in the Ministry of Interior — both district governors and those in the central offices — occupied a middle position.

These results are somewhat surprising, particularly when compared with the data of Table 9-2. The groups complaining about friction with politicians were not the same groups which evaluated politicians so negatively. The individual inter-item correlations reinforce this statement. The items presented in Table 9-2 were intercorrelated with each other, as were the items in Table 9-3. However, the relationships between items in Table 9-2 and those in Table 9-3 were weak or nonexistent. For example, contact with peasants and politicians is unrelated either to an individual's perception of political pull or to his evaluation of the politicians' contribution to national development.

Such findings suggest that two largely separate processes are at work. Many attitudes are dependent upon the individual's experience at his place of work. In Chapter 7 place of work was seen to be an important determinant of job satisfaction or dissatisfaction. Some selective leaving took place, but reasons for satisfaction tended to change when the respondent moved from one organization or position to another. We hypothesize that answers to the items concerning interaction and friction were also shaped by the administrator's day-to-day work experience. The type of job situation in which the respondent found himself was a primary determinant of his interaction and friction with peasants and politicians.

On the other hand, selective recruitment to various types of organizations may also take place. Individuals might have sought employment in the new ministries and state economic enterprises to try to avoid dealing with politicians who would annoy them. We suggest that selective recruitment is largely responsible for the data reported in Table 9-3; respondents critical of politicians have been particularly attracted to jobs in the new, noncentral organizations.

Socialization versus Recruitment — Political Attitudes

These questions of socialization and recruitment can be clarified by the following diagram.

Socialization

Membership in an organization ⟶ Attitudes

Selective Recruitment

Attitudes ⟋ Joining an organization
⟍ Leaving an organization and joining another

Are many of the attitudes of graduates shaped by their work experience? Do graduates with different attitudes tend to enter different types of organizations? Our data can be used in several ways to investigate these questions.

Events have forced the Ministry of Interior to cooperate with local politicians in a number of ways. The power relationship between administrator and politician changed markedly after the ruralizing election of 1950; work as a district governor is probably aided by psychological acceptance of these changes. Thus, as Cyert and Mac-

Crimmon have noted, "compatibility between organizational goals and those of participants often increases over time." Attitude change is one way this can be done: "The goals of individuals who remain in . . . situations of potential conflict are sometimes modified in such a way that they become more compatible with the organizational goals . . . Another common mechanism conducive to more compatibility over time is turn-over. An individual who cannot resolve a conflict leaves or is removed from his role." [12]

The feelings of district governors hoping to move into the private sector were generally intermediate between the attitudes of those already in the noncentral organizations and the attitudes of district governors planning either to remain in the Ministry of Interior or to change ministries. This finding indicates the significance of turnover and differential recruitment, but does not undermine the possible importance of adult socialization as a determinant of attitudes toward politicians. Since most of the older graduates in the new, noncentral organizations originally worked in the Ministries of Interior or Finance, the attitudes of respondents in the newer organizations could have been formed by unpleasant experiences with politicians while working in the central ministries.[13]

Some of the attitudinal differences among organizations appear linked to factors independent of previous job experience in the central ministries. Table 9-4 shows the attitudinal differences between 1958–1961 graduates serving as district governors and those in the new, noncentral organizations. The great majority of the 1946–1955 graduates who were district governors (51 out of 56) had more than five years' experience in their jobs. The 1958–1961 graduates in the Ministry of Interior all had less than five years' experience as district governors; the average was between two and three years. Since the 1958–1961 graduates have moved directly into positions in the new organizations, most of them never worked in the central ministries. Although

12. Richard M. Cyert and Kenneth R. MacCrimmon, "Organizations," in Gardner Lindzey and Elliot Aronson, eds., *The Handbook of Social Psychology* (Reading, Mass., Addison-Wesley, 1968), I, 573.

13. This analysis concentrates on the attitudes toward politicians held by graduates in the Ministry of Interior, since there were few differences between the opinions of graduates in the Ministry of Finance and those of respondents in noncentral organizations. This supports the hypothesis forwarded in Chapter 7: "Attitudinal differences between those who leave an organization experiencing severe stress and those who stay are likely to be greater than differences between leavers and stayers in other organizations."

172

Table 9-4: Attitudes of Younger and Older Graduates toward Politicians

Attitudes of respondents	Younger graduates (Classes of 1958–61)[a]		Older graduates (Classes of 1946–55)[b]	
	District governors (%)	In noncentral organizations (%)	District governors (%)	Left Ministry of Interior for noncentral organizations (%)
Politicians hinder national development	25	46	14	50
Index of negative feelings toward interest groups:				
Medium	50	42	25	19
High	0	19	2	19
Political pull is important	33	46	32	56
Number of respondents	24	26	56	16

[a] Differences were significant at the .05 level for the index of negative feelings toward interest groups.

[b] Differences were significant at the .05 level for all variables.

only one of the relationships was statistically significant, the attitudinal differences were suggestive.

Table 9-4 also illustrates the importance of selective leaving. The attitudes of the younger district governors (1958–1961 graduates) were intermediate between those of the older district governors and those of the older graduates who left Interior to work in the new, noncentral organizations. The more experienced district governors were more favorably inclined toward politicians and other groups than were their counterparts with less experience. The older graduates in the new, noncentral organizations were more hostile toward politicians. Over the course of their first few years as district governors, the more alien-ated administrators may have left the Ministry of Interior. Such selec-tive leaving would help account for the attitudinal differences discussed here; the remaining district governors would tend to be dispropor-tionately favorable to politicians.

The 1956 survey of district governors suggests that less experienced administrators were more likely to mention harmful political inter-ference than were their counterparts with more experience. Moreover, district governors with less than five years' experience were more likely to report political party members as intermediaries than ad-ministrators with more than five years' experience. The attitudes of the administrators who left in the 1956–1965 period appear most similar to those of the governors with less than five years' experience. These differences may reflect the actual pressures upon the adminis-trators or just the particular sensitivities of younger governors assigned to the more difficult districts.[14]

Finally, an effort was made to combine the surveys and construct a joint index of concern about political interference. Three questions, each from a different survey, were used to build an index of political interference.[15] Leaving the Ministry of Interior in the 1956–1965 period was associated with this index of political interference. Twenty-seven percent of the 1956 district governors with a high degree of con-cern for political interference had taken outside jobs by 1965, while only 6 percent of those with a low score had done so. Overall, the data

14. Fifty-nine percent of the district governors ($n = 166$) with less than five years' experience reported that they sometimes experienced harmful political interference. Corresponding figures for those with between five to ten years' ex-perience ($n = 83$) and more than ten years' experience ($n = 31$) were 48 and 33 percent respectively. Controlling for the developmental status of the district somewhat reduced the strength of this relationship.

15. The questions related to (a) dissatisfaction because of political inter-ference (1956 Political Science Faculty survey); (b) the presence of harmful political interference (1956 district governor survey); and (c) the importance of "political pull" (1965 Political Science Faculty survey). This index was corre-lated with the data on intermediaries. Eighty-two percent of the district gover-nors reporting a low score on the index of political interference ($n = 33$) men-tioned that over 80 percent of the citizens with grievances presented their own requests, while only 62 percent of the governors with a high score made this statement ($n = 33$). The use of an index compiled from three independently conducted surveys increased the reliability of the results, helping to avoid the instability connected with the use of single items. This index is discussed further in Appendix C.

accord with an emphasis upon the selective leaving of district governors who dislike political pressures.[16] The possibility of attitude change among the more experienced governors cannot be eliminated; such processes might supplement the differences due to selective leaving.[17]

Careers and Group Feelings

The respondent's place of work and variables closely associated with organizational recruitment, such as section at the Political Science Faculty, were consistently the best predictors of the attitudes discussed here: contribution and prestige of various professions, interaction and friction with peasants and politicians, and feelings toward politicians.[18] Specifying causal relationships is more difficult, particularly with respect to feelings toward politicians. Organizational socialization may still lead to attitudinal differences, but the data emphasize the importance of selective recruitment to and selective departure from different organizations. Graduates with negative opinions of politicians may have particularly disliked the politicized interaction with local leadership required in the district governor's work. These individuals would be expected to avoid the Ministry of Interior, and if obligated to enter this ministry because of scholarship aid, to leave as soon as possible. Such behavior probably constitutes individual adaptation to the pressures of control by rurally based politicians.

The most unfavorable feelings toward politicians were found outside the Ministry of Interior; they did not depend solely upon experiences in the Ministries of Interior or Finance. The new organizations have been attracting graduates with negative feelings toward

16. The provincial governors, almost all of whom had been promoted from the ranks of district governors, were extremely close-mouthed about political interference.

17. Some American data indicate that, in a politicized environment, experience with political pressures may lead to an increased acceptance of these pressures. Wahlke and his collaborators found that the longer the legislative service, the more favorable the attitudes toward political pressures. John C. Wahlke, et al., "American State Legislators' Role Toward Pressure Groups," *The Journal of Politics,* 22 (May 1960), 203–227.

18. Other independent variables considered were participation in decision-making at home and in school, region of work, region of birth, father's occupation, date of university graduation, salary and rank, administrative versus professional work, opinions of democracy, and desired curriculum changes. Several different proportional-reduction-in-error measures were used for this comparison.

politicians directly from the Political Science Faculty. However, even the 1958–1961 graduates had been working for several years by 1965; the respondents could have been influenced toward adopting attitudes characteristic of the organization in which they worked.

Thus, socialization within various organizations might have contributed to the negative opinions of politicians.[19] As discussed earlier, graduates whose work was concerned with rational production, fiscal measures, and economic planning may become embroiled in — or at least be affected by — disputes with politicians. The contact with politicians does not involve day-to-day interference in the bureaucrat's work (as it does with district governors), but higher-level political decisions which may go against the recommendations and interests of administrators in the Ministry of Finance or in the new, noncentral organizations. The interests of graduates in such varied organizations as the Ministry of Finance, state economic enterprises, banks, and private enterprise are often in conflict with each other, but the politicians who must mediate the disputes and make the decisions receive little appreciation from the individuals affected.

The thrust of this analysis is different in some respects from that presented in Chapter 7. Two separate processes seem to be involved. Here, selective recruitment to various organizations has been put forward as a critical determinant of certain attitudinal differences among ministries. The causal factors responsible for these attitudes — the orientations toward politicians stressed in this chapter — were unclear but may well have been formed before the respondent entered the job market. On the other hand, one set of politically relevant attitudes — those dealing with job satisfaction — were almost certainly caused by the conditions and organizations associated with the work experience.

These data also shed light on the much-discussed bureaucrat-politician conflict. The attitudinal information suggests that feelings toward politicians vary significantly from one organization to another. Administrators play different roles in different kinds of organizations, and an awareness of these roles may be reflected in selective recruitment. Even such negative feelings as irritation and hostility need not go together within the same organization. Further studies of this bureaucrat-politician conflict would be aided by a better specification of types of politician than was attempted here.

19. Other investigators have stressed the importance of such adult socialization. See Donald D. Searing, "The Comparative Study of Elite Socialization," *Comparative Political Studies,* 1 (January 1969), 471–500.

176

Feelings toward politicians must be considered within the general attitudinal framework of graduates working in the new, noncentral organizations. Since these individuals were generally satisfied with their work and optimistic about their futures, these negative attitudes were not expressed in vigorous political action. Even within the Ministry of Finance, 60 percent of the respondents reported being satisfied with their jobs. Satisfactory career possibilities would be expected to lower the tensions associated with disagreement among elite groups. Turkish economic growth between 1965 and 1969 may have helped maintain these career possibilities and thus aided stability. By the same token, the slowdown in rates of growth in 1970 appears to have had negative implications for stability.

More generally, the data suggest that social change can affect attitudes in rather unexpected ways. The greatest hostility toward politicians and interest groups was found outside the organizations most hurt by ruralizing election. These findings may have been partially attributable to resentment on the part of individuals forced to change career patterns because of new status and power relationships within Turkey.

Finally, the bureaucrats' reserved feelings toward the military should be reiterated. Such data are of particular interest as indicators of the loosening of the bonds between the bureaucracy and the military which have endured since the founding of the Turkish Republic. As of 1965, there was no widespread awe of the military's uniquely valuable contribution to Turkey. Although both the civil servants and the military had been under similar pressures in the late 1950's, few enduring psychological ties between these two groups were noted in the 1965 survey data. The tie between administrator and military officer may have been eroded by social change and the experience of military rule.

10

Administration, Politics, and Development

The relationships among administrators, local leaders, and villagers form the basis for many discussions of modernization. Riggs, for example, has stressed that government officials are likely to hinder rural development efforts; local initiative can be stifled by bureaucrats oriented toward the central government.[1] Various sorts of attitudes may be important. Silberman has argued that Japan's successful efforts toward economic development were due to a similar value structure, shared by both the social and bureaucratic elites.[2] Perhaps administrators from rural backgrounds, because of attitudinal similarities with local elites, are more successful in development efforts than their counterparts raised in an urban elite tradition.

Other factors may influence the effectiveness of the rural administrator. An area's level of development may be related to the kind and quality of local demands upon the district governor. Eisenstadt has suggested that social, economic, and cultural modernization all combine to produce new types of political pressures with which the central political institutions must deal.[3] One group of scholars has argued that increased political pressures upon administrators have positive effects upon performance, forcing the administrators to make decisions, to obtain services, and to treat individuals on a more-or-less equal basis. Thus political pressures push administrators into a service orientation.[4]

Another perspective is provided by considering the bureaucrat-citizen relationship from the villagers' point of view. Contact with govern-

1. Fred W. Riggs, "Bureaucrats and Political Development: A Paradoxical View," in Joseph La Palombara, ed., *Bureaucracy and Political Development* (Princeton, N.J., Princeton University Press, 1963), pp. 120–167.

2. Bernard S. Silberman, "Criteria for Recruitment and Success in the Japanese Bureaucracy, 1868–1900: 'Traditional' and 'Modern' Criteria in Bureaucratic Development," *Economic Development and Cultural Change,* 14 (January 1966), 171–172.

3. S. N. Eisenstadt, "Bureaucracy and Political Development," in La Palombara, ed., *Bureaucracy and Political Development,* pp. 102–103.

4. Riggs, "Bureaucrats and Political Development." See also Lucian W. Pye, "The Political Context of National Development," in Irving Swerdlow, ed., *Development Administration: Concepts and Problems* (Syracuse, N.Y., Syracuse University Press, 1963).

178

ment officials may be seen as a significant form of political participation. When peasants and townsmen approach an administrator, they cross important status barriers in an effort to improve their conditions and opportunities. Official responsiveness aids individual and group mobility, demonstrating that democracy can help the low-status villager.

A very different case is made by those who fear that economic development is accompanied by a greater capacity for group organization and by increased group demands. If the government is unable to satisfy these increased demands, dangerous social frustration and political instability may result.[5] Others, particularly administrators themselves, feel that the constant intervention of elected officials and politicians adversely affects administrative efficiency, often fostering graft and corruption.[6]

Turkish Local Administration

The changing nature of Turkish rural administration has been discussed in several parts of this book. During the authoritarian single-party period, the district governor was an official commanding respect, accountable only to his superior, the provincial governor, and to the central office of the Ministry of Interior. At that time much of the district governor's activity was directed toward settling disputes and ensuring compliance with the laws. Although the governor was also responsible for supervising the modernization of villages, there was no great thrust toward local development. The administration was satisfied with token compliance with the law.[7]

With the advent of multi-party politics, however, the administrator's responsibility for village development took on a new meaning. Parties won votes by listening to the grievances of the rural masses and by promising concrete improvements. No longer did the provincial governors represent both the party and the administration. Under the

5. Samuel P. Huntington, *Political Order In Changing Societies* (New Haven, Conn., Yale University Press, 1968), p. 50.
6. See Aydĭn Yalçĭn, "Turkey: Emerging Democracy," *Foreign Affairs,* 45 (July 1967), 711, for a report on how administrators have reacted. This thesis is also presented by Joseph Szyliowicz in *Political Change in Rural Turkey-Erdemli* (The Hague, Mouton, 1966), pp. 132–135.
7. Szyliowicz, *Political Change,* p. 38.

stimulus of political pressure the bureaucrat was to assume a new role as an agent of change. Moreover, development had at least partially to meet the demands of the awakened peasantry. As might be expected, the change in roles increased the importance of satisfactory relations between elite and mass.

Relations between the university-educated bureaucratic elite and the less educated citizenry pose numerous problems and opportunities. Successful interaction can benefit elite and mass. Communication patterns between the elite administrator and the local leadership serve vital instrumental and intelligence functions for the elite, aiding it both in achieving support and in evaluating "the ever-changing content of citizen demands." At the same time, communicative relationships may (or may not) help motivate the citizen to participate in government programs.[8]

Problems connected with the elite–mass gap hamper relations between district governors and villagers in several ways. The villagers' ability to pressure the district governors has taken many forms, most of which the district governors have found objectionable. Local politicians often accompany the citizen to help present his views to the administrator or otherwise intervene to plead the individual's case. The town mayors and village headmen play a prominent role in pressuring the district governors. Both mayor and headman are typically elected, although only the former is allowed to campaign openly on a party platform. At the village level formal political party organizations are prohibited, but many of the headmen have informal party affiliations.

These local officials are not the social equals of the administrator; for this reason their pressures may have seemed particularly onerous. In Turkey, education is the primary determinant of social status.[9] District governors are not only university graduates, but for the most part graduates of one of the most prestigious faculties — the Political Science Faculty. The educational level of mayors and headmen falls far below this. In 1958 only 8 percent of the mayors were university graduates; these better-educated mayors were concentrated in provin-

8. Samuel J. Eldersveld, "Bureaucratic Contact with the Public in India," *Indian Journal of Public Administration*, 11 (April–June 1965), 216.

9. For a discussion of this, citing a number of other authors, see Frederick W. Frey, *The Turkish Political Elite* (Cambridge, Mass., M.I.T. Press, 1965), pp. 29–72.

180

cial centers rather than in the smaller towns under the district governors' jurisdiction.[10] The mayors with whom the district governor came into contact were largely primary or middle-school graduates.[11] The village headmen were an even less educated group. According to the 1962 village survey, only 68 percent of the headmen were literate, and only 43 percent had attended school.

A deterioration in the prestige and economic status traditionally associated with the position of district governor has also accompanied the increase in responsibility and political interference. This has led to a reluctance to go into the provincial administration and to substantial job dissatisfaction among district governors. Graduates who have entered the Ministry of Interior over the last decade are likely to be upwardly mobile individuals — sons of farmers and minor officials — obligated by scholarship support to work in this ministry.

Local Administration: Social Structural Variables

The importance of the district governor to rural modernization has been discussed above. Another individual playing a crucial role in the implementation of many rural development programs is the village headman. This elected official has obligations to the central government and as well as to his own villagers. Poor communication between the locally elected village headman and higher administrative officials, all of whom are centrally appointed, can create problems. Feedback along the administrative chain is often lacking, and appointed officials are sometimes unresponsive.[12]

10. Provincial and district centers — whatever their population — and cities of over 2,000 population constitute municipalities. In municipalities, the elected mayors represent the populace in dealing with the district governor. Mayors are elected directly by the people for a four-year term and run for office as members of political parties. "As a chief executive, the mayor carries out regulations, puts into effect the decisions of the (elected municipal) council and committee and controls the work of the municipal departments" — Arslan Başarïr and Dundar Karaşar, "Local Government in Turkey," in Frederick T. Bent and Louise L. Shields, eds., *The Role of Local Government in National Development* (Ankara, CENTO, 1968), p. 45.

11. In 1964 10 percent of the mayors were university graduates, 53 percent primary school graduates, and 20 percent middle school graduates. Mayors were predominantly from commercial and agricultural occupations (averaging over 30 percent from each group). Ruşen Keleş and Cevat Geray, *Türk Belediye Başkanlarï* [Turkish mayors] (Ankara, Ayyïldïz Matabaasï, 1964), p. 17.

12. John F. Kolars, *Tradition, Season, and Change in a Turkish Village* (Chicago, Ill., University of Chicago Press, 1963), p. 87.

The district governor's relationship with this local figure and the headman's feeling toward the central governmental representative are matters of real concern. If the district governor sees the headman as a threat or a nuisance, the administrator may bypass him and attempt to set up his own power structure in the village. Thus Befu has declared that in the modernizing state, "the government begins to affect more and more areas of life, gradually replacing the traditional political structure of the village with a structure of its own creation." [13] On the other hand, the district governor may decide to work through the local power structure, thus strengthening the headman's position. The headman also has several options: he can obstruct the district governor's efforts, trying to minimize the bureaucrat's authority in village affairs; or he can cooperate with the administrator, perhaps winning some patronage useful in intra-village affairs.

The administrative elite's assessment of the role played by village headmen was measured by the following question: "In your opinion do the village headman and the council of elders help, hinder, or are they unimportant to Turkey's development?" [14] Although the overall evaluation of the headman was relatively favorable, the more familiar the administrator was with rural problems, the higher he ranked the headman's contribution to national development. Thus, having a great deal of contact with villagers — being employed as a district governor — was associated with considering the village headman helpful to development. Fifty percent of the district governors said the headman was helpful. The percentage from this one subgroup within the Ministry of Interior was considerably higher than that found in any of the other organizations. Most of the respondents outside of the Ministry of Interior considered village headmen unimportant to the development process. Past experience as a district governor seems to have affected responses to this question. Former district governors, both those promoted to other positions in the ministry and those who left it for higher-paying work, had almost as favorable opinions of village headmen as did the 1965 district governors.

The communications problem between the village official and the central government representative was noted earlier in this section.

13. Harumi Befu, "The Political Relation of the Village to the State," *World Politics*, 29 (July 1967), 601–620.

14. The council of elders is generally agreed to be of rather minor importance in village decision-making. This item was asked on the 1965 survey of Political Science Faculty graduates.

182

District governors from less privileged backgrounds tended to have a relatively favorable view of village headmen, but the data were of marginal statistical significance. Two related indicators of rural background — being born in a district center (or smaller town) and being the son of a farmer — seemed correlated with a positive evaluation of the village headmen's role, but the findings were not statistically significant. The possibilities of selective recruitment mentioned in Chapter 9 are reinforced by the fact that certain groups of respondents seem particularly hostile toward the village headman. Thus only 29 percent of those who had left the Ministry of Finance for jobs in the new, noncentral organizations — and only 12 percent of the younger graduates in these organizations — evaluated the headman favorably.[15]

Just as district governors generally evaluated the village headmen favorably, so were the village headmen disposed toward acknowledging the administrator's power. Both villagers and headmen were asked which people were influential with respect to various local issues. On a general question of influence over village affairs, the headmen were not averse to recognizing their own privileged position, but they discriminated more sharply than the ordinary villager between different kinds of power. In the area of farming leadership, headmen viewed their villagers as likely to turn either to the district governor[16] or to a government technical expert such as an agricultural agent. The village headmen were also less prone to see themselves as providing leadership in a land dispute and more likely to see the district governors in such a role.

The tendency for district governors to be relatively favorably disposed toward the village headman and the village headman's respectful evaluation of the administrator's position would seem to permit fruitful communication between these two power figures (Table 10-1). However, communication may be hindered by attitudinal differences. On both the 1965 elite survey and the 1962 village survey, a similar

15. A number of other factors were compared with the item evaluating the headman. Such variables as age, job satisfaction, holding an administrative versus a professional job, and socialization experiences were not regularly associated with the evaluation of the headman. Among the district governors, no consistent relationships were found between evaluation of the village headman and the administrator's time-budgeting pattern — whether he spent time on administrative matters, village touring, public works projects, and so on.

16. This seems unlikely and may simply illustrate the deference of the headmen to their administrative superiors, the district governors.

Table 10-1: Assessment of Leadership at Local Level

	In opinion of	
Assessment	Village headmen	Male villagers
Individual seen as:		
Most influential in village		
Village headman	78%	74%
District governor	1	1
Agricultural leader in village[a]		
Village headman	18	48
District governor	31	13
Other government official	41	28
Leader with regard to land disputes[a]		
Village headman	32	45
District governor	53	42
Number of respondents	424	3,022

Source: The data on village headmen and male villagers were provided by Frederick W. Frey from the 1962 Turkish village survey.

[a] Differences for these variables were significant at the .01 level.

series of items dealt with peasants' problems and possible responses to them. The initial question read: "In your opinion, what is the most important problem that faces the peasants today?" The respondents then were asked what could be done to solve the problem. The rural administrative elite's diagnosis of peasant problems differs substantially from the peasants' own feelings on the subject.

It is perhaps not surprising that administrators who have spent at least their university years in the relative comfort of Ankara should find the poverty and low intellectual level of the villagers overwhelming. Contact with villagers seems to have sharpened the bureaucrats' perceptions, but the effects of such contact are not cumulative (see Table 10-2). Although district governors were somewhat closer to the villagers in their perception of village problems than were other elite administrators (for example, 71 percent of the respondents in the Ministry of Foreign Affairs mentioned education), the district governor's perception of peasant problems was related neither to his own social background nor to his length of service as a district governor. As mentioned earlier, the elite generally see education as the key

184

Table 10-2: Elite and Mass Perceptions of Villagers' Problems[a]

Most important problem	District governors (%)	Village headmen (%)	Male villagers (%)
Need for education	29	7	5
Poverty	31	8	10
Need for roads	3	22	20
Need for water	1	27	31
Need for land	8	13	15
Need for occupational equipment	8	4	1
Need for health care	0	0	0
Villagers' own characteristics	6	0	0
No problems	0	2	7
Other	15	5	6
No answer; don't know	0	2	5
Number of respondents	80	424	3,022

Source: The data on village headmen and male villagers were provided by Frederick W. Frey from the 1962 Turkish village survey.

[a] Differences between the perceptions of the district governors and those of the village headmen and the male villagers were significant at the .01 level.

to solving rural problems. Thus one district governor stated that villagers must realize their need to achieve a certain level of education if standards of living are to be raised.

Apparently a major elite-mass gap exists concerning this very important issue. Education and the problem of "general poverty" are simply very low on the villagers' list of priorities. The villagers emphasize more tangible needs — water, roads, and land. It should be noted that the village headmen were not at all in accord with the perceptions of their administrative superiors. The headmen echoed their constituents' priorities, stressing programs for improving water supplies and road conditions.

This would appear to be a potentially unhealthy situation. The administrators might initiate programs for which there was very little peasant support, and against which considerable opposition might be mobilized. Here there is a real paradox; the actual ongoing programs which district governors mentioned were quite different from what would be predicted from their attitudinal data. In fact, district governors tended to spend their time on projects dealing with roads and water — the two top priorities of the peasants — rather than on projects related to education. Forty-five percent of the 1956 district governors reported projects dealing with roads, 39 percent noted projects dealing with water, and only 28 percent had projects dealing with local educational needs. It is apparent that the elite-mass gap is being bridged. Peasants' desires are being communicated to the district governor, no matter how urban and elite his background.

Political Pressures and Administrative Response

At the administrative level, local political influence, and its implications for bureaucratic careers, can keep the elite from imposing its views upon the villagers. The case study material gives numerous examples of how local politicians, often working through party executive committees, have pressured administrators into carrying out programs desired by their mutual constituents. One party chief stated this process very plainly:

> . . . our organization, in order to enable us to come into contact with people directly, has different echelons. This facilitates our getting in touch with the local populace, our learning of local needs, and enables us to convey news of the wise and legal needs to the government.[17]

Conversations with villagers confirmed the importance of political factors linked to the ruralizing election. If asked when real improvement of their own living conditions started, the typical villager response was "under the Democrats," or "from Menderes." Political pressures upon bureaucrats have encouraged an administrative responsiveness to peasants which would not be expected under other circumstances.

Survey data indicate that most of the mediators between citizen and administrator had political connections; when asked to identify the intermediaries used to present requests to the district governor, the 1956 governors responded as shown in Table 10-3. Intermediaries were either characterized simply as politicians, or incumbents of a

17. This report (to the Democratic Party provincial congress in Mersin in 1957) was obtained and translated by Szyliowicz, *Political Change,* pp. 177–178.

Table 10-3: Intermediaries between the Public and the District Governor

Intermediaries[a]	Percentage of district governors reporting
Politicians	65
People of importance (agas, beys, etc.)	30
Legal representatives	17
Mayors and other municipal officials	15
Citizens' relatives and friends	14
Village headmen and council of elders	13
Members of Parliament	11
Friends of the district governor	7
Provincial General Assembly members	6
Number of district governors	306

Source: 1956 survey of district and provincial governors.

[a] Often more than one type of intermediary was mentioned.

partisan office — mayors and municipal officials, members of Parliament, and members of the provincial general assembly.

One measure of political pressure was derived from the survey data. This index was based upon the number of intermediaries mentioned by the district governor.[18] The level of reported political pressure would seem to be influenced by two factors: the objective characteristics of the given district and the subjective perceptions of the administrator himself. This index of political pressure appears related to other important aspects of the administrator's overall performance.

District governors who perceived themselves under heavy political pressure from their constituents seemed more involved with development projects and with programs at the top of the villagers' priority list. The differences are not as large as expected; perhaps by 1956 district governors were taking their cues from a national government which backed many of the same programs (public works with an

18. Four intercorrelated items regarding intermediaries were used to make up this index. Twenty-nine percent of the district governors were operating under conditions of low political pressure; they did not mention contact with any of the (four) intermediaries. Similarly, 35 percent of these bureaucrats mentioned one intermediary and 35 percent noted two or more intermediaries. This index is discussed in Appendix C.

Table 10-4: Correlation between District Governors' Activities and Degree of Political Pressure

Activities of district governors[a,b]	Degree of political pressure		
	Low (%)	Medium (%)	High (%)
Mentioned having program for:			
Roads	42	37	55
Water	33	32	50
Involvement in development projects:			
Low	23	7	13
Medium	38	52	44
High	39	41	44
Frequency of problems with laws and their interpretation:			
Low	10	7	8
Medium	68	41	46
High	22	52	45
Frequency of interorganizational conflict:			
Low	37	31	16
Medium	37	34	35
High	27	35	49
Number of district governors	104	127	75

Source: 1956 survey of district and provincial governors.

[a] Indices used in this table are described in Appendix C.

[b] Differences were significant at the .05 level for all variables.

emphasis on road construction and improving water supplies) most popular with the peasants.

The district governors who felt themselves under political pressure appear to have been particularly impatient with the restrictions imposed by certain legal and administrative procedures. These bureaucrats were also more likely to report conflicts with officials representing such other organizations as the judiciary, the military, and the municipalities. The district governors also reported conflict with such

188

organizations as State Economic Enterprises, the Agricultural Banks, the Office of Monopolies, the Post Office, and the Highway Department. The Forestry Department, the Water Works Department, the Soil Products Office, and officers from the Ministry of Finance were also mentioned.

The descriptions of these conflicts suggest several reasons why administrative conflict may be more intense in more heavily politicized districts. Municipalities with their popularly elected mayor not only have a responsibility to but also are dependent upon the voting public. The public's conception of what the municipality should do may differ from the district governor's conception of what is appropriate. This is reflected in one bureaucrat's comment: "The main goal of the municipality is to get more votes in the upcoming elections and not to lose any that they have already won. Therefore they neglect to apply some laws and they do not act impartially in the application of others." Where the district governor felt under pressure from politicians pushing the claims of their constituents, his attempts to pursue these claims may have caused conflict with other departments. For example, one district governor mentioned the Forestry Department's failure to deliver the villagers' allotment of wood on time. Another district governor complained that the Ministry of Public Works kept its best technicians at the center, assigning their less capable men to the districts.

Political Sensitivity and Administrative Careers

As stressed above, the district governors have been subject to considerable political pressure. These pressures may lead insecure incumbents of bureaucratic positions to resort to such dysfunctional behavior as "excessive aloofness, ritualistic attachment to routines and procedures, insistence on rights of authority and status, and resistance to change." [19] In a democratic system, a bureaucrat's style — how he exerts his authority — is obviously important for his career. A highly authoritarian leadership style, which might have been successful before 1950, seemed much less appropriate after the ruralizing election. A number of propositions from organization theory suggest how a successful bureaucrat might behave.[20] The propositions can be used to

19. Robert L. Peabody and Francis E. Rourke, "Public Bureaucracies," in James G. March, ed., *Handbook of Organizations* (Chicago, Rand McNally, 1966), p. 812.

20. Cultivating support within one's department is important for professional

structure the Turkish findings. The relevance of these propositions to rural development is of particular interest because they have their origin in research conducted in (American) industrial organizations.

The successful leader:

1) mediates organizational requirements to personal needs in ways which are organization-enhancing;[21]

2) adapts own interpersonal style to needs of others, helping to generate among group members a resultant strength of motivation for the achievement of group and organizational goals;[22]

3) reduces ambiguity and feelings of threat in his relations with group members;[23]

4) avoids arbitrariness in his relations with group members;[24]

5) consults with members of the group before making decisions;[25]

6) represents to his superiors the needs of the people below him;[26]

7) understands how his superiors are likely to act because of their organizational position, and how those below them are similarly motivated and limited by their placement in the organization.

In a politicized environment the satisfaction of the bureaucrat's subordinates — the villagers and village leadership — may be crucial. Several related propositions concerning the satisfaction of subordinates also help to organize the data:

1) Satisfaction of subordinates is associated with working under influential superiors. Influential superiors, as compared with noninfluential superiors, will be better able to satisfy the needs of their subordinates.[27]

2) Satisfaction of subordinates is associated with the degree to

---

success in all political systems, but the importance of the linkages between the administrator and the citizen may be less in more authoritarian systems. See Fred W. Riggs, *Thailand: The Modernization of a Bureaucratic Polity* (Honolulu, East-West Center Press, 1966), p. 384.

21. Daniel Katz and Robert L. Kahn, *The Social Psychology of Organizations* (New York: Wiley, 1966), p. 325.

22. *Ibid.*, p. 326.

23. Derived from Barry E. Collins and Harold Guetzkow, *A Social Psychology of Group Processes for Decision-Making* (New York, Wiley, 1964), p. 163.

24. Derived from *ibid.*, p. 163.

25. Derived from Victor H. Vroom, *Work and Motivation* (New York, Wiley, 1964), pp. 226–227.

26. This proposition and the following are derived from Katz and Kahn, *Social Psychology of Organizations*, p. 321.

27. Vroom, *Work and Motivation*, p. 115.

190

which they are permitted an opportunity to participate in making decisions.[28]

3) Satisfaction of subordinates is related to the consideration or employee orientation of their superiors.[29]

These data permit correlating bureaucratic success with the attitudes of both the local leadership and the district governors themselves. Some of the propositions presented above seem particularly applicable to this analysis. Such a focus can add significantly to the previous discussion of how job satisfaction at the university was associated with promotion within the Ministry of Interior. We can ask: what types of interaction with local leadership distinguish the successful from the unsuccessful district governor? These interaction patterns are particularly important because local leadership seems to have played a critical role in the administrative selection process. Case study data indicate that local politicians have exerted a negative influence on certain bureaucrats' careers. In 1957 local leaders in Erdemli successfully approached the Ministry of Interior about disputes with their district governor. Moreover, as a result of angering the local Democratic Party machine, one administrator had earlier been transferred from a neighboring district to Erdemli in the middle of his term.[30]

Much of the data on the relationship between bureaucratic success and the attitudes of local leadership is summarized in Table 10-5. The attitudinal variables are all indices based on the responses of the eighty-three village headmen serving under fifty-six 1962 district governors still working in the Ministry of Interior (either as district governors or in higher positions) in 1965. The interaction between bureaucrat and village headman is particularly critical when governmental services are involved.[31] The villagers' desire for services, as well as

28. *Ibid.,* p. 115.
29. *Ibid.,* p. 110.
30. Szyliowicz, *Political Change,* p. 132.
31. The index of "governmental services wanted" is based on a series of items asking how important it was that the government do a number of things, among them, improve village schools, provide more agricultural credit, provide more seed and fertilizer, improve village mosques, etc. The index expresses the tendency to rate each of these items as "very important." This index is described in Frederick W. Frey, Allan R. Kessler, and Joan E. Rothchild, *Index Construction and Validation* (Cambridge, Mass., M.I.T. Center for International Studies, 1967). The "governmental services wanted" index and the index of "educational and occupational aspiration" were moderately correlated (.32 by a product-moment coefficient) with each other, but essentially uncorrelated with the "perceived concentration" index.

Table 10-5: Administrative Success and Village Headman's Attitudes

| | Association with district governor's success[a] | |
Orientations of headmen	Gamma coefficient[b]	Product-moment correlation coefficient[b]
Governmental services wanted[c]	.48	.28
Educational and occupational aspiration[c]	.38	.20
Perceived concentration in one person of village power and wealth[c]	.34	.20
Other indices:		
Sense of communal responsibility	−.01	.00
Political empathy	−.13	−.02
Tolerance of deviance	.16	.08
Subjective poverty	−.15	−.09
Politicization	−.26	−.11
Desire for political participation	.02	.01
Attitudinal modernity	−.11	−.05

Source: The data on village headmen were provided by Frederick W. Frey from the 1962 Turkish village survey. The indices constructed for the village headmen are described in Frederick W. Frey, Allan R. Kessler, and Joan R. Rothchild, *Index Construction and Validation* (Cambridge, Mass., M.I.T. Center for International Studies, 1967).

[a] The administrator's success was dichotomized according to his remaining a district governor or being promoted in the 1962–1965 period. There were 83 matches between the bureaucrat and village headman data.

[b] A positive coefficient indicates a positive association between the headman's index score and the district governor's being promoted.

[c] Relationships for these variables were significant at the .05 level.

the potential for difficulties, has been documented by a number of authors. Organizational theorists have noted that such demands upward, "demands that flow contrary to status lines — from lower to higher status — create conflicts." [32] Successful district governors may raise the level of expectation of the village headmen with whom they

32. Peter M. Blau and W. Richard Scott, *Formal Organizations* (San Francisco, Chandler, 1962), p. 83.

work. Forty-six percent of the village headmen serving under district governors who were not promoted expressed few demands for governmental services; only 11 percent of the headmen under administrators who were promoted had such a low level of demands.

Even given the high level of expectations among their village headmen, the successful bureaucrats may have been unusually adept at satisfying local demands. Although the differences were not statistically significant, 20 percent of the headmen under the more successful administrators versus 42 percent of those under less successful governors complained that the authorities do not bother with their problems. On the other hand, the more successful district governors may have encouraged the villagers to participate in programs of little local interest. Twenty-nine percent of the headmen under successful governors mentioned that the authorities pushed projects with which villagers refused to cooperate. Fifteen percent of the headmen under governors who were not promoted had a similar complaint.

The coefficients in Table 10-5 also suggested an association between the headman's feeling that power and wealth in his village were concentrated in the hands of one person and the bureaucrat's later success. District governors who were later promoted may have reinforced the headman's conviction that village power is concentrated in his own hands. Case study material accords with such an interpretation; headmen have often used their ties with government officials to bring benefits to the village.[33] Efforts by the administrator to work through local leadership aid the headman's self-image and reduce perceived threats to his authority. Despite the possible political influence of local leaders, the district governor has both status and formal power which can affect the headman.

This interaction between people of diverse backgrounds is of general relevance. Several studies have shown that "personal dissimilarities, such as background, values, education, age, social patterns lowered the probability of interpersonal rapport" between the representatives of different units within the same organization.[34] Collins and Guetzkow note that "increasing heterogeneity of personality (within a group)

33. Kolars, *Tradition, Season, and Change*, p. 85, and Ayşe Kudat Sertel, "A Study of Power Conceptions in a Turkish Village," unpub. master's thesis, Harvard University, Cambridge, Mass., 1968, p. xiii.

34. Richard E. Walton and John M. Dutton, "The Management of Interdepartmental Conflict: A Model and Review," *Administrative Science Quarterly*, 14 (March 1969), 77.

will increase the difficulty of building interpersonal relations." [35] In the Turkish context, successful district governors probably reduce tension by exhibiting a lack of arbitrariness and by consulting with local political leadership. Such consideration on the part of the administrator may be good politics and at the same time lead to more cooperative, effective performance on the part of the villagers.

As is seen in Table 10-6 headmen serving under bureaucrats who were promoted perceived themselves as considerably more influential than their counterparts under less successful district governors. Ordinary villagers did not seem to share the sentiments of their headmen; the villagers' perception of the local power structure was not greatly affected by the type of bureaucrat responsible for their district. The successful bureaucrats appeared to elicit the cooperation of the village headmen and thus helped make the headmen feel influential. In turn, the village headmen supported the district governor and refrained from the vigorous complaining through political channels which could injure a bureaucrat's career. From a more theoretical perspective, the interaction between a district governor and a village headman can act to facilitate "the progress of each of the persons toward the attainment of his goals." [36] Successful administrators tried to aid the headman in reaching his goals, thereby advancing their own.

Promotion within the Ministry of Interior was correlated with several other variables from the 1956 district governor survey. Bureaucratic success seemed associated with participation in popular programs. Given the villagers' interest in obtaining better water and better roads for themselves, a concern with public works could be expected to be very popular. Fifty-five percent of the 1956 district governors who by 1965 had been promoted to provincial governor (one of the highest positions in the Ministry of Interior) mentioned public works projects as one of the activities taking up the most time. Only 34 percent of the district governors not promoted in the 1956–1965 period noted such public works activity.

Case study data from Erdemli district further support these findings. In Turkey, as in other modernizing nations, the government has provided much of the impetus for rural development. The district governor can play an important innovating role in the rural environment, particularly since local leaders generally lack the training, im-

35. Collins and Guetzkow, *Social Psychology of Group Processes*, p. 101.
36. Vroom, *Work and Motivation*, p. 124.

Table 10-6: Correlation between Administrative Success and Local Opinion on Village Leadership

	Status of 1962 district governor	
Opinions of villagers	Remained district governor in 1965	Promoted in 1962–1965 period
Leader in agricultural matters:[a]		
Headman	50%	56%
Local landlord	2	2
District governor	19	12
Other government official (Agricultural agent, etc.)	14	14
Other and no answer	15	16
Leader concerning land disputes:		
Headman	42	45
Local landlord	2	1
District governor	43	42
Other government official	6	6
Other and no answer	8	7
Number of bureaucrat-villager matches	808	344

	Status of 1962 district governor	
Opinions of headmen	Remained district governor in 1965	Promoted in 1962–1965 period
Leader in agricultural matters:[a]		
Headman	15%	36%
Local landlord	0	0
District governor	36	11
Other government official (Agricultural agent, etc.)	36	46
Other and no answer	13	7
Leader concerning land disputes:[a]		
Headman	27	46
Local landlord	0	0
District governor	56	50
Other government official	2	0
Other and no answer	15	4
Number of bureaucrat-headman matches	55	28

Source: The data on village headmen and villagers were provided by Frederick W. Frey from the 1962 village survey.
[a] Differences for these variables were significant at the .05 level. For the headmen data it was necessary to collapse categories in order to obtain an adequate number of "expected" respondents in each category.

agination, and resources to initiate community projects.[37] In the "bureaucratic polity" conceptualized by Riggs, such a pattern characteristically deprives the local citizenry of meaningful political participation and tends to increase the power of the central bureaucracy at the expense of political forces within the society.[38] During the 1950–1965 period the strength of local political forces kept this from happening in Turkey. The district governor was under sustained pressure to convince the villagers that his projects were worthwhile. In actual practice, satisfactory cooperation was often elicited through compromise resulting in fewer projects than might otherwise be completed.

The district governor's relationship with his superior, the provincial governor, has been particularly important because of the scarcity of funds available for rural development.[39] One of the provincial governor's most important functions has been the preparation of the annual budget. The provincial governor thus decides which district gets what funds. Although the Council of Ministers reviews the budgets prepared by the governors, in actual practice few changes are made.[40] The provincial governor's ability to submit special budgetary requests to appropriate central agencies is another important power. Since local sources of revenue are insufficient to support provincial development, the resourcefulness and initiative of the provincial governor in obtaining sources of additional funding are critical.

The discussion thus far has stressed the activist role played by the successful district governor, but several qualifications must be made. First, there were few differences in overall activity between the more successful and less successful governors. The activity of the administrators who were promoted seemed focused in a few special areas. Secondly, district governors may be too demanding and alienate the citizens under their jurisdiction. The 1956 governors who depended on mandatory labor to accomplish local jobs tended not to be promoted in the 1956–1965 period.[41] In contrast to this, Table 10-7 shows that

37. Szyliowicz, *Political Change*, pp. 122–124.
38. Riggs, "Bureaucrats and Political Development," pp. 120–167.
39. One analysis has shown that in 1962 in a relatively rich province (Adana) only approximately 50 cents per villager was available for village services such as public works, health, etc. H. Teoman Baykal and Nurittin Yağanoğlu, "Meeting Problems of Social and Economic Development in Rural Areas," in Bent and Shields, eds., *The Role of Local Government*, p. 88.
40. Şerif Tüten, "The Role of Local Governments in Development," in *ibid.*, p. 62.
41. Difficulties with using coercive measures in local development projects

Table 10-7: Correlation between Administrative Success and Performance in Office

	Status of 1956 district governor			
	Remained a district governor (or equiv-alent) in 1965	Intermediate Promotions[a]		Promoted to provincial governor by 1965
Performance in Office[b]		Lower positions	Higher positions	
Emphasized public works projects	34%	38%	52%	55%
Independent funding of local jobs[c]	27	38	34	45
Number of respondents	132	40	21	20

Source: 1956 survey of district and provincial governors.

[a] Within the Intermediate Promotions Group, the Higher category included legal advisor (in provincial administration), and assistant general director. The Lower category included office chief, assistant legal advisor, member of research committee, inspector, and assistant provincial governor. Roughly equated with the district governor's job were those of section director and public prosecutor in district administration. Career success within the Ministry of the Interior was measured according to two scales — one attributional and one based on the average salary associated with a particular position held in 1965 by a 1956 district governor. The attributional and salary scales correlated 0.78; the data presented here are based upon the attributional scale. The information on behavior is taken from the reports of the bureaucrats themselves.

Dichotomizing the promotional data (between the respondent's remaining a district governor and his being promoted) produced gamma values of .29 for the public works projects variable and of .22 for the payment of local jobs variable.

[b] Differences for the independent variables in this table were significant at the .05 level.

[c] The district administration financed 61–100 percent of local jobs.

the bureaucrats who were promoted were more successful in independently financing their projects and thus being able to pay villagers for their work. The more influential district governors (superiors) seemed better able to satisfy the needs of the villagers (their subordinates).

Being promoted to a provincial governor is not only one of the highest promotions which a person in the Ministry of Interior can receive, but it is also a highly politicized appointment. After a review by a high-level committee within the Ministry, provincial governors are nominated by the Minister of Interior, then appointed by the cabinet with the approval of the President. The decisions to appoint a new governor, to transfer a governor from one province to another, or to bring a provincial governor back to an assignment in the Ministry of Interior's central offices are all heavily influenced by political considerations. Although efforts have been made to rationalize the appointment and transfer of district governors, no attempt has been made to remove political considerations from appointments at the provincial governor's level. It is significant, therefore, that the individuals most capable of combining administrative and political success were both active in promoting public works projects and yet able to accomplish these projects without using levies of local labor. District governors satisfying both these criteria were the most likely to be promoted.[42]

There are several mutually compatible interpretations of these findings. One interpretation emphasizes the administrator's influence with his superiors; the other stresses the administrator's influence with his subordinates. The district governor who can get extra money for projects in his area might obtain extra "visibility" in the administration, thus facilitating his promotion. The administrator may have been rewarded for behavior which is only imperfectly measured in this study; the correlations between villager responses and bureaucratic behavior may have been spurious. On the other hand, local political leadership has possessed considerable administrative influence. Successful con-

have been stressed by Herbert H. Hyman, Gene N. Levine, and Charles R. Wright, *Inducing Social Change in Developing Communities* (New York, United Nations Research Institute for Social Development, 1967), pp. 87–92.

42. Twelve percent of the 1956 district governors who were interested in public works and who paid for over 40 percent of the local jobs ($n = 96$) were promoted to provincial governor status by 1965. Of the governors who met neither criterion ($n = 40$), none achieved the rank of provincial governor.

198

tacts between politicians and the Ministry of Interior about disputes with the district governor were reported in the Erdemli case study. The debureaucratization accompanying multiparty politics may have gone hand in hand with an administrator's de-emphasizing unpopular directives. Any activity by the district governor which alienated local leadership (such as requisitioning village labor) could have most unfortunate effects on the bureaucrat's career. The work of popular district governors seems likely to have been mentioned through both administrative and political channels.

Successful district governors appear similar to successful middle managers. They understand "how those above them are likely to act because of their organizational position and how those below them are similarly motivated and limited by their placement in organizational space." [43] From a slightly different viewpoint these administrators must be concerned with interunit relationships, with "mixed-motive situations which require high behavioral flexibility to manage optimally." [44] District governors appear aware of the demands upon them. They were the group of Political Science Faculty graduates who most emphasized the need for social science training in their curriculum.

The data presented in Table 10-7 reflect on the criteria for bureaucratic promotion in a democratic society.[45] The performance of a district-level administrator is obviously difficult to measure. The successful management of development projects, among other factors, seems to be associated with promotion. Amicable interaction with local leadership appears causally related to the bureaucrat's career success. Concepts of performance and effectiveness in local administration must take into consideration the bureaucrat's ability to deal with the local power structure. It seems that successful bureaucrats must both exercise consideration for local feelings and be oriented toward initiating development projects. On the other hand, the need for both affective and instrumental leadership on the part of the district governor increases the demands of the role. The dissatisfaction which many dis-

43. Katz and Kahn, *Social Psychology of Organizations,* p. 320.
44. Walton and Dutton, "Management of Interdepartmental Conflict," p. 77.
45. Few variables helped predict which district governors were likely to leave the Ministry of Interior. Despite the fact that about 25 percent of the 1956 district governors had taken jobs outside the Ministry of Interior by 1965, only the previously discussed job satisfaction and social background variables seemed to be related to the probability of an individual's leaving this ministry.

trict administrators feel may be inevitable in jobs which require the individual to assume both instrumental and affective leadership.[46]

The overall picture demonstrates the necessity of Turkish bureaucrats' attending to the needs of their villagers. Katz and Kahn have noted that organizations in which influence is widely shared tend to be most effective. "The reasons for this are in part motivational, having to do with implementation of decisions, and in part nonmotivational, having to do with the excellence of decisions." [47] The use of democratic leadership methods may lead to the formation of group norms favorable to the successful execution of the decisions in which group members have had influence.[48]

There are several ways in which participation by local leadership can improve decision-making. From a general perspective, Collins and Guetzkow stress that increasing the heterogeneity of personality within a group tends to increase the group's problem-solving potential: more alternatives are forwarded, errors and biases are more likely to be eliminated, and so on.[49] As is stressed earlier, the "felt needs" of the villagers were markedly different from the needs perceived by the administrators. This is particularly important because many experts recommend "action according to the desires expressed by the people themselves, and not necessarily according to the aims of the project or to needs that may objectively exist but are not recognized by the people." [50]

Given the differences in priorities between administrator and peasant, it is probably beneficial that district governors are rewarded at least partially according to their responsiveness to local demands. Ashford notes the need for such responsiveness when he states:

> It is the unavoidably arbitrary character of the developmental process that may, in turn, represent the greatest threat to effective adaptation to modern life. Without constant and informed atten-

46. See the discussion of the role of the foreman in Amitai Etzioni, *A Comparative Analysis of Complex Organizations* (New York, Free Press, 1961), pp. 121–125.

47. Katz and Kahn, *Social Psychology of Organizations,* p. 332.

48. Vroom, *Work and Motivation,* p. 228.

49. Collins and Guetzkow, *Social Psychology of Group Processes,* p. 101. Note the previous reference that heterogeneity also increases the difficulty of building interpersonal relations.

50. Hyman et al., *Inducing Social Change,* pp. 85–86.

200

tion to the reconciliation that must take place at the local level, the massive efforts of many developing countries may be largely wasted.[51]

In a competitive political system local pressure helps ensure that the benefits of development are distributed to the people and that arbitrariness is minimized.

But forcing the elite to respond to local political demands does have its disadvantages. The dissatisfaction felt by many district governors has been a major problem with this system. Moreover, although the on-the-job behavior of administrators from privileged backgrounds was not markedly different from that of their less privileged counterparts, the former's psychic turmoil seems to have been much greater.[52] During the 1960's moving out of the Ministry of Interior provided an outlet for such frustration; but, if these difficulties are an almost inevitable consequence of the ruralizing process, continuing opportunities for mobility are important.

51. Douglas E. Ashford, *National Development and Local Reform* (Princeton, N.J., Princeton University Press, 1967), p. 210.

52. Some differences between district governors from privileged and less privileged backgrounds were mentioned in this chapter, but social background factors were not good predictors of a number of behavioral variables relating to the administrator's work. These background factors were, however, the best predictors of satisfaction and mobility.

11
Conclusion

The changes which have taken place in Turkey over the last several decades are relevant to an understanding of the wider issues of political modernization. Relationships between elected officials (the politicians) and appointed officials (the bureaucrats) are sources of friction and conflict in most countries, developed and undeveloped. Pressures generated by the spread of technology and new methods of production are changing patterns of behavior and social mobility around the world. The challenges of older elites by younger elites seem incessant. Finally, there is the question of whether competitive party systems have any future in the developing countries. Chaotic politics, revolutionary unrest, and military coups have made the future of democracy in the Third World seem bleak indeed.

By focusing upon the consequences of one kind of election, this work has emphasized the problems which may accompany the replacement of one elite by another. A ruralizing election has major effects upon the urban elite and upon administration in general.[1] Basic to the concept of a ruralizing election is a decline in bureaucratic participation in representative institutions. The dramatic nature of this change suggests that the decline may be more rapid at higher levels of authority than at lower. The concept of ministerial autonomy is helpful in judging which ministries are likely to be affected more and which less. Turkish data suggest that those ministries most dependent for their work upon the country's internal environment will be those affected most by the change in political leadership. Thus, Ministries of Interior with their high levels of interaction with the public are likely to suffer disproportionately from a ruralizing election; considerable debureaucratization is likely to result in such ministries.

The ruralizing election process can be conceptualized in terms of intergroup relations. This study has focused upon the urban bureau-

1. It has been suggested to me that in some modernizing countries, particularly those influenced by the British colonial tradition, the urban elite and the bureaucracy may be much more widely separated than in Turkey. New elites which gain power may then move toward a single-party system, fusing party and bureaucracy in order to better rule the society. Parallels here may be with the earlier, single-party days of Atatürk.

cratic elite, the group which lost the electoral competition. As Schein has pointed out, "the net effect of the win-lose situation is often that the loser is not convinced that he lost, and that intergroup tension is higher than before the competition began." [2] The loser may be particularly tense and eager to find someone to blame. In political terms, the losers of a ruralizing election seem especially prone to find fault with the regime which replaced them. Objective difficulties and mistakes by new elite groups are compounded in the eyes of the losers. The tensions produced by conflicts between winners and losers — between new elites and old — have frequently manifested themselves in coups and chronic instability.

It is valuable to separate that which may be common to general processes following a ruralizing election from that which may be unique to Turkey. The pressures upon the administrative elite might be distinguished from the responses made by this elite. The pressures may be common after a ruralizing election, while the responses may be unique to Turkey. Such distinctions help generate hypotheses which might be further tested in comparative studies after having been suggested by the Turkish analysis.

By definition, in a ruralizing election the political power and representation of the rural masses increases; the power of an urban-based, bureaucratic elite declines. If we assume that the influence of various sectors of the society is dependent upon their access to political leadership, a number of propositions can be suggested.

1. A disproportionate loss of parliamentary representation will be felt by the less autonomous ministries, particularly those exerting direct influence in the rural areas.

2. Fusion between bureaucracy and political party will break down. The old, modernizing party which dominated in the single-party system will be under real pressure to disassociate itself to some degree from the bureaucracy in order to compete electorally.

3. Relationships between the bureaucracy and client groups will change markedly and be characterized by considerable debureaucratization.

2. Edgar H. Schein, *Organizational Psychology* (Englewood Cliffs, N.J., Prentice-Hall, 1965), p. 82. Some most interesting data on winners and losers are provided in Chong Lim Kim, "Political Attitudes of Defeated Candidates in an American State Election," *American Political Science Review*, 64 (September 1970), 879–887. Despite high overall levels of support for the democratic rules of competition, losing candidates in an American state election were less supportive of these rules than were the winners.

4. The status of the less autonomous ministries will be lowered in the eyes of numerous groups.

5. Connected with this loss of status will be difficulties in recruitment and turnover. Because individuals from advantaged backgrounds may tend to avoid a vulnerable ministry, opportunities for social mobility may be created in those ministries which have suffered most from the ruralizing election.

6. Younger individuals will tend to avoid work in these ministries.

7. Problems of maintaining their position vis-à-vis other organizations will be particularly acute for these ministries.

a. Question of conflicting jurisdictions and salary inequities will increasingly arise; organizations will make vigorous efforts to increase their resources in order to compete.

b. There will be attempts on the part of the affected ministries to expand their functions and modify their internal operations to better deal with the new situation.

8. Successful organizations will emphasize their remunerative power ("based on control over material resources and rewards through allocation of salaries and wages, commissions and contributions, etc.")[3] rather than normative considerations.

At the individual level, several attitudinal and behavioral changes may take place as a result of a ruralizing election:

1. Job dissatisfaction and the desire to change jobs may become so marked that various organization theory propositions do not hold; i.e., job satisfaction may not increase with the length of time an individual remains in an organization. This may partially be due to status incongruence.

2. Within an affected ministry, achieving a promotion which tends to insulate one from the public will result in a dramatic rise in job satisfaction.

These two propositions seem especially likely to hold in other nations which have experienced a ruralizing election; such other countries include Ceylon, Burma, Jamaica, and Lesotho. They seem to logically follow from the redistribution of power accompanying such an election. Other propositions are dependent upon additional independent variables. Such factors as economic growth and moderate

3. The definition is taken from Amitai Etzioni, *A Comparative Analysis of Complex Organizations* (New York, Free Press, 1961), p. 5.

leadership may help generate some of the social changes compatible with political and economic progress:

3. Many individuals in affected ministries will come to lose faith in their unique role as modernizers of the country.

4. Operations of affected ministries will in time change in response to political realities.

5. Operations of political parties will in time change in response to political realities. In particular, the fusion between bureaucracy and political party will break down. The old, modernizing party which dominated in the single party system will be under real pressure to at least partially disassociate itself from the bureaucracy in order to compete electorally.

6. Administrators will tend to take a more calculating attitude toward the government and their own careers. There may be substantially greater willingness to move out of traditional jobs into other work offering greater financial rewards.

7. A realignment of occupational prestige will accompany changes in the elite occupational structure.

Unsatisfactory economic conditions and vindictive political leadership will tend to increase political instability. Among the changes accompanying this "political decay" are

8. Members of various elites, including the bureaucrats, may become so dissatisfied as to be alienated. Such alienation (as perhaps occurred in Turkey in the period before the 1960 coup) augurs ill for stability.

9. Individuals' moral commitment to particular policies (i.e., to the policies of a one-party regime dominated by the urban elite) may increase when they are forced out of power.

10. Group structure of the administrative elite may become more cohesive, and membership in the bureaucracy may become increasingly important to the individual.

11. Members of the administrative elite may refuse to grant status to new elites and occupations.

The problems involved in applying such a formulation in a predictive way are obvious. The 1965 data suggest that Turkey was following a path relatively favorable for development. "Pure" examples of successful development may be impossible to find; the military coup of 1960 and the military intervention in 1971 demonstrate the problems which Turkey has had. Social changes have proceeded rapidly. As of 1971, Tachau has noted that

. . . the traditional outlook of rural village and provincial town is more openly expressed through the parties than has been true in the past. This outlook has always been opposed to the more cosmopolitan and modernist view of the urban-based bureaucratic and military elite which dominated the country under the Republican Party.[4]

Localism has continued, and the actions of right-wing dissidents have reinforced fears of a revival of traditionalism.

Despite these difficulties the social changes of the 1960's helped many members of the old elite to adapt to their loss of political influence. These changes are reflected in this analysis, which has emphasized occupational mobility, opportunity structures, and economic growth. Because of the lack of adequate longitudinal data extending back beyond 1956, many of the propositions put forward here cannot be adequately treated. The following propositions are in accord with the survey data, although the more general propositions cannot be tested by such data.

1. A ruralizing election will tend to lead to the founding of new organizations and new organizational structures.

2. Economic growth will tend to increase occupational mobility.

3. Economic growth will tend to increase the demand for technical skills.

4. Economic growth will tend to lead to the founding of new organizations and new organizational structures.

5. Occupational mobility will tend to increase "cross-pressures" among individuals who move from one post to another.

6. Occupational mobility will tend to aid economic growth.

7. The possibilities for occupational mobility will tend to be greater for individuals with technical training than for those without such training.

8. The possibilities for occupational mobility and the increased demand for technical skills will tend to reduce tensions within the political system by:

    a. Allowing for movement of dissatisfied individuals out of various organizations.

    b. Preventing downward mobility when particular or-

4. Frank Tachau, with the assistance of Mary Jo Good, "The Anatomy of Political and Social Change: Turkish Parties and Parliaments, 1960–1970," *Comparative Politics*, forthcoming.

ganizations no longer enjoy their previous status.

c. Acting to lower political participation by providing more satisfactory career opportunities — both inside and outside the bureaucracy.

The Turkish Model of Elite Development

The Turkish pattern of social mobility described here might be called elite pluralism. Members of the established elite have moved from their traditional stronghold of power and prestige — the central ministries — into organizations which are a product of the economic developments of the past two decades. Their exit has opened new opportunities to upwardly mobile groups in Turkish society.

Several "organizing principles" which have fostered the development of such mobility patterns come to mind.[5] These factors are political, economic, and social. Turkey has never had a political system which proscribed private industry and foreign companies. Similarly important, Turkey has never had a centralized system of control over recruitment to bureaucratic agencies. The ability of each agency to set the rules for recruiting its own personnel built a certain flexibility into the system and meant that new organizations were able to compete effectively with the central ministries for talented personnel. They could offer high salaries which proved competitive with the power and prestige associated with positions in the central ministries.

Changing political structures have also had a significant impact on the attractiveness of ministerial careers. The democratic political system has challenged the autocratic authority which bureaucrats traditionally wielded; much of the prestige and power which bureaucratic careers once offered has been undermined. Atatürk's exchange of populations also significantly affected subsequent inter-elite relations. This acted to remove the monopoly held by Greeks, Armenians, and Jews on the Turkish business sector. Turkey does not now have the problem of the "pariah entrepreneurial class" which plagues many developing societies. Businessmen — both in public and private enter-

5. This discussion of "organizing principles" was suggested by the analytical framework proposed in Neil J. Smelser and Seymour Martin Lipset, "Social Structure, Mobility and Development," in Neil J. Smelser and Seymour Martin Lipset, eds., *Social Structure and Mobility in Economic Development* (Chicago, Aldine, 1966), pp. 12–17.

prise — are overwhelmingly Turkish.[6] The "Turkishness" of the business community facilitates an elite mobility into and out of the private sector which might not otherwise be possible.

Because individuals from privileged backgrounds have been more likely to move into newer ministries, state economic enterprises, and the private sector, the tendency for the urban official elite to constitute a unified social group seems to have been reduced. The 1965 survey data show how economic pressures have helped cause a shift into new jobs on the part of elite individuals; this aided in reducing the conflict between older elites and new social groups. Contacts and linkages among different sectors of the society seem to be on the increase. A graduate working in a bank whose father had been employed in the Ministry of Interior is not likely to be overly hostile toward the central ministries. In accordance with the well-known hypothesis of "cross pressures," individuals being pulled in different directions by various tendencies might be expected to adopt relatively moderate opinions.

The relationships between class, ideology, and occupational mobility have further implications for Turkey. On the one hand, officials have tended to support an elitist political ideology and favor etatist economic policies. At the same time, the occupational mobility data imply that it is the individuals with privileged backgrounds who have abandoned careers in the central ministries (Finance, Interior, and Foreign Affairs) to seek opportunities in the new, noncentral organizations. People from the middle and lower classes, with their ideology favoring a populist democracy and private enterprise, have become increasingly represented in important ministerial positions.

These 1965 survey findings pointed toward at least short-term stability in Turkish politics. The relative calm in the 1965–1969 period

6. One survey of 138 entrepreneurs reports the following ethnic breakdowns: 83 percent Turkish, 9 percent Jewish, 7 percent Greek and 2 percent unknown. Arif Payaslıoğlu, *Türkiyede Özel Sanayi Alanındaki Müteşebbisler ve Teşebbüsler* (Political Science Faculty-Financial Institute, 1961), p. 22. Our argument is almost the obverse of that often made. Thus, Holt and Turner argue from historical data that, when an entrepreneurial class is prevented from entering the land-holding aristocracy, economic development is aided. We suggest that after a ruralizing election the entry of a bureaucratic elite into various types of businesses is likely to facilitate both political stability and economic development. See Robert T. Holt and John E. Turner, *The Political Basis of Economic Development* (Princeton, N.J., Van Nostrand, 1966), p. 318.

may have been a partial reflection of such tendencies. Many cosmo- politans were drawn out of the central ministries into organizations where their potential for implementing ideological biases was dimin- ished. Lipset has suggested that "the chances for stable democracy are enhanced to the extent that groups and individuals have a number of crosscutting, politically relevant affiliations . . . the greater the iso- lation from heterogeneous political stimuli, the more the background factors 'pile up' in one direction, the greater the chances that the group or individual will have an extremist perspective." [7]

This theory of cross-pressures implies that cosmopolitans (sons of officials born in Ankara, Istanbul, or Izmir) working in the noncentral organizations would support the etatist Republican People's Party (toward which they were predisposed by virtue of their social back- ground) but be more tolerant of business; a comparison of attitudes of the cosmopolitans in new, noncentral organizations with the atti- tudes of their counterparts remaining in the older ministries supports such an hypothesis. Those working in the noncentral organizations rated the businessman's contribution to national development higher and granted a business career slightly more prestige. In addition, cos- mopolitans outside the central ministries had a much less favorable view of the civil servant and his contribution than that held by their counterparts in the older ministries. The patterns were less clear-cut for the more explicitly political attitudes. Although cosmopolitans in the noncentral organizations supported a more populist interpretation of democracy, they were no more favorable in their assessment of poli- ticians than the cosmopolitans working in the older ministries. While the small number of respondents in each category (14 cosmopolitans in the noncentral organizations and 40 in the older ministries) makes these findings inconclusive, the 1965 data suggested pluralism rather than polarization.

Such patterns of circulation might also have encouraged communi- cation and understanding between three of the often hostile power centers in Turkish society — businessmen, politicians, and officials.[8]

7. Seymour Martin Lipset, *Political Man* (New York, Doubleday, 1963), pp. 77–79. Lipset notes that in contemporary Germany, a working-class Cath- olic pulled in two directions will probably vote Christian-Democratic, but may be more tolerant of the Social Democrats than the average middle-class Cath- olic.

8. One important power center which has been neglected in this analysis is the military. At present the attitudinal and social background data necessary to assess the relative standing of this group are unavailable, and its status in con-

There has been constant tension among these social groups, with the demands of the military complicating affairs. In the years immediately following 1965, the sorts of elite circulation described here might have helped moderate the ever-present tendencies toward violent conflict in Turkish society.[9]

Status and Mobility

In a rapidly changing social environment, defining status is always difficult. Individual and organizational status interact. The preceding analysis has stressed status incongruence, discussing the reactions of high-status individuals to employment in organizations adversely affected by social change. But the status of an organization is influenced by the status of the individuals working in it. By moving into the new, noncentral organizations, Political Science Faculty graduates helped to reinforce the newly found status of these organizations.

The general pattern of findings is important in suggesting a flexible status orientation on the part of an important segment of the Turkish elite. In 1956 relatively few Political Science Faculty graduates entered the economic enterprises which were starting to play an important part in Turkish society. But the Political Science Faculty graduates from the classes of 1958–1961 seem to have responded to the new opportunities wholeheartedly. Almost half of the younger survey respondents from official backgrounds entered the new, noncentral organizations.

Another consequence of the movement of individuals with elite backgrounds to jobs outside the central ministries had favorable implications for political stability. Movement out of the Ministries of Interior and Finance helped create openings for upwardly mobile individuals. The data indicate that Political Science Faculty graduates going into — and staying in — these ministries have been those with less privileged backgrounds. The new opportunities engendered by economic growth can be expected to increase the demand for trained personnel. As people switch from one job to another, this demand

---

temporary Turkish society is difficult to judge. The military intervention in 1971 demonstrated the power of the military, but the long-term consequences of this are unclear.

9. For a discussion of the "low tolerance of deviance" in Turkish society, see Şerif Mardin, "Opposition and Control in Turkey," *Government and Opposition*, 1 (May 1966), 375–387.

210

should filter down and affect other, less desirable positions. Since increased opportunities for employment raise the number of job possibilities acceptable to university graduates, the pull of the new organizations produces vacancies in the central ministries which must be filled. During the nineteen sixties this process seems to have helped Turkey deal with the continuing problem of providing satisfactory employment for its educated individuals.[10]

Economic development and the results of ruralizing elections tend to affect all the criteria of social status — power, wealth, and prestige. The transfers out of the Ministries of Interior and Finance aided in reassigning status as well as in facilitating social mobility. Suzanne Keller has pointed out the dangers associated with status systems which "become ends in themselves instead of means to the fair distribution of abilities, responsibilities, and rewards."[11] Both inefficiency and ritualism are likely results when status systems do not bear a reasonable correspondence to social needs.

One danger is that upwardly mobile groups may feel that they have not been accorded adequate status. For example, the position of the businessman in Turkey has been rapidly changing over the past two decades. The officials' willingness to change their occupations and move into the more growth-oriented sectors has helped boost the status associated with work in the newer organizations and in the private sector. One indication of the new status situation is seen in the fact that 25 percent of the 1965 district governors preferred employment in the private sector. The movement of sons of officials into these organizations should reduce the "status discrepancy" — the gap between status allocated by society and position achieved by the individual — felt by businessmen in the state and private sectors.

The previous discussion has emphasized that major changes in recruitment to different types of organizations have taken place. The implications of such processes have been summarized by S. N. Eisenstadt:

The continuous absorption of change necessarily entails the development of social processes which tend on the one hand to break

10. See Fred W. Riggs, *Thailand: The Modernization of a Bureaucratic Polity*, (Honolulu, East-West Center Press, 1966), pp. 388–389, for a discussion of this problem in Thailand.

11. Suzanne Keller, *Beyond the Ruling Class* (New York, Random House, 1963), p. 242.

up any fixed, freezing ascriptive arrangements of groups and power structure, while on the other hand they facilitate the continuous restructuring of the distribution of power, wealth, and prestige and the rearrangement of different social groups and roles within common institutional frameworks.[12]

It is especially important that so many of the younger respondents from official backgrounds have joined the new organizations and taken advantage of the opportunities produced by change.

National Policies and Organizational Status

Particular political and economic policies affect not only individuals' possibilities for changing organizations but also the status of the organizations themselves. From a larger perspective, it is the failure to satisfy organizations rather than the failure to satisfy individuals which often leads to political instability. The events of 1971 have emphasized the need for "moderate" governmental policies — policies which do not rapidly alter the status of the major organizational groupings within Turkish society.

For example, abolishing the State Planning Organization might tend to substantially increase the influence of private sector organizations at the expense of other interest groups. Such a move would be widely interpreted as a return to the free-wheeling economy which characterized the Democratic Party regime; the anxiety of administrators in other sectors would be increased by the destruction of the Planning Organization. In the 1965–1969 period the Justice Party's handling of the planning issue was quite sophisticated. The influence of State Planning Organization in the highest councils of government declined, and major personnel changes were made within the organization. The organization's output also changed. The Second Five Year Plan (beginning in 1968) emphasized the role of the private sector and represented a substantial shift from the developmental strategy outlined in the First Plan.[13]

Governmental policies have been directed toward gradually increas-

12. S. N. Eisenstadt, *Modernization: Protest and Change* (Englewood Cliffs, N.J., Prentice-Hall, 1966), p. 151.

13. See C. H. Dodd, *Politics and Government in Turkey* (Berkeley, University of California Press, 1969), pp. 67, 75–76, 232, for a discussion of the politics associated with the State Planning Organization.

ing the power of groups competing with the still powerful bureaucracy. Fostering competition among organizations, if such competition can be kept at a moderate level, may promote administrative efficiency. Thus, Ilchman has noted that an administration "which can meet changing and increasing demands is more likely if competing institutions exist." [14] Riggs has also stressed that "the degree of administrative efficiency of a bureaucracy varies inversely with the weight of its power" and that an administration suffers when the "bureaucracy provides a primary channel for access to elite status." [15]

Thus far we have considered economic development as an external input affecting organizations and politics, but organizational competition may have real implications for growth. The distribution of educated personnel among the different sectors of the society — the relationship between those processes of occupational mobility and future economic changes — is of particular interest. Is economic growth aided or hindered by the flow of talent out of the central ministries? Is it more important for the directly productive parts of the economy to recruit the best talent or does Turkey need more effective individuals to staff the government regulatory and administrative structures? We believe that a continuation of the flow of able graduates away from the Ministries of Interior and Finance would have favorable implications for economic development.

A reciprocal relationship between occupational mobility and economic development is suggested here. As economic growth has increased the rate of occupational mobility, increased mobility can promote development. A lack of managerial talent has been one of the factors most frequently cited as contributing to the poor performance of the state economic enterprises. Structural changes have been made in the state economic enterprises to encourage them to produce more effectively;[16] these enterprises need talented individuals in order to translate these changes into more efficient production. Although the central ministries would certainly benefit by maintaining or improving the quality of their personnel, the marginal contribution which able

14. Warren F. Ilchman, "Rising Expectations and the Revolution in Development Administration," *Public Administration Review,* 25 (December 1965), 323.

15. Fred W. Riggs, *Administration in Developing Countries* (Boston, Houghton Mifflin, 1964), pp. 263–266.

16. Nuri Eren, "Financial Aspects of Turkish Planning," *Middle East Journal,* 20 (Spring 1966), 192.

administrators can make by working in the productive sectors would seem to be much greater than in local administration, budgetary work, and regulation of business.

The questions of efficiency and national interest may be phrased in terms of the possibilities for occupational mobility. Is it in Turkey's best interests to have an occupational structure which encourages individuals to move from one sector to another as opportunities present themselves? The answer to this question is affirmative for several reasons. Such a system helps prevent stagnation and inertia within particular organizations. In the past, the slow promotions and security-oriented environment of the central ministries have proved stifling to graduates lacking the opportunities to move to jobs in other sectors of the society. Even in 1965, many of the working conditions within the Ministries of Interior and Finance did not seem to differ in any substantial way from those prevailing in 1956.

Organizational competition aids the "expert" in his struggle against the generalist and would seem to facilitate the more efficient use of highly trained manpower. Despite the widely recognized need for technical input, entrenched interests within organizations often prove unwilling to adapt to such changes. Several authors have stressed that modern bureaucracies are characterized by an "imbalance between the technical specialists and the incumbents of hierarchial position." [17] Individuals with technical training are likely to give professional advice and at the same time to have career expectations which are at variance with the ideas of their administrative superiors. In Turkey the opening up of opportunities outside the old-line ministries strengthens the position of technical specialists by providing them with new occupational possibilities. Able individuals are less likely to be ignored within one organization when it is relatively easy for them to move to another sector.

This growth of demand for technically trained experts in various sectors and the shifts of highly trained manpower away from traditionally powerful ministries have led to some salary increases in the Turkish central ministries, but the amount of the increases has not reestablished the competitive position of the affected ministries. Further pressures for salary increases in the central ministries seem inevitable.

17. Robert L. Peabody and Francis E. Rourke, "Public Bureaucracies," in James March, ed., *Handbook of Organizations* (Chicago, Ill., Rand McNally, 1966), p. 816. Peabody and Rourke are referring specifically to the work of Victor A. Thompson, *Modern Organization* (New York, Knopf, 1961).

214

It is questionable, however, whether salary increases alone will solve the recruitment problems of the Ministries of Finance and Interior. Political Science Faculty graduates' awareness of opportunities outside the central ministries undoubtedly makes the more able individuals less willing to tolerate jobs which do not utilize their full abilities. The pull of bright graduates out of the central ministries has not resulted in subjectively better working conditions inside these ministries. Overall job satisfaction remained remarkably similar between 1956 and 1965; the lower levels of political interference in 1965 seem to be a result of societal changes rather than ministerial efforts.

Some undesirable consequences may result from the loss of many of the brightest university graduates from the central ministries. Several authors have stressed that "high rates of turnover have . . . been broadly associated with low organizational efficiency." [18] High organizational efficiency can hardly be expected when many talented individuals avoid or leave these organizations. Not only is efficiency affected, but the more traditional ministries are weakened by such an exodus. Dill has noted that organizations seeking "personnel who do not feel threatened by change, who have high levels of aspiration, and who are easily dissatisfied will be better able to adapt than organizations who seek other kinds of personnel." [19]

These data can profitably be discussed using a framework proposed by Hirschman, who stresses two major responses to organizational decline: exit and voice. An individual may leave an organization which he perceives as having difficulties. By exit, "the market is used by the individual to defend his welfare or to improve his position." Exit also helps set in motion "market forces which may induce recovery on the part of the firm that has declined in comparative performance." [20] Voice is defined as "any attempt at all to change, rather than to escape

18. Jose A. Silva-Michelena, "The Venezuelan Bureaucrat," in Frank Bonilla and Jose A. Silva-Michelena, eds., *A Strategy for Research on Social Policy* (Cambridge, M.I.T. Press, 1967), p. 92. For a summary of the literature bearing on this topic see Daniel Katz and Robert L. Kahn, *The Social Psychology of Organizations* (New York, Wiley, 1966), p. 338.

19. William R. Dill, "The Impact of Environment on Organizational Development," in S. Mailuk and E. Van Ness (eds.), *Readings in Administrative Behavior* (Englewood Cliffs, N.J., Prentice-Hall, 1961), pp. 13–14.

20. Albert Hirschman, *Exit, Voice, and Loyalty* (Cambridge, Mass., Harvard University Press, 1970), pp. 15–16.

from, an objectionable state of affairs." [21] Voice is direct and straight-forward; it implies articulation of critical opinions.

Our analysis has suggested that the existence of the exit option is important for political stability. Voice is not lacking in developing countries; indeed, the level of criticism and discord may be extremely high. But, particularly after a ruralizing election, it may be impossible for the bureaucratic elite to use voice effectively. Newly elected politicians are likely to be insensitive to the criticisms of the elite whose representatives have just been voted out of political office.

If the exit option is relatively difficult, bureaucrats and other fixed-income groups may become increasingly dissatisfied. Voice, other than that expressed in a successful coup or revolution, provides few possibilities for reform or meaningful change. When a suitable exit option is available, much of the discontent may be siphoned off. In Turkey, as we have seen, the exit options in 1965 appear to have been substantially greater than those available in 1956. The ability of individuals dissatisfied with their work in the Ministries of Interior and Finance to find better jobs outside the central ministries probably helps reduce tensions within the public bureaucracy. Occupational mobility can make a direct contribution to stability by providing adequate rewards for those who have suffered from the results of political change.

The survey data suggest that such conflict between bureaucrats and politicians was more marked during the mid-fifties than during the mid-sixties. Since this bureaucrat–politician conflict has been emphasized by a number of students of development, it seems worthwhile to discuss its meaning in the Turkish context. The data suggest that unbalanced growth can exacerbate the conflict between the bureaucracy and other sectors of a developing society. An inflationary situation, combined with conspicuous consumption by certain groups, can lead to frustration among the fixed-salaried groups. In Turkey during the 1950's politicians moved into the domain of the bureaucrats before new technical opportunities opened up. This lag between the time when new enterprises were founded and the time when trained bureaucrats could respond to the new opportunities may have been particularly unsettling. These conditions of high frustration may well have contributed substantially to the bureaucrats' reported support for the 1960 coup.

The military intervention in 1971 has suggested that several addi-

21. *Ibid.*, p. 30.

216

tional factors should be taken into account in an analysis of Turkish stability. In addition to the violent activities of student and terrorist groups, other political parties seem to have been frustrated by their lack of ability to influence or replace the Justice Party. Such frustration, coupled with tactical errors on the part of the Justice Party, helped support the high levels of Parliamentary conflict and contributed to the military intervention. But economic factors have remained important; besides their implications for mobility, development policies have been a source of considerable disagreement. Although adequate data were not available in early 1971, the time of this writing, there is some evidence that 1970 was characterized by relatively high rates of inflation and slipping economic growth.[22]

We have emphasized the influences of economic growth upon politics. Disaffected groups may plot during periods of economic progress, particularly if inflation and a lack of job mobility hinder their adaptation to new circumstances. On the other hand, economic growth eventually tends to produce new opportunities for skilled individuals. But politics can also affect economics; political turbulence may well directly influence the economy. Such major political events as the opening up of the one-party system in 1946 and the military coup in 1960 seem to have significant implications for economic efficiency. Empirical data on the performance of the state economic enterprises suggest how disruptive conflict and instability can be. The state enterprises make relatively good progress during periods of calm, but political turmoil appears to substantially affect their efficiency. Figure 11-1 shows that the large declines in the value added/capital stock ratio occur during politically unsettled periods: 1946–1950 and 1960–1962. The value added/employment ratio shows a similar drop in 1946–1950, but rises slightly during 1960–1962. Peaks of efficiency were reached in 1957, but the record during the last years of the Menderes period was rather mixed.[23]

22. Preliminary data suggested an accelerating rate of inflation in the 1968–1970 period — from about 5 percent annually in 1968 to perhaps 9 percent in 1970. Per capita income appeared to grow at about a 4 percent/year rate in 1968 and 1969; available data implied a much lower rate of growth for 1970. Statistics are from *Turkish Economic Review*, 1969 and 1970 and from *OECD Economic Surveys — Turkey* (Paris, Organization for Economic Cooperation and Development, 1970).

23. The data presented in Figure 11-1 are from James W. Land, *Economic Accounts of Non-financial Public Enterprises in Turkey, 1939–1963* (Ankara, State Institute of Statistics, 1969). Deflated capital stock is measured in millions

217

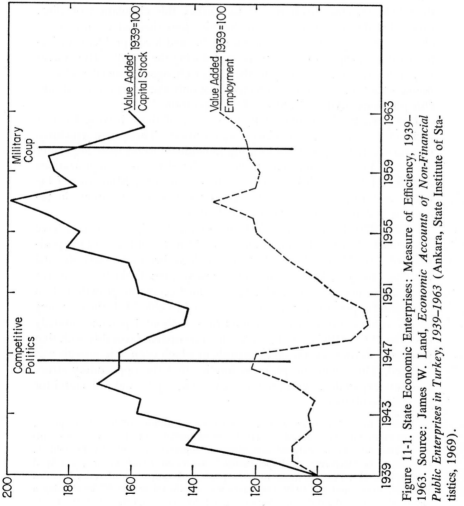

Figure 11-1. State Economic Enterprises: Measure of Efficiency, 1939–
1963. Source: James W. Land, *Economic Accounts of Non-Financial
Public Enterprises in Turkey, 1939–1963* (Ankara, State Institute of Statistics, 1969).

218

Elite Circulation and the National Opportunity Structure

In the broadest sense, much of this work has been concerned with "the processes whereby individuals or groups gain access to or lose their hold on elite positions." [24] In Turkey this circulation of elites proceeded during a period when the elite jobs themselves have been changing rapidly. At least at the most educated level, problems of bureaucratic unemployment were averted during the 1960's. The system responded relatively flexibly to the recent changes in social and economic structure which have affected "not only the types recruited into elite positions but the very bases of these positions." [25]

It is particularly significant that so many of those leaving Interior and Finance moved to the newer organizations. These new structures had relatively few problems locating individuals to fill their important positions. Both the financial incentives offered by these organizations and the relatively high levels of dissatisfaction in the Ministries of Finance and Interior undoubtedly aided the new organizations in recruiting and maintaining a high level of talent.

Since 1950 changes in the Turkish social and political structure have particularly downgraded the status of the Ministry of Interior; the positions of a sizable number of bureaucrats have been adversely affected by these changes. At the same time, however, the Turkish system was reasonably successful in producing sustained economic growth and an expanding opportunity structure. As is seen in Table 11-1, the economy seems to have grown at a per capita rate of about 4 percent annually over the 1962–1967 period, a rate which compares favorably with that generated during several other periods in which economic growth was stressed. This economic progress implies that the opportunity structure was expanding, since growth creates more jobs and a demand for the skills to fill them.

---

of Turkish lira, while value added is measured in millions of lira, 1962 prices. Month-by-month data would clearly be most useful, but these were unavailable. The data were analyzed according to suggestions made by Donald T. Campbell, in "Reforms as Experiments," *American Psychologist,* 24 (April 1969), 409–429. For the value added/capital stock ratio the difference between the 1947 figure and the 1939–1946 data was significant at the .07 level using a single Mood test; the difference between the 1961 figure and the 1950–1960 data was significant at better than the .05 level. Differences in the value added/employment ratio for the same periods were not significant.

24. Keller, *Beyond the Ruling Class,* p. 228
25. *Ibid.,* p. 235.

Table 11-1: Turkish Rates of Economic Growth

	1935–1939	1950–1955	1962–1967
Per capita average annual increase (in percent)	4.0	3.9	4.2

Source: Rates of growth for 1935–1939 and 1950–1955 are from Dwight Simpson, "Development as a Process — The Menderes Phase in Turkey," *Middle East Journal*, 19 (Spring 1965), 145. The 1962–1967 data are from Lawrence A. Mayer, "A Roundup of the World Economy," *Fortune*, 78 (September 15, 1968), 28. Shorter and Hershlag have suggested that such estimates of Turkish growth rates may be exaggerated. See F. C. Shorter, "Military Expenditures and the Allocation of Resources," in F. C. Shorter, ed., *Four Studies on the Economic Development of Turkey* (London, Frank Cass, 1967), pp. 43–44, and Z. Y. Hershlag, *Turkey — The Challenge of Growth* (Leiden, E. J. Brill, 1968), pp. 284–296.

Changes in a nation's opportunity structure can affect both political and economic modernization. Mondale has stressed that national development "requires a transformation of its opportunity structure just as much as it demands more education, increased capital investment, a sound agricultural base, expanded exports, progress toward national unity, and all the other goals of which experts rightly speak." [26] One of the most important features of a national opportunity structure concerns its implications for social mobility. An expanded opportunity structure has helped prevent downward mobility by making it possible for individuals to enter more satisfying jobs in the newer sectors of the economy.[27]

Forestalling possible downward social mobility has undoubtedly been important for the Turkish political system. Lipset and Smelser have stressed that one of the potentially disruptive consequences of mobility is the creation of individuals and groups which have been forced to move downward by virtue of changes in the social structure.[28]

26. Walter F. Mondale, "The Cost of the Brain Drain," *The Atlantic*, 220 (December 1967), 69.

27. Fox and Miller, using data from 12 countries, found that high levels of economic development are closely associated with lower levels of downward mobility. Thomas G. Fox and S. M. Miller, "Economic, Political, and Social Determinants of Mobility: An International Cross-Sectional Analysis," *Acta Sociologica*, 9 (1965), 91.

28. Smelser and Lipset, *Social Structure and Mobility*, p. 16.

220

Such downward mobility could be particularly destabilizing politically because Political Science Faculty graduates have been through a competitive, elitist educational experience. Collins and Guetzkow have stressed the problems created "when the status which a person deserves on one dimension — educational level, for instance — differs from the status he deserves on the basis of his accomplishments in another dimension." [29] Another facet of social mobility has been emphasized by Huntington, who posits that opportunities for mobility in the economic sphere can act to lower levels of political participation.[30]

These new economic opportunities siphoned off able, dissatisfied individuals from the Ministries of Interior and Finance. By providing more satisfying work for members of the administrative elite, the newer organizations aided the cause of political stability. These possibilities have been important because defeated elites may become more active, rather than withdrawing from politics.[31] Without these channels of individual mobility, many of the graduates who moved might have been providing leadership for bureaucrats disgruntled with economic conditions.

This employment function of state economic enterprises has been neglected in the literature. The inefficiencies of state enterprises have been a target of economists, but one important political function — that of providing a safety valve for downward mobility — deserves further research.[32] The opportunity to change one's individual circumstances helped prevent overt mobilization of the bureaucratic elite against Justice Party dominance in the 1965–1969 period. Economic growth and the structural changes accompanying this growth aided the bureaucratic elite in adjusting to the problems presented by in-

29. Barry E. Collins and Harold Guetzkow, *A Social Psychology of Group Processes for Decision-Making* (New York, Wiley, 1964), p. 98.

30. Samuel P. Huntington, *Political Order in Changing Societies* (New Haven, Conn., Yale University Press, 1968), p. 54.

31. Kim, "Defeated Candidates," p. 887, has suggested that "the higher the cost of defeat, the greater the likelihood that a losing candidate withdraws his support for the democratic rules of the game and shows a low inclination to political activity." But there are other possibilities; the same social groups, if not the same individuals, may continue to be active. Moreover, there are likely to be major differences among countries in this regard.

32. As Wildavsky has stressed in the American context, budgets have many functions other than providing for greater outputs, more efficiency in government, and so forth. Aaron Wildavsky, *The Politics of the Budgetary Process* (Boston, Little, Brown, 1964).

creased rural participation and the dominance of new elite groups. The opportunities for individual mobility have helped lessen demands for the restoration of the bureaucratic group to its former position of influence. The Turkish case provides some support for the proposition that "rapid economic growth creates new opportunities for entrepreneurship and employment and thereby diverts into money-making ambitions and talents which might otherwise go into coup-making." [33]

The survey data suggest that the Turkish political situation in 1965 was considerably different from that prevailing in 1956. The decline in reported political interference is consistent, even among groups recording similar levels of job satisfaction in 1956 and 1965. An increase in mutual understanding between politician and bureaucrat may have occurred. A recognition of the importance of working together may have replaced some of the antagonism at the local level. District governors in particular appear to have been more disposed toward taking suggestions from local leaders in 1965 than in 1956. Given the central role of bureaucrat-politician conflict in recent formulations of Turkish politics, this finding may have major significance for the political system. Even with the Justice Party dominating the coalition government, political pressures upon bureaucracy in 1965 seem to have been less than those prevailing during the Democratic Party period.

The presence in 1965 of new institutions like the State Planning Organization may have aided this decline in political influence. Because development priorities are being set by such organizations, they act as a buffer between the politician and the bureaucrat. Complaints about the lack of local facilities may be referred elsewhere than to the Ministry of Interior. Thus, an organization which has restricted the power of the Ministry of Interior may indirectly aid it by taking some of the political pressure off the Ministry.

On the other hand, in 1970 and 1971 pressure was put on the government by various nonbureaucratic groups. Extremists of the left and right, with their allies among the religious groups, added to the tension inherent in the Turkish sociocultural climate. Political parties have been unstable, and the level of discourse increasingly shrill. Rising demands from both villagers and urban dwellers have increased pressures for performance by various elites. The political leadership tried to steer a middle course, playing one group off against another, but the Justice Party government proved unable to keep order and satisfy the

33. Huntington, *Political Order*, p. 49.

222

military. This analysis hypothesizes that economic growth had a stabilizing influence upon the political system during the 1960's. Inflation and economic difficulties contributed to the military intervention in 1971.

The social and political situation which has characterized Turkey in recent years obviously did not emerge overnight.[34] When one considers the more immediate historical antecedents of the present system, it is hard to disagree with Simpson's judgment:

> The "Menderes Phase" (the Democratic Party government between 1950 and 1960) is still difficult to evaluate, partly for the political partisanship attached but equally for the many paradoxes it brought to existence. For instance, the great doses of inflation that seriously imperiled the economy at the same time brought to it a new dynamism, volatile yet potentially creative. An investment and entrepreneurial class grew rapidly, knowledge of industrial techniques became much more widespread and a glimpse of the potentialities of the development process was afforded to many hitherto unseeing elements of the population.[35]

Political, economic, and social changes in Turkey over the last two decades have contributed to a breaking down of older styles of behavior and provided new stimuli for the development enterprise. The changes can be summarized in terms of the problems confronting the administration in the two time periods. In 1956 the Turkish administration was struggling with social and political change, and the atmosphere was highly politicized. The conflict was between bureaucrat and politician, each representing different social groups. Although these conflicts have been only partially resolved, technical change has also posed a major problem to the administration. New organizational structures and increased demand for the expert rather than the old-line generalist have been transforming the bases of power and status within the Turkish bureaucracy. New issues have been superimposed upon older problems, and — despite progress — many paradoxes remain.

34. For an interesting analysis, see Ismet Giritli, "Turkey Since the 1965 Elections," *Middle East Journal,* 23 (Summer 1969), 351–363.

35. Dwight Simpson, "Development as a Process — The Menderes Phase in Turkey," *Middle East Journal,* 19 (Spring 1965), 152.

Appendices

Bibliography

Index

Appendix A. The Design of the Study

Much has been written about the process of development; yet longitudinal studies of change in the developing areas are rare. Since much of this research focused on the Turkish administrative elite's reaction to its changing economic and political environment, gaining a time perspective on this phenomenon was essential. The basic research design was that of a panel study with two waves of questionnaires (1956 and 1965). These data were supplemented by information from additional surveys, particularly research conducted by other investigators in 1956 and 1962. Such work from various data sources represents an effort to extend secondary analysis beyond its previous uses.

We have relied extensively upon several surveys of elite groups carried out in Turkey in the mid-1950's. One of the most interesting of these was conducted in 1956 by Fahïr Armaoğlu and Guthrie Birkhead. Armaoğlu and Birkhead attempted to contact all graduates of the Political Science Faculty from the classes of 1946–1955. Their research was aimed at determining how well the Faculty was serving its students and at bringing the Faculty up to date on the changing training needs of governmental employees.[1] Thus, Armaoğlu and Birkhead focused on graduates' attitudes towards training at the Faculty, on their career histories since leaving the Faculty, and on the aspects of their work which contributed to job satisfaction or dissatisfaction.

The 380 signed questionnaires from this survey were obtained along with the expressed interest of Professor Armaoğlu in seeing the survey repeated.[2] The respondents to the 1956 questionnaire were used as the basis for the panel study. Information was obtained concerning the university grades and 1965 occupations of almost all of these 380 graduates. This material helped serve as a check on nonresponse bias for the 1965 survey, since our new questionnaires were not returned

1. Fahir Armaoğlu and Guthrie Birkhead, *Graduates of the Faculty of Political Science, 1946–1955* (Ankara, Public Administration Institute for Turkey and the Middle East, 1957), p. 3.

2. Twenty-four questionnaires from the Armaoğlu and Birkhead study were not used because we were unable to determine the names of the respondents. Of the 508 questionnaires used in the 1956 study, over a hundred could not be located when we returned to Turkey in 1965.

226

by all the 380 people who had responded to the Armaoğlu and Birkhead survey.[3] In addition, these data aided in the study of factors related to promotion and job change during the 1956–1965 period.

Finally, another group of Political Science Faculty graduates from the classes of 1958–1961 was sampled. This permitted both an age level analysis, comparing the 1956 responses of the classes of 1949–1952 with the 1965 responses of the 1958–1961 graduates, and a limited trend analysis, since the classes of 1958–1961 had been surveyed in 1958 while they were still students at the Faculty.[4] A number of the questions which had been included on the 1956 questionnaire were repeated on the 1965 questionnaire. Additional items directed toward the values and occupational mobility of the graduates were used in 1965.

Two hundred forty-one Political Science Faculty graduates who returned questionnaires in 1956 responded to the 1965 panel study. Sixty-nine of the graduates from the classes of 1958–1961 returned their questionnaires. The 63 percent response rate among the panel respondents compares relatively favorably with that reported for one well-known American study.[5] The response rate for the 1958–1961 graduates was 54 percent, if we include only the 126 graduates for whom addresses were available in this calculation. There were also 11 graduates who would have been sent questionnaires, but whose addresses could not be found.

A second 1956 survey was also analyzed. This survey was sponsored by the Political Science Faculty, and was concerned with the social backgrounds, time-budgeting, communication patterns, and activities of Turkish district and provincial governors.[6] The results of

3. Old home addresses (from Political Science Faculty files) were used in an effort to locate the graduates for whom job information was not available.

4. For a description of this survey see Herbert H. Hyman, Arif Payaslïoğlu, and Frederick W. Frey, "The Values of Turkish College Youth," *Public Opinion Quarterly,* 22 (Fall 1958), 275–291. Some of the trend analysis is reported in Leslie L. Roos, Jr., Noralou P. Roos, and Gary R. Field, "Students and Politics in Contemporary Turkey," in S. M. Lipset and P. G. Altbach, eds., *Students in Revolt* (Boston, Houghton Mifflin, 1969), pp. 257–282.

5. The group at the Michigan Survey Research Center reported about 68 percent of those interviewed in their 1956 election study who were still living four years later were also interviewed in the 1960 study. Angus Campbell, Philip E. Converse, Warren E. Miller, and Donald E. Stokes, *Elections and the Political Order* (New York, Wiley, 1966), p. 80.

6. Turhan Feyzioğlu, Arif Payaslïoğlu, Albert Gorvine, and Mümtaz Soysal,

this study were originally published in Turkish; the data from the 1956 survey have been extensively reworked for the present book.

The questionnaire used in the survey of district and provincial governors was distributed to all the districts and provinces in Turkey. The response rates are illustrated in Table A-1. The overall response rate was that used by original investigators in their account of the survey results. On inspection of the data in 1965, it was determined that some of the questionnaires were filled out by assistant district governors (or assistant provincial governors) rather than by the governors themselves. These questionnaires answered by someone other than the governor were eliminated from consideration; this elimination process is reflected in the figures for "response rate, after screening."

Table A-1: Response Rates for 1956 Survey of District and Provincial Governors

	District governors	Provincial governors
Overall response rate	71%	68%
Response rate, after screening	62%	67%
Number of possible respondents	493	66

Although it was not possible to contact the respondents to this 1956 survey a second time, several additional items of information concerning these individuals were collected. Respondents who were still district governors in 1962 were identified and their 1962 district recorded. This procedure permitted linking the district governor data with that obtained in a 1962 nationwide sample survey of Turkish villagers.[7] In addition, the respondent's 1965 occupation — whether inside or outside of the Ministry of Interior — was recorded; this enabled us to consider the factors associated with promotion or with leaving the ministry in the 1956–1965 period.

Finally, this survey of provincial and district administrators included 97 Political Science Faculty graduates who answered the 1956 ques-

Kaza ve Vilayet Idaresi Üzerinde Bir Araştırma [An investigation concerning district and provincial administration], (Ankara, Ajans-Türk Matbassí, 1957).

7. This study is described in Frederick W. Frey, "Surveying Peasant Attitudes in Turkey," *Public Opinion Quarterly,* 27 (Fall 1963), 335–355.

tionnaire distributed by Armaoğlu and Birkhead. Sixty-seven of these individuals answered all three surveys — the 1965 panel survey and the two 1956 studies. Merging the data from the various surveys made it possible to obtain information in depth for a reasonable number of respondents. At various points in the analysis the results of cross-tabulation across several surveys will be presented.

An overview of the representativeness of the surveys used in our analysis would seem particularly desirable. In the following pages, the representativeness of the Political Science Faculty survey data will be considered in terms of its fit with available information on the total population of Political Science Faculty graduates. After this relatively general presentation, some of the more specific problems of bias will be discussed.

Representatives of Various Samples

Although the 25 percent sample of the 1958–1961 graduates could be drawn from available class lists, we were committed to surveying a panel of 1946–1955 graduates initially selected by other investigators. The situation was complicated by the fact that 128 of the questionnaires gathered by Armaoğlu and Birkhead could not be located or were otherwise unusable for our purposes. The questionnaires obtained from the Armaoğlu and Birkhead study, as well as the subsample who participated in the 1965 panel study, have been compared with data on all Political Science Faculty graduates in the 1946–1955 period. As is seen in Table A-2, the available survey data overrepresent the older graduates at the expense of the younger.

This overrepresentation of older graduates should not be especially important for the interpretation of most of the attitudinal data. Attitudinal differences between the classes of 1946–1950 and those of 1951–1955 were very slight for almost all the items included on the 1956 and 1965 surveys.

It was also possible to compare the distribution of graduates of different sections of the Political Science Faculty among both the total population and the various samples. The sections have somewhat different course requirements and tend to lead to positions in different ministries: the administration section to the Ministry of Interior, the financial section to the Ministry of Finance, and the political section to the Ministry of Foreign Affairs.

Table A-2: Distribution by Classes of Political Science Faculty Graduates

	Faculty Graduates, Classes of 1946–1955			
Classes	Total population	Total number in 1956 study	Coded from 1956 study	In 1956–1965 panel study
1946–1950	50%	50%	56%	59%
1951–1955	50	50	44	41
No answer	—	—	1	—
Number of graduates	1,062	508	380	241

Source: Fahir Armaoğlu and Guthrie Birkhead, *Graduates of the Faculty of Political Science, 1946–1955* (Ankara, Public Administration Institute for Turkey and the Middle East, 1957), pp. 34. Another source is Ali Çankaya, *Mülkiye Tarihi ve Mülkiyeliler* [History of the Civil Service School and its graduates], vol. 2 (Ankara, Örnek Matbaasi, 1954). This publication reports that 46 percent of the graduates were in the classes of 1946–1950 and 54 percent were in the classes of 1951–1955; the number of graduates was given as 1,141. Part of the discrepancy could lie with different methods of reporting individuals who have to repeat particular years due to poor academic performance.

Table A-3: Distribution by Section of Political Science Faculty Graduates in Various Groups

	Faculty Graduates, Classes of 1946–1955			
Section at PSF	Total population	Total number in 1956 study	Coded from 1956 study	In 1956–1965 panel study
Administration	45%	47%	46%	49%
Financial	45	44	42	39
Political	9	9	10	12
(No answer)	—	—	1	—
Number of graduates	1,062	508	380	241

230

As is seen in Table A-3, the distribution of graduates by section in the surveys was fairly close to that found in the total population. The somewhat lower representation of graduates of the financial section in the 1956–1965 panel study is due to problems of nonresponse in the Ministry of Finance. These will be discussed later in this appendix.

Some basic comparisons between the findings from the 508 respondents surveyed by Armaoğlu and Birkhead and the 380 questionnaires available for coding can also be made. Fifty-one percent of the 508 respondents said their fathers were officials; 50 percent of the subgroup of 380 gave this reply. Armaoğlu and Birkhead coded the data on job satisfaction somewhat differently from the way we did and assigned 16 percent of the respondents to an intermediate category of "satisfied due to certain reasons and unsatisfied due to others." In the final coding scheme, these respondents were recorded as satisfied or dissatisfied according to the relative number of reasons for satisfaction or dissatisfaction they gave. Thus, in the subgroup of 380 individuals, 55 percent were found to be satisfied, 43 percent dissatisfied, and 2 percent gave no answer. The figures for the 508 graduates were 47 percent satisfied, 35 percent dissatisfied, 3 percent no answer, and 16 percent in the intermediate category described above.

Political Science Faculty Graduates and Government Employment

The panel of graduates and the sample of 1958–1961 graduates do appear to be generally representative of Political Science Faculty graduates who work for the government — the majority of our respondents. In Table A-4, the occupational distribution of those who responded to our survey is presented.

Column 1 shows the occupational distribution of our respondents in 1965, and this can be compared with the estimated 1965 occupational distribution of all Political Science Faculty graduates which is given in column 2. Column 3 lists the proportion of graduates of all different university faculties in Turkey who were employed in the various organizations in 1963. We have then computed the relative prominence of Political Science Faculty graduates (number of PSF graduates as a proportion of all faculty graduates) in each of the organizations. These figures are given in column 4. Thus in the Ministry of Foreign Affairs in the 1960's, Political Science Faculty graduates made up approximately 63 percent of all graduates employed in this Ministry.

Table A-4: Occupations of 1965 Respondents, Political Science Faculty
Graduates, and All Faculty Graduates

Organization	(1) Roos respond- ents (1965)	(2) Living graduates, Political Science Faculty (1963)	(3) Living graduates, all Faculties (1963)	(4) Propor- tion of PSF Graduates to all Faculty Graduates
Ministry of Interior	37%	31%	1.6%	82%
Central offices	11	11	.5	85
District governors	26	20	1	80
Ministry of Finance	15	19	1.8	47
Ministry of Foreign Affairs	11	10	0.6	63
Other ministries and organizations	15	18	29	3
pre-1950	11	13	26	2
post-1950	4	6	2	11

State economic
  enterprises, banks,
  and private sector
	21	22	66	1

Number of graduates	310	2,328	52,973	

Source: *Devlet Personel Sayïmï I Genel ve Katma Bütçeli Kurumlar* [State
Personnel Census, I, General and Attached Budget Organizations] (Ankara,
Devlet Istatistik Enstitüsü, 1965), pp. 13–19. For a fuller explanation of how
the calculations were made, see Appendix B.

A quick glance down column 4 shows that Political Science Faculty
graduates made up a very substantial proportion of the three central
ministries — Interior, Finance, and Foreign Affairs. In the Ministry of
the Interior, where fully 82 percent of all university graduates are from
this one faculty, they were distributed almost equally between the provincial and central organizations.

Outside these three central ministries, the Political Science Faculty graduates were rather widely dispersed. The 428 people in the non-central ministries were working in 45 different organizations. However, they were likely to be found in the older ministries, with 59 working in the Ministry of Commerce and 34 in the Council of State (Danĭştay). As Table A-4 indicates, only a few of the Political Science Faculty graduates have found work in the newer organizations. However, several very high-level officials were included among those working in these organizations — the head of the State Institute of Statistics and the General Director of the Department of Highways, among others.

Since data from the personnel census of state economic enterprises were not collected until 1965, and comparable information on private sector employees is not easily obtained, these two sectors were treated together and provided only rough estimates of the distribution of graduates. The estimate presented in Table A-4 was made by subtracting the known number of Political Science and other faculty graduates in government from the totals of these groups presented in the population census.[8] The results support the observation that Political Science Faculty graduates have not ordinarily sought employment outside the central ministries — Interior, Finance, and Foreign Affairs.

Although Table A-4 suggests no underrepresentation of graduates working in noncentral organizations, tests presented later in this appendix point toward such bias. These two findings are compatible if several factors are taken into consideration. First of all, age was closely related to place of employment: the younger the graduate, the more likely he was to have found a job outside the central ministries. Since the 1965 sample of Political Science Faculty graduates excludes both the larger older group graduating before 1946 and the smaller younger group graduating between 1956 and 1958, the comparison of our sample with the overall distribution of graduates might show no differences, despite a bias towards underrepresentation of nongovernmental employees. This is true because there were more pre-1946 Political Science graduates living than there were living graduates from the three classes graduating between 1956 and 1958; these older graduates are likely to be found in disproportionate numbers in government service. Other calculations show the number of Political Science Faculty graduates who responded to our survey relative to the number of Faculty graduates in any given organization varying only from a low of 10 percent in the Ministry of Finance to a high of 16 percent in the Ministry of the Interior.

8. See Appendix B for the details of this calculation.

While our sample is basically representative of Political Science Faculty graduates employed in the different types of organizations, it is much more limited in its representativeness of the organizations themselves. Political Science Faculty graduates constitute only 5 percent of the university graduates in the Turkish work force. However, since these graduates made up such a large percentage of the higher echelons of a few key ministries (Interior, Finance, and Foreign Affairs), describing the attitudes of Political Science Faculty graduates in these ministries provided an estimate of the attitudes held by the bulk of the high-level employees in these ministries. Such significance is lacking when the attitudes of Faculty graduates working outside these central ministries are discussed.

The overall representativeness of the Political Science Faculty surveys seems reasonably good, but there were several possibilities of bias. The remainder of this appendix will focus upon the investigation of these possibilities in the various studies.

Only 65 percent of the graduates from 1946 to 1955 were located by the researchers for the Armaoğlu and Birkhead survey in 1956. Since the study was a mail questionnaire, mainly dependent upon the availability of ministerial address lists, those working in private enterprise were probably underrepresented in the sample. Nonresponse bias was also a possible problem, since 26 percent of those receiving questionnairs did not return them. Although the lists used by Armaoğlu and Birkhead were not available, other kinds of checks were possible.

In 1956 Dr. Armaoğlu had to work alone without help from a central alumni agency with up-to-date files. By 1965 the Political Science Faculty Alumni Association had an active office in Ankara, and for certain classes, particularly the class of 1951, the association could provide an almost complete list of current addresses. This complete 1951 list could be compared with the 1965 occupational distribution of graduates responding to the Armaoğlu and Birkhead questionnaire. Actually, since the number of graduates answering the Armaoğlu and Birkhead questionnaire varied greatly among classes graduating in the 1950–1952 period, it was decided to make the comparison with the 1950, 1951, and 1952 graduates who had answered the questionnaire. When the 1950–1952 addresses were compared with the list from the Alumni Association, an underestimation of private sector graduates was noted. Only 7 percent of the 1950–1952 graduates surveyed in 1956 were in the private sector nine years later, as opposed to 14 percent from the class of 1951 list. Similar differences between survey and list were found with respect to the proportion of Political Science Faculty graduates working in state economic enterprises.

This type of bias was expected, and in attempting to relocate the original panel, people working outside the central ministries were found to be the hardest to trace down. Checks on the representativeness of the original samples and the sample of younger graduates suggest a related bias; graduates located in the 1956 and 1965 mail surveys were less likely to have had fathers in business than were Political Science Faculty students in general.

The previously mentioned student survey of the classes of 1958–1961 was used for this comparison; this questionnaire was administered in 1957 to all students in attendance at the Faculty on a given day.[9] While such a study probably underrepresents those less likely to attend classes, it is not subject to the same biases noted for mail questionnaires. As seen in Table A-5, the main differences between studies relate to the representation of sons of officials, businessmen, and professionals. Sons of officials made up 55 percent and 71 percent of the respondents to the two graduate surveys, but only 49 percent of those answering the student survey. Twenty-three percent of the students mentioned that their fathers were businessmen, while sons of professionals constitute 8 percent of the respondents to the student survey. These percentages were substantially higher than those recorded on the graduate survey for the classes of 1958–1961, and slightly higher than those for the classes of 1946–1955.

There are several possible explanations for this discrepancy between student and graduate data. Sons of officials might be much more likely than sons of businessmen to complete their work and eventually graduate from the Political Science Faculty. It is more likely, however, that the problems already noted in locating individuals in the private sector were responsible for these differences between surveys. Since sons of businessmen and professionals have been more likely than other students to enter the private sector, these individuals were probably more difficult to locate than were the sons of officials.

In summary, important social background differences are suggested by the comparisons among the various samples. The fathers of students at the Faculty were more likely to have worked in the private sector than were fathers of the graduates located by Armaoğlu. If sons of people who work in the private sector were more likely themselves to

9. Results of this survey are discussed in Hyman, Payaslioğlu, and Frey, "The Values of Turkish College Youth."

Table A-5: Graduate and Student Surveys[a]

	Classes of 1946–1955	Classes of 1958–1961	
	Graduate survey (%)	Graduate survey (%)	Student survey (%)
Father's occupation:			
Official	55	71	49
Business	20	10	23
Farmer	15	13	11
Professional	5	1	8
Other	4	3	3
No answer	2	1	6
Number of respondents	380	69	399

Source: The student data were from the survey described in Herbert H. Hyman, Arif Payaslioğlu, and Frederick W. Frey, "The Values of Turkish College Youth," *Public Opinion Quarterly*, 22 (Fall 1958), 275–291.

[a] Differences were significant at the .05 level for comparisons involving the graduate data from the classes of 1958–1961.

find jobs in this sector, the two tests of bias would seem to reinforce each other. The original panel probably underrepresents both graduates who work in nongovernmental positions and those whose fathers were not employed by the government.

Nonresponse Bias in the 1965 Political Science Faculty Survey

The preceding section has dealt with possible biases in the original 1956 survey by Armaoğlu and Birkhead. Another test of possible bias in the 1965 panel research can be made by comparing the 1956 data on the 1965 respondents and nonrespondents. The 241 graduates who answered both the 1956 and 1965 questionnaires can be compared with the 139 graduates who responded in 1956 but not in 1965. Since — in addition to attitudinal items from 1956 — information is available on the university grades and 1965 jobs of almost all the 380 respondents to the Armaoğlu and Birkhead survey, a number of comparisons are possible.

236

Table A-6 presents only those items and alternatives for which there was a substantial difference between 1965 respondents and non-respondents. There were few differences between the two groups with respect to such variables as place of residence at university entrance, university grades, course choices, and job success.

Table A-6: Differences Between 1965 Respondents and 1965 Nonrespondents

	1965	
	Respondents (%)	Nonrespondents (%)
Father's occupation:[a]		
Official	59	46
Business	16	26
1956 position:[a]		
Ministry of Finance	27	38
1956 type of work:		
Administrative	37	33
Executive	27	17
Clerical	2	3
Professional	34	46
1956 Job satisfaction:[a]		
Satisfied	51	62
1956 Reasons for satisfaction:[a]		
Enough authority	34	45
Enough pay	20	35
Few transfers	10	23
1965 position:[a]		
Ministry of Finance	17	33
1965 type of work:		
Administrative	42	27
Executive	21	16
Clerical	0	0
Professional	36	48
Number of 1956 respondents	241	139

[a] Differences for these variables were significant at the .05 level.

As seen in Table A-6, the major problem with nonresponse bias occurs in the Ministry of Finance; this was the only ministry in which there was some hostility toward the questionnaire. Although generally adequate, the response rate was somewhat lower in that ministry. That is, 51 percent of those in the Ministry of Finance responded in 1965, compared with 70 percent of those in the Ministry of Interior, 60 percent in the Ministry of Foreign Affairs, and 60 percent of those in the noncentral organizations. The panel response rate was 63 percent. As noted earlier, there were 241 panel respondents and 69 respondents from the classes of 1958–1961.

Further analysis was performed to determine the degree of similarity among 1965 respondents and nonrespondents within the Ministries of Interior and Finance. Respondents and nonrespondents in the Ministry of Interior were very similar; however, differences between respondents and nonrespondents in the Ministry of Finance are primarily responsible for the overall differences between the respondents and the nonrespondents. Thus, 76 percent of the 1965 respondents and only 39 percent of the nonrespondents in the Ministry of Finance were sons of officials. Even more important, while 59 percent of the 1965 respondents in the Ministry of Finance reported being satisfied with their jobs in 1956, 78 percent of the 1965 nonrespondents said they were satisfied. Response rates among the 1958–1961 graduates in the Ministry of Finance raise similar problems. Although the overall response rate was 54 percent, only 33 percent (4 out of 12) of those approached in the Ministry of Finance responded to the 1965 questionnaire. This contrasts with 50 percent response (4 out of 8) in the Ministry of Foreign Affairs and 76 percent (26 out of 34) in the Ministry of Interior.

Because of these differences, particular caution is necessary in comparing 1956 and 1965 data from the Ministry of Finance. Longitudinal comparisons will emphasize the panel study data from this ministry; using the findings from those who cooperated in both 1956 and 1965 helps eliminate some of the problems of nonresponse bias. However, the fact that these panel respondents are clearly not representative of Political Science Faculty graduates within the Ministry of Finance does complicate problems of generalization.

Checks across Surveys

Various checks on the validity of the survey data can be made by comparisons between several of the studies.[10] If the results of tabula-

10. Relatively little information was available to permit direct checks on

tions done within two or more surveys are similar, we can have additional confidence in the validity of the data. The most important comparison to be made between the survey data involves the two 1956 studies. This comparison is between:

> 1) Political Science Faculty graduates surveyed in the 1956 Political Science Faculty study who were district governors at that time, and
>
> 2) District governors surveyed on the 1956 district and provincial governor study who were Political Science Faculty graduates.

The respondents to be compared should be very similar. There is only one notable difference between the two samples: the district governor survey included a few Political Science Faculty graduates (6 percent of the sample) who had been district governors for over 10 years. Since the sample used in the 1956 Political Science Faculty study was made up of individuals who graduated between 1946 and 1955, the older district governors were not included in this survey.

As is seen in Table A-7, there were few actual differences between the two samples with regard to father's occupation, the only item available for comparison. The reasons for the discrepancy between the percentages of sons of professionals in the two surveys are not clear.[11]

Checks across surveys can also provide more direct information on nonresponse bias. The respondents to the survey of provincial and district administrators included graduates of the Political Science Faculty between 1946 and 1955 who apparently did not answer the Armaoğlu and Birkhead questionnaire. (Since these graduates occupied important positions in the Ministry of Interior, it is likely that their names were on the lists originally used by Armaoğlu and Birkhead.) On the other

---

nonresponse bias among the 1956 district governors studies at the time. One set of comparisons was made using data on the 1965 occupations of both respondents and nonrespondents to the 1956 survey of district governors. Of those still in the Ministry of Interior, only 37 percent of respondents to the 1956 survey of district governors ($n = 219$) had been promoted (according to an attributional ranking) since 1956. However, 50 percent of the nonrespondents ($n = 92$) had been promoted. This finding for the 1956 administrators contrasts with the data from the 1956–1965 Political Science Faculty study, where no differences in job success were found between 1965 respondents and nonrespondents.

11. There was also a close relationship between the 1956 Political Science Faculty survey data on the governor's region of residence (before coming to the university) and the 1956 district governor survey data on region of birth. This comparison could be made because individuals typically move to the capital of their province — rather than outside the province — for lýcee schooling.

Table A-7: A Comparison of 1956 Survey Findings Concerning Father's Occupation[a]

| | Political Science Faculty graduates who were district governors (1956) | |
	Political Science Faculty survey (%)	District governor survey (%)
Father's occupation:		
Official	45	42
Business	21	18
Farmer	22	22
Professional	2	6
Other	8	6
No answer	2	7
Number of respondents	126	250

[a] Differences were not statistically significant.

hand, 38 provincial and district administrators responded to the Political Science Faculty questionnaire but not to the longer administrative survey. The comparison of the two groups of "one-time" responders with those who answered both questionnaires can help isolate nonresponse bias. An analysis of the social backgrounds of district administrators responding only to the Political Science Faculty questionnaire indicates that, at least for this variable, nonresponse bias was minimal. The social backgrounds of these "one-time" respondents were very similar to those of the district administrators who responded to both questionnaires.

Date of Questionnaire Return

One additional way to estimate bias is to use the date of questionnaire return to infer characteristics of nonrespondents. The basic assumption here is that the respondents who return the questionnaires only after a relatively long period are more similar to the nonrespondents than are those who reply promptly. There is some doubt as to whether this assumption is correct for our Turkish data. The 1965 nonrespondents returned their 1956 questionnaires about as quickly as did the graduates who replied to both surveys. On the other hand, since this use of data of response is a well-established technique for checking on possible nonresponse bias, it seemed worthwhile to briefly consider some of the correlates of promptness of response to the various questionnaires.

Table A-8: Date of Return of 1956 Political Science Faculty Questionnaire[a]

	Early (%)	Inter-mediate I (%)	Inter-mediate II (%)	Late (%)
Father's occupation:				
Official	58	59	56	44
Business	16	18	18	26
Residence before entering university:				
Ankara, Istanbul, Izmir	46	31	30	22
1956 position:				
Ministry of Interior	34	39	50	61
Ministry of Finance	22	44	35	18
Ministry of Foreign Affairs	20	7	11	4
Year of graduation:				
1946–1950	71	66	43	39
1951–1955	27	33	57	60
Number of respondents	77	107	97	72

Individuals who responded between January 1 and January 27 were placed in the Early category. Those responding between January 28 and February 3 were assigned to the Intermediate I category, and between February 4 and February 17, to the Intermediate II category. Graduates responding after February 17 were assigned to the Late category.

[a] Differences were significant at the .05 level.

Several points are illustrated in Table A-8. First of all, the fact that Political Science Faculty graduates from business backgrounds were likely to return their questionnaires later than graduates from official social backgrounds lends a measure of additional support to the hypothesis that graduates in business were underrepresented among the respondents to the 1956 survey. Secondly, the fact that respondents from more elite backgrounds were more likely to respond earlier seems to have been partly a function of accessibility.[12] Graduates from less privileged backgrounds were more likely to have been in the Ministry of Interior and been posted to remote areas as district governors.

Additional analysis of the survey and discussion with the original authors of the 1956 study indicated that the graduates from the classes of 1946–1950 seem to have been sent questionnaires before the younger graduates. Controlling for year of graduation reduces many of the relationships between date of return and such variables as father's occupation, place of residence, and 1956 position. Thus, with the exception of the minor point regarding business mentioned above, it seems unlikely that further implications regarding possible nonresponse bias can be drawn from the data.

Table A-9: Date of Return of 1956 District Governor Questionnaire[a]

	Early (%)	Intermediate (%)	Late (%)
Report substantial political interference	71	51	50
Report substantial conflict with other groups	46	38	34
High score on public works orientation	54	39	36
Number of respondents	117	66	50

Questionnaires returned in February 1956 were classified as early and those returned in March as intermediate. Only Political Science Faculty graduates are included in these tabulations, but similar results were obtained for the district governors as a group.

[a] Differences were significant at the .05 level.

The 1956 data on district governors were also examined in terms of the date of questionnaire return. Several differences between early and late respondents were noted in this study. The largest differences of this type are presented in Table A-9.

12. The fact that Armaoğlu and Birkhead did not send questionnaires to graduates outside of Turkey is partially responsible for the rapid response within the Ministry of Foreign Affairs.

242

As seen in Table A-9, individuals who return their questionnaires early appear to have had more complaints about political interference and to have pushed harder for public works programs than did their counterparts who answered the survey later. The respondents who were particularly interested in pressing their points of view thus seem to have been motivated to answer sooner than the other district governors; such individuals with "axes to grind" may have been overrepresented in the survey. Finally, it should be noted that the social background differences associated with date of return in the 1956 Political Science Faculty study were not found in the district governor study.

A final check on bias using date of questionnaire return was performed with the 310 respondents from the 1965 study. Because the questionnaires were sent to the graduates of the classes of 1958–1961 slightly later than to the other respondents, date of return was run against the graduates' attitudes and positions, controlling for year of graduation. For the 1965 respondents there were no systematic differences in responses associated with the date on which the questionnaire was returned.

Summary

The data used in this study can be presented as a diagram showing the interconnection among the surveys. Figure A-1 shows how three basic surveys of the Turkish administrative elite provide the core of the information for this research. The previous discussion has evaluated the representativeness of the sample survey data collected in 1956 and 1965. The most important sources of bias in the Political Science Faculty surveys are summarized in Table A-10. The probability that the sons of businessmen are somewhat underrepresented is made clear by this table. Both sets of data on nonresponse bias in the 1965 Political Science Faculty survey also indicate the underrepresentation of graduates in the Ministry of Finance.

Problems of nonresponse bias pose threats to internal validity when the 1956 and 1965 data are compared without the proper controls.[13] Such comparison may suggest that a change has taken place when, in fact, the marginals differ because of nonresponse bias. Controlling for

13. Both internal and external validity are discussed in Donald T. Campbell, "Factors Relevant to the Validity of Experiments in Social Settings," *Psychological Bulletin,* 54 (July 1957), 297–312.

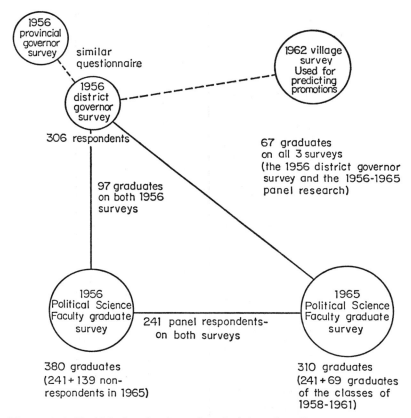

Figure A-1. Turkish data bank on the administrative elite.

ministry and looking at both panel respondents and at nonrespondents helps deal with this question of internal validity.

External validity concerns the question: "To what populations, settings, and variables" can our findings be generalized? [14] We think that our findings are, by and large, relevant to all Political Science Faculty graduates in 1956 and 1965. At the same time, we discuss elite attitudes and behaviors in several different types of ministries and organizations, thus generalizing from our data to organizational leadership as a whole. But authors have clear biases. The tables presented in this chapter

14. *Ibid.,* 297.

Table A-10: Biases in the Surveys

Problem	Probable bias in 1956 Political Science Faculty survey	Nonresponse bias in 1965 Political Science Faculty survey (panel comparison)	Nonresponse bias in 1965 Political Science Faculty survey (1958–1961 graduates)	Estimate from information on date of response — 1956 Political Science Faculty survey	Estimate from information on date of response — 1965 Political Science Faculty survey
Sons of businessmen underrepresented	Yes	Yes	Yes	Yes	No
Ministry of Finance underrepresented	No information	Yes	Yes	No	No
Job satisfaction underrepresented	No information	Yes	No information	No	No
Metropolitan areas overrepresented	No information	No	No information	Yes	No

should make it possible for the reader to evaluate the external validity of this study for himself.[15]

It is clear that the data from the Ministry of Interior present the fewest problems of nonresponse bias; moreover, Political Science Faculty graduates made up over 80 percent of the university graduates in Interior. Likewise, the Ministry of Foreign Affairs posed few difficulties; the response rate was high, and Political Science Faculty graduates constituted almost two-thirds of this ministry's university-educated employees. Although Political Science Faculty graduates were well represented in the Ministry of Finance, the substantial nonresponse bias in this ministry suggests the need for considerable caution in interpreting the 1965 data from Finance. Finally, Political Science Faculty graduates make up a small proportion of the university graduates in the new organizations, in state economic enterprises, and in the private sector. This fact necessitates speaking specifically of Political Science Faculty graduates in these organizations, rather than of the organizational leadership as a whole.

15. From a theoretical perspective, it is important to note that the under-representation of sons of businessmen (and possibly of individuals in the private sector) should not cause difficulties for the arguments made here. Although consistent, the absolute percentages involved are small, particularly in comparison with the percentages of 1958–1961 graduates working outside the central ministries.

Appendix B. The Occupational Distribution
of Political Science Faculty Graduates

The figures presented in Table A-4 were derived as follows: The total numbers of Political Science Faculty graduates in the various organizations were approximated by using relevant data from the 1963 State Personnel Census.[1] Categories in this census included the Ministries of Interior, Finance, and Foreign Affairs, as well as old (founded before 1950) and new (founded after 1950) ministerial organizations. Since the personnel census did not separate district governors from other administrators in the Ministry of Interior, an estimate of Political Science Faculty graduates who were district governors was made using findings reported by Gorvine and Payaslĭoğlu.[2] In 1963 there were 571 districts, while Gorvine and Payaslioglu noted that 81 percent of the 1956 district governors were Political Science Faculty graduates. Extrapolating from these data, we assumed that about 457 governors were from the Political Science Faculty; this left 258 of these graduates working in the Ministry of Interior.

A further effort was made to calculate the total number of Political Science Faculty graduates. The 1960 Population Census reported that there were 2,038 graduates of this faculty. Roughly 580 people graduated from the Political Science Faculty between 1960 and 1963, but, because Turkey enforces a system of universal military service, approximately half of these graduates were assumed to be in the service at the time of the 1963 personnel census.

These data can be used to estimate the number of Political Science Faculty graduates working in the state economic enterprises and private sector. From the above figures we calculated that there were 2,328 Political Science Faculty graduates employed outside of the army in 1963. From this sum we subtracted the graduates reported working for the government in the 1963 personnel census. This left an estimate of

1. *Devlet Personal Sayĭmĭ, I, Genel ve Katma Bütçeli Kurumlar* [State Personnel Census, I, General and Attached Budget Organizations] (Ankara, Devlet İstatistik Enstitüsü, 1965).

2. Albert Gorvine and Arif Payaslĭoğlu, "The Administrative Career Service in Turkish Provincial Government," *International Review of Administrative Sciences*, 22 (1957), 467–474.

513 Political Science Faculty graduates employed in the state economic enterprises or the private sector.

A check on these figures was available from another source. The 1965 State Personnel Census recorded a total of 359 Political Science Faculty graduates working in state economic enterprises.[3] Given that several classes would have graduated from the Faculty in the 1963–1965 period, our 1963 estimate of 513 graduates from the Political Science Faculty in state economic enterprises and the private sector seems reasonable. This would suggest that by 1965 there were 150–200 Political Science Faculty graduates working in the private sector.

Information on the number of living graduates of all faculties was obtained by summarizing data from the 1960 population census. Only the figures given on "faculty" graduates were used, and not those from other institutes, academies, or schools. Since faculty graduates could not be distinguished from graduates of institutions in the "other" category, this category was excluded from the calculations. Also, the figures in Table A-4 on the Ministry of Interior do not include employees of the General Directorate for Security, which is attached to this ministry, even though one of our respondents worked in this organization.

3. *Devlet Personel Sayĭmĭ, III, Kamur Iktisadĭ Teşebbüsleri* [State Personnel Census, III, State Economic Enterprises] (Ankara, Devlet Istatistik Enstitüsü, 1967).

Appendix C. Measurement and Models

All three of the surveys used in this study were coded under the direction of the authors by a team of six Turkish research assistants. During their training period, the coders worked on the same questionnaire; differences of opinion concerning open-ended items were resolved through discussion. Between 5 and 10 percent of the questionnaires were coded twice to check on reliability during the course of the coding; overall reliability among the coders was over 0.90.

Checks on reliability are particularly desirable when the basic source of information is self-administered questionnaires. The research design provided a number of such reliability checks. Because many individuals answered more than one questionnaire, direct checks for consistency were possible for such items as father's occupation, place of birth, and job history. In no case did there seem to be any misrepresentation on the part of the respondents. When asked their fathers' occupations, several sons of military doctors checked "professional" once and "military" another time; this discrepancy was handled by classifying the occupation as "professional." Occasionally an item left blank in one survey was filled in on another questionnaire answered by the same individual; the fact that several questionnaires were available minimized the missing data problems.[1]

Two other sources were particularly useful for cross-checking and for resolving missing data problems. Biographical data on graduates of the Political Science Faculty, the former Civil School, were available in a work entitled *The History of the Civil Service School and Its Graduates*.[2] Unfortunately, the class of 1950 was the most recent class included in this directory. The records of the Political Science Faculty were generously made available for our research. These records were

1. The nature of our highly educated sample was probably responsible for the lack of problems in classifying occupations. Other studies in the United States have reported disagreement on the order of 17–22 percent between reinterview studies on the reliability of reports on occupation. See Peter M. Blau and Otis Dudley Duncan, *The American Occupational Structure* (New York, Wiley, 1967), p. 15.

2. Ali Çankaya, *Mülkiye Tarihi ve Mülkiyeliler* [History of the Civil Service School and its graduates] (Ankara, Örnek Matbaasĭ, 1954), 2 vols.

used for obtaining information on the graduates' grades at the Faculty, for checking the accuracy of the social background data and for identifying respondents to the 1956 survey of district and provincial administration.

The names of the district governors were not on the questionnaires from the 1956 survey of district and provincial administration; thus various sources were used to make this identification. Data from the Ministry of Interior were of great help in identifying these respondents. Transfer notices in the Ministry of Interior's official publication (*Resmi Gazete*) aided in this process and in matching district governors with villages surveyed in the 1962 village study. Definitive identification (cross-checked using two or more sources) was available for 248 (81 percent) of the 306 administrators on the 1956 district governor survey. The other 58 respondents were identified according to the data supplied by the Ministry of Interior.

A substantial effort has been made to use sources other than just the basic questionnaires in identifying respondents' place of employment in 1956 and 1965 and in matching questionnaires. Such efforts were important because "it is a common experience in test and measurement research that any two items in the same questionnaire tend strongly to correlate more highly than do the same two if in separate questionnaires." [3] Within a given survey, the relationship between employment variables and attitudes might be spuriously high due to misclassification of variables dealing with job position and problems in re-identifying former respondents. Although the need to fill in missing data did not permit obtaining employment information completely independent of the attitudinal data, every effort was made to avoid error.

Additional features of the research operation imply a high level of reliability.[4] The social background and job satisfaction items were put in the same positions in both the 1956 and 1965 questionnaires, although the 1965 questionnaire was considerably longer. The 1956 and 1965 surveys were coded independently by different individuals before the panel study respondents were linked. After the code sheets were brought together, the checks described above were carried out.

3. Donald T. Campbell and Julian C. Stanley, *Experimental and Quasi-Experimental Designs for Research* (Chicago, Rand McNally, 1967), p. 67.

4. See the discussion of reliability in Eugene J. Webb, et al., *Unobtrusive Measures: Nonreactive Research in the Social Sciences* (Chicago, Rand McNally, 1966),

250

Although previous analysis of one survey may bias the findings of a subsequent survey, we do not believe that this was a major problem with these Turkish data. The Armaoğlu and Birkhead writeup of the 1956 material was limited by the fact that the data were not put onto IBM cards. The controls by ministry which form the basis for much of our analysis were not run by Armaoğlu and Birkhead. Thus, the collection of the 1965 data was not influenced by a detailed knowledge of the 1956 results.

Reliability

Naturally, the reliability of the attitudinal items was more difficult to check than the social background information. Several lines of evidence, however, support the reliability of our measurements. First of all, items from a single survey were intercorrelated in the expected ways; a number of reliable indices were possible from the questions included on the 1965 survey of Political Science Faculty graduates. A second check on the attitudinal items involved a comparison of items across surveys and across time. Despite problems in obtaining a high degree of association among items on different surveys, questions concerning similar issues were correlated across the 1956 and 1965 surveys. These correlations are presented in Table C-1.

A discussion of the relationships among items allows the reader to evaluate the several indices used in this study. The index of negative feelings toward interest groups suffers from the fact that few Political Science Faculty graduates believed that peasants, headmen, administrators, or professionals hindered national development. Only two items, those dealing with foreigners and interest groups, could be suitably intercorrelated; the other items did not contribute significantly to the index. Although the correlation between the interest groups item and the overall index was .20, the correlation between the "foreigners" item and the overall index score was just .06.

The "concern about political interference" index utilized data from 67 graduates responding to all three surveys — the 1956 district governor study, the 1956 Political Science Faculty study, and the 1965 Faculty study. The measures of item interassociation were very sensitive to the cutting points selected and the number of categories used. For several association gamma scores varied between .20 and .50, while phi coefficients varied between .02 and .16, depending upon the cutting points. This "concern about political interference" index was

Table C-1: Association among Items from 1956 and 1965 Surveys

Issue area	No. of 1956 items used	No. of 1965 items used	No. of associations with absolute value of gamma greater than .30	No. of associations with absolute value of gamma greater than .40
Needs of villagers:				
Education	2	3	5 (83% of possible associations)[a]	1 (17%)
Land	1	4	3 (75%)	3 (75%)
Political interference	4	2	3 (38%)	3 (38%)
Opinion of peasants and local politicians	4	1	3 (75%)	2 (50%)

[a] The percentages were derived by comparing the number of associations meeting the statistical criterion with the total possible number of associations across time (number of 1956 items used multiplied by the number of 1965 items used). There were 67 respondents who replied to both the 1956 district governor survey and the 1965 survey of Political Science Faculty graduates.

not used extensively, but rather to provide an additional check on hypotheses tested using information from a single survey.

Another index dealt with political pressure; the 1956 district governor survey was used to generate a measure of political pressure. As discussed in Chapter 10, this index was based on a count of some of the different types of individuals whom the district governor reported as intermediaries used to present requests to the administration.

Further analysis indicated that items dealing with four types of intermediaries — politicians, people of importance, mayors, and members of the Provincial General Assembly — were those correlating most strongly with overall indices constructed from various sets of alternative responses. The correlations of these four individual items with the index constructed from them ranged between .22 and .37. Although four items are too few for a Guttman scale, testing these items with the appropriate program produced a coefficient of reproducibility of .92 and a coefficient of scalability of .62.[5]

5. Guttman scaling is described by William A. Scott, "Attitude Measurement," in Gardner Lindzey and Elliot Aronson, eds., *Handbook of Social Psy-*

252

Several indices from the 1956 district governors' survey were run against the index of political pressure. Three questions concerning problems with the laws and their interpretation were combined into a single index. The specific items dealt with whether or not regulations reached the administrator on time, with the applicability of the regulations, and with their relevance to current problems. Correlations between the index and the individual items varied between .06 and .25.

The index of involvement in development projects was compiled from three items from the 1956 district governors survey dealing with the district governors' activities regarding public works, village business, and agricultural development. The correlations between individual items and the overall index of activity were rather weak, ranging between .05 and .19.

Four items from the 1956 survey concerning the district governors' conflict with representatives of other organizations made up the index of interorganizational conflict. These items — referring to conflict with the military, with the judiciary, with municipalities, and with other organizations — were substantially intercorrelated; correlations between the individual items and the overall index ranged between .25 and .32.

An Index of Job Satisfaction

The data on job satisfaction permit supplementing the discussion in Chapters 6 and 7 by generation of an index based on the reasons for

chology, vol. 2 (Reading, Mass., Addison-Wesley, 1968), pp. 204–273 and by Norman H. Nie, Dale H. Bent, and C. Hadlai Hull, *Statistical Package for the Social Sciences* (New York, McGraw-Hill, 1970), pp. 196–207. The definitions used in Nie, et al. are: the coefficient of reproducibility is "a measure of the extent to which a respondent's scale score is a predictor of his response pattern." The minimum marginal reproducibility is the "minimum coefficient of reproducibility that could have occurred for the scale given the cutting points used and the proportion of respondents passing and failing each of the items." The coefficient of scalability is:

$$\frac{\text{coefficient of reproducibility} - \text{minimum marginal reproducibility}}{1 - \text{minimum marginal reproducibility}}$$

Nie, et al. note that the coefficient of scalability "should be well above .6 if the scale is truly unidimensional and cumulative." These coefficients have recently been criticized by Brent M. Rutherford, Donald G. Morrison, and Donald T. Campbell, "Sensitivity and Bias of Scalogram Indices and Tests of Significance," unpublished manuscript, Evanston, Illinois, 1970.

satisfaction and dissatisfaction. Each reason for satisfaction was scored +1, while each reason for dissatisfaction was given a −1. The index score was computed starting from a base of 12 (satisfied), 11 (no answer-no further computation), or 10 (dissatisfied). The data are presented in Table C-2. The first score provided for each group is the raw score for each time period. The second score is the standardized score, calculated using the data from the appropriate year — 1956 or 1965.

The standardized scores are particularly important because the mean for the entire sample is higher in 1965 than in 1956. We believe this suggests greater satisfaction in 1965 than in 1956; the rise in satisfaction seems to have resulted from movement out of central ministries rather than from substantial improvements within these ministries. But there is at least one other plausible hypothesis: measurement error might have been responsible for some or all of the differences between the 1956 and 1965 scores. By assuming that such error was distributed randomly across our sample, we can compare the standard scores, looking at the changes within each group while controlling for overall changes between 1956 and 1965.[6]

The most important results summarized in Table C-2 concern the respondents leaving the Ministries of Interior and Finance. The differences in standard scores indicate that, even controlling for changes in mean respondent scores between 1956 and 1965, leaving the Ministries of Interior and Finance was associated with a higher score on the index of job satisfaction. The change in job satisfaction seems real and not due solely to differences in measuring procedures used at the two points in time. A final point concerns the 1965 data from the younger respondents; the raw scores for the 1958–1961 graduates in the Ministry of Interior (9.7) and in the new, noncentral organizations (14.4) approximated the 1965 scores for their older counterparts. This close relationship between the scores of the one-time and those of the two-time respondents suggests that the experience of answering the 1956 questionnaire had little effect on the answers in 1965.

Finally, we can consider measurement error, using the typology of mobility of job satisfaction presented earlier. If our measurement procedure were reliable, we might expect the highest (test–retest) correlation between 1956 and 1965 attitudes among those respondents who

6. For the 1956 panel respondents, the mean index score was 11.37, with a standard deviation of 6.09. In 1965, the mean score was 13.10, with a standard deviation of 5.09.

Table C-2: Alternate Conceptions of Mobility and Job Satisfaction

Position in		1956 scores	1965 scores	Number of respondents
1956	1965			
STAYING				
Assistant district governor	District governor	8.2, −.52	8.2, −.96[a]	20
District governor	District governor	10.1, −.22	9.7, −.66	35
Ministry of Finance	Ministry of Finance	12.3, .16	13.6, .10	38
Ministry of Foreign Affairs	Ministry of Foreign Affairs	16.4, .82	15.2, .42	26
New, noncentral organizations	New, noncentral organizations	14.9, .58	15.9, .55	10
MAJOR PROMOTION				
District governor	Higher level in Ministry of Interior	9.7, −.27	12.9, −.03	27
MOVING				
Assistant district governor and district governor	Other old organizations	7.5, −.64	15.7, .51	10
Assistant district governor and district governor	New, noncentral organizations	7.2, −.69	14.4, .25	16
Ministry of Finance	New, noncentral organizations	12.4, .18	15.7, .51	21

[a] The first figure is the raw score on the index of job satisfaction; the second figure is the standard score calculated from the raw data for the appropriate year.

did not markedly change their job situation or place of work. As is seen in Table C-3, prediction was generally borne out, although the findings from the Ministry of Foreign Affairs are worth noting. Since almost all of these respondents were rotated from one embassy to another over the nine-year period and satisfied in both 1956 and 1965, these results suggest that the attractions of work in this ministry varied markedly according to where a diplomat was stationed. Diplomats changed their job situation rather differently than the administrators who experienced major promotions or a change of organization.

Table C-3: Mobility, Job Satisfaction, and Test–Retest Correlations

Position in		Test–retest corre-lation between 1956 and 1965 scores (index of job satisfaction)	Number of respondents
1956	1965		
STAYING			
Assistant district governor	District governor	.36[a,b]	20
District governor	District governor	.49[a]	35
Ministry of Finance	Ministry of Finance	.63[a]	38
Ministry of Foreign Affairs	Ministry of Foreign Affairs	−.11	26
New, noncentral organizations	New, noncentral organizations	.61[a]	10
MAJOR PROMOTION			
District governor	Higher level in Ministry of Interior	.20	27
MOVING			
Assistant district governor and district governor	Other old organizations	.26	10
Assistant district governor and district governor	New, noncentral organizations	.18	16
Ministry of Finance	New, noncentral organizations	.41[a]	21

[a] Correlations were significant at the .05 level.
[b] The measure of association was the product-moment correlation.

Guttman Scaling and Factor Analysis

The simple additive index presented in Table C-2 summarizes some of the information included in the reasons for job satisfaction or dissatisfaction. Another approach involves looking both at the relationships among these reasons and at the relationships between individual reasons and a cumulative index score. Because of their dependence on the basic choice of satisfaction or dissatisfaction, each set of reasons was analyzed separately; all 241 panel respondents were included in

Table C-4: Correlations between Individual Items and Cumulative Index — Reasons for Satisfaction and Dissatisfaction

	1956	1965
Reasons for satisfaction:		
Pay	.63[a]	.58[a]
Political factors	.66	.58
Self-realization		
Opportunity to increase knowledge	.77	.70
Job interest	.66	.52
Autonomy		
Authority	.75	.64
Responsibility	.67	.62
Prestige	.72	.54
Security	.50	.48
Other reasons		
Promotional opportunities	.50	.46
Geographical location	.43	.40
Reasons for dissatisfaction:		
Pay	.73	.63
Political factors	.55	.55
Self-realization		
Opportunity to increase knowledge	.58	.57
Job interest	.46	.32
Autonomy		
Authority	.57	.70
Responsibility	.52	.66
Prestige	.43	.52
Security	.62	.49
Other reasons		
Promotional opportunities	.54	.55
Geographical location	.44	.40

[a] The measure of association was the product-moment correlation. The relationships for these 241 panel respondents were statistically significant, but the correlations were inflated by the wording of the items.

each run. Because of the wording of the satisfaction–dissatisfaction questions, the correlations are artificially inflated. As is seen in Table C-4, several of the items exhibited markedly lower correlations with the cumulative index than did the others. Inspection of the matrix of item intercorrelations identified these same questions as possessing lower correlations with the other individual items.

The fact that the same items generally showed the lower correlations in both 1956 and 1965 suggest the general stability of these reasons for satisfaction and dissatisfaction over time. Similar patterns were obtained among the 1958–1961 graduates surveyed in 1965. Reasons for satisfaction and dissatisfaction form a generally coherent stable set despite the substantial mobility during the nine-year period under consideration. This generalization is supported by factor analyses of the matrices of inter-item correlations for satisfaction and dissatisfaction. The first factors generated by principal components analysis accounted for between 40 to 50 percent of the communality; second factors accounted for about 12 percent.

The reasons for satisfaction and dissatisfaction were examined further by Guttman scaling techniques. As discussed above, job security, promotional opportunity, and geographical location were not included

Table C-5: Reasons for Satisfaction and Dissatisfaction
as Guttman Scales

	Statistics on Guttman Scales		
	Coefficient of reproducibility	Minimum marginal reproducibility	Coefficient of scalability
1956			
Reasons for satisfaction	.881	.702	.602
Reasons for dissatisfaction	.853	.748	.417
1965			
Reasons for satisfaction	.832	.659	.507
Reasons for dissatisfaction	.923	.870	.409

258

in the "reasons for job satisfaction" scale. In similar fashion, prestige, geographical location, and job interest were not used in the "reasons for job dissatisfaction" scale. Factor analyses of the reasons for job satisfaction and dissatisfaction at both points in time led to a rejection of the same reasons eliminated by the strictly correlational analyses. Table C-5 summarized the results obtained by the Guttman scaling procedure with the above reasons eliminated. Although the coefficients of scalability in Table C-5 suggest that there may be more internal coherence among the reasons for satisfaction than among the reasons for dissatisfaction, the theoretical rationale for this is unclear.

Two Indicators at Two Points in Time

Standard procedures for index construction are used in the above discussion of reliability. Some newer techniques have been proposed by Blalock as applicable for use with two indicators at two points in time.[7] These are particularly valuable because of the general desirability of moving away from a single indicator approach toward a multiple-indicator perspective. Among other things, these techniques provide a method of testing whether several indicators can be combined assuming only random measurement error.

In Chapter 6, the data on job position, organizational mobility, and satisfaction were approached using a single indicator of job satisfaction — responses to the question, "Are you satisfied with your job?" A second indicator — answers to the item, "Would you recommend attending the Political Science Faculty?" — is available, but this indicator of job satisfaction lacks the face validity of the first. This question on recommending the Political Science Faculty has a sort of "would you do it again" component which seems a little different from the usual indicator of job satisfaction, although there may be considerable shared meaning. Table C-6 shows the synchronous correlations between these two indicators of satisfaction for several related sub-

7. H. M. Blalock, Jr., "Estimating Measurement Error Using Multiple Indicators and Several Points in Time," *American Sociological Review*, 35 (February 1970), pp. 101–111. A more general discussion of this problem is included in H. M. Blalock, Jr., "A Causal Approach to Nonrandom Measurement Errors," *American Political Science Review*, 64 (December 1970), pp. 1099–1111.

samples. This item on the Political Science Faculty might be used to increase confidence in our findings.

The correlational data reported in Table C-6 suggest that, on the basis of the 1956 information alone, the two items might well be used to build an index. But the 1965 data are somewhat different. In 1965 there was a slight tendency for dissatisfied respondents in the Ministry of Finance to recommend the Political Science Faculty, perhaps because their (financial) education provided them with fairly good opportunities for moving out of undesirable positions.

Table C-6: Two Indicators of Satisfaction at Two Points in Time (Synchronous Correlations)[a]

	Job Satisfaction 1956 — Recommend Faculty 1956 $r_{S_1F_1}$	Job Satisfaction 1965 — Recommend Faculty 1965 $r_{S_2F_2}$
Respondents remaining in:		
Ministry of Interior (80)[b]	.75, .40	.47, .25
Ministry of Finance (36)	.71, .41	−.26, −.11
Stayers and movers:		
Ministry of Interior — New, noncentral organizations (105)	.62, .33	.46, .24
Ministry of Finance — New, noncentral organizations (65)	.71, .40	−.30, −.11

[a] The measures of association were gamma and the product-moment correlation.

[b] The number of panel respondents are indicated in parentheses.

Blalock has derived a pair of testing equations to be used to determine whether several indicators can be combined; the quantities on each side of the equation should be approximately equal if only random measurement error can be assumed. Data relevant to the Blalock formulation are presented in Table C-7; testing equations and results for respondents remaining in the Ministry of Interior are presented below. Translating from Blalock's notation to that used throughout this book, the testing equations are:

Equations	Results (for respondents in Interior)
$r_{S_1F_2} = r_{S_2F_1}$	$.04 \neq .23$
$r_{S_2S_1} = r_{F_1F_2}$	$.34 \neq .24$

The product-moment correlation coefficients are presented in the equations. Since similar results are obtained for respondents with other career patterns, it is clear that the two indicators cannot be combined without violating the assumptions concerning measurement error.

Finally, the question on recommending the Political Science Faculty can be analyzed in the same way as the item on job satisfaction. Leav-

Table C-7: Two Indicators of Satisfaction at Two Points in Time
(Horizontal and Cross-Correlations)[a]

	Job satisfaction 1956 — Job satisfaction 1965 $r_{S_1S_2}$	Job satisfaction 1956 — Recommend Faculty 1965 $r_{S_1F_2}$	Job satisfaction 1965 — Recommend Faculty 1956 $r_{S_2F_1}$	Recommend Faculty 1956 — Recommend Faculty 1965 $r_{F_1F_2}$
Respondents re- maining in: Ministry of Interior (80)[b]	.63, .34	.08, .04	.44, .23	.46, .24
Ministry of Finance (36)	.89, .60	.14, .07	.69, .39	.62, .31
Stayers and Movers: Ministry of Interior — New, noncentral organizations (105)	.62, .32	.11, .06	.40, .20	.46, .24
Ministry of Finance — New, noncentral organizations (65)	.78, .44	.14, .06	.59, .28	.54, .25

[a] The measures of association were gamma and the product-moment correlation.

[b] The number of panel respondents are indicated in parentheses.

ing the Ministries of Interior and Finance in the 1956–1965 period was associated with an increased probability of recommending the Faculty. For example, graduates of the Political Science Faculty who left the Ministry of Interior for new, noncentral organizations were more likely to recommend the faculty in 1965 (75%) than in 1956 (50%). On the other hand, several cross-lagged panel analyses for these data produced very ambiguous results. Clear-cut differences between the cross-lagged correlations were not found.

To summarize, an effort has been made here to explore the relationship between two indicators at two points in time. It was hoped that the use of a second indicator would provide further backing for the discussion in Chapters 6 and 8. This indicator — the item "would you recommend attending the Political Science Faculty" — showed a number of similarities with the job satisfaction item, but the two items did not consistently move together in the same way. For this reason, other career patterns, it is clear that the two indicators cannot be sumed. The previous discussion cannot be significantly buttressed by a multiple indicator approach which uses the Political Science Faculty item. The next section will suggest how a further analysis of the reasons for job satisfaction can help support the arguments made in Chapters 6 through 8.

Causal Models

The standard scores can also be used to supplement the cross-lagged panel analysis presented in Chapter 8. As is seen in Table C-8, the overall evidence that moving to a new, noncentral organization causes the change in job satisfaction is stronger for respondents leaving the Ministry of Interior than it is for those leaving the Ministry of Finance. A further analysis controlling for the administrator's social background illustrates the extent to which the overall relationships depend upon the mobility of the respondents from privileged backgrounds. Although some differences in the expected direction were obtained for the Ministry of Interior data on respondents from less privileged backgrounds, no differences were found for the Ministry of Finance. These findings suggest that the respondent's social background was a significant causal factor, affecting both job satisfaction and the choice of organization.

Problems of measurement have been treated by Duncan, who has developed a series of models for two-wave, two-variable panel data which take reliability into account. Such formulations make explicit

Table C-8: Organizational Mobility and Job Satisfaction (Standard Scores)

	Horizontal correlations		Synchronous correlations		Cross-lagged correlations	
	1956 organ.–1965 organ.	1956 job satisf.–1965 job satisf.	1956 organ.–1956 job satisf.	1965 organ.–1965 job satisf.	1956 organ.–1965 job satisf.	1956 job satisf.–1965 organ.
	$r_{o_1o_2}$	$r_{s_1s_2}$	$r_{o_1s_1}$	$r_{o_2s_2}$	$r_{o_1s_2}$	$r_{o_2s_1}$
Ministry of Interior— New, noncentral organizations						
All respondents (n = 113):	.57[a]	.31[a]	.31[a]	.36[a]	.26[a,b]	.06
Privileged backgrounds (n = 23)	.52[a]	.13	.42[a]	.54[a]	.33[c]	−.16
Less privileged backgrounds (n = 89)	.57[a]	.37[a]	.29[a]	.26[a]	.21[a]	.14
Ministry of Finance— New, noncentral organizations						
All respondents (n = 69):	.46[a]	.54[a]	.15	.22[a]	.11	.07
Privileged backgrounds (n = 22)	.59[a]	.58[a]	.20	.29	.27	.17
Less privileged backgrounds (n = 42)	.39[a]	.48[a]	.12	.11	−.01	−.04

Note: The measure of association was the product–moment correlation.

[a] These relationships were significant at the .05 level.

[b] Differences between the cross-lagged correlations (between $r_{o_1s_2}$ and $r_{o_2s_1}$) just missed statistical significance at the .05 level.

[c] Differences between the cross-lagged correlations (between $r_{o_1s_2}$ and $r_{o_2s_1}$) were statistically significant at the .05 level for these graduates from privileged backgrounds.

the way different assumptions about measurement error can affect the choices among competing causal models. Duncan uses "a general model for the causal linkages that may be present in a set of 2W2V (two-wave, two-variable) data." [8] Particular models are derived from the general model by assuming that certain paths and correlations are equal to zero.[9]

Although the various sets of models do not explicitly deal with the problem of the direction of causality, they do treat problems of measurement reliability and questions of simultaneous-versus-lagged causation. It was possible to explore the Turkish panel data in terms of these models forwarded by Duncan. To summarize, the information from the Ministry of Interior presented a number of problems; they fit none of the various models forwarded by Duncan. The results from the Ministry of Finance showed that several models implying the "simultaneous causal influence" of organization upon job satisfaction would be appropriate; various assumptions about the reliability of measurement could not be separated.

Some other approaches to panel data emphasize the necessity of going beyond the analysis of two variables at two points in time. The analysis of two-wave, two-variable data is hindered by the fact that causation, as indicated by assymetrical cross-lagged correlations, "can be rivally explained as violations of stationarity." [10] Stationarity assumes that the causal parameters of the measured variables remain constant over time; if this is not true, "assymetrical cross-lagged correlations may not be an indication of causality." [11] Thus, the possibility of change in an important cause common to both variables poses a rival hypothesis to inferences about causation generated from panel studies.

8. Otis Dudley Duncan, "Some Linear Models for Two-Wave, Two-Variable Panel Analysis, with One-Way Causation and Measurement Error," *Psychological Bulletin,* 72 (1969), p. 177.

9. It did not seem worthwhile to reproduce these models for this appendix; the general model is discussed in Duncan, "Some Linear Models." In a revised form, both the general and specific models used here are treated in Otis Dudley Duncan, "Some Linear Models for Two-Wave, Two-Variable Panel Analysis, with One-Way Causation and Measurement Error," unpub. manuscript, Ann Arbor, Michigan, 1970.

10. David A. Kenny, "Common Factor Model with Temporal Erosion for Panel Data," paper presented at Social Science Research Council conference on structural equation models, Madison, Wisconsin, November 12–16, 1970, p. 6.

11. *Ibid.,* p. 5.

One solution to this problem is to gather additional data to try to rule out this rival hypothesis concerning the misspecification of the causal model. Kenny has suggested that either analyzing more variables from two points in time or sampling more time points can help in building models with assumptions weaker than those of stationarity. After suggested correction procedures, new cross-lagged correlations accounting for shifts in communality can be compared. Asymmetric crosslags may then be considered evidence for causation, although questions of measurement error posed by Duncan and Blalock remain important.[12]

Since two-wave panel data on a third variable — whether or not the respondent would recommend the Political Science Faculty — were available, correction procedures accounting for shifts in communality were used with the Ministry of Interior — new, noncentral organizations data. Such procedures were not appropriate for the Ministry of Finance because of a mixed pattern of positive and negative correlations. The corrections for communality for the Interior — new, noncentral organizations data resulted in greater differences between the cross-lagged correlations than were found without incorporating the corrections. Thus, the rival hypothesis of stationarity is not plausible for the mobility-satisfaction data from the Ministry of Interior.

Another approach has been proposed by Bohrnstedt, who stresses the difficulties in comparing cross-lagged correlations without taking into account initial states of the two variables.[13] This is particularly likely to cause problems when the horizontal correlations (the over-time correlations for the two variables) differ substantially. One suggestion involves the use of partial correlation coefficients, in order to remove the effect of S_1 from S_2. Partial correlation coefficients may also illustrate mutual causation more clearly than do zero-order cross-lagged correlations.

Although the horizontal correlations are not markedly different, one appropriate comparison for our Turkish data involves $r_{o_1s_2 \cdot s_1}$ and $r_{o_2s_1 \cdot o_1}$. Such a comparison turns out to be more stringent than the cross-lagged comparison. For the various data sets from the Ministry of Finance, there were essentially no differences between these

12. *Ibid.* See the treatment of measurement error in Blalock, "A Causal Approach," pp. 1099–1111.
13. George W. Bohrnstedt, "Observations on the Measurement of Change," in Edgar F. Borgatta, ed., *Sociological Methodology 1969* (San Francisco, Jossey-Bass, 1969), pp. 113–133.

two partial correlation coefficients. This suggests that we cannot really make causal statements about the relationship between job mobility and job satisfaction for the respondents from the Ministry of Finance — new, noncentral organizations.

The data from the Ministry of Interior showed another pattern. The $r_{o_1 s_2 \cdot s_1}$ correlations were significantly greater than the $r_{o_2 s_1 \cdot o_1}$ correlations for the Interior — new, noncentral organizations sample as a whole; these differences held true when both the index of job satisfaction and the single dichotomized variable were used. These findings were, however, primarily due to the data from the respondents from relatively privileged backgrounds; for these data, $r_{o_1 s_2 \cdot s_1}$ equalled .28, while $r_{o_2 s_1 \cdot o_1}$ was −.51. Thus, controlling for the initial states of the variables does not eliminate the differences between the cross-lagged correlations.[14]

Such findings reinforce the proposition that — at least for the respondents from privileged backgrounds — mobility out of the Ministry of Interior led to job satisfaction in the new, noncentral organizations. In addition, the results of the various testing models have suggested that:

1 — Two-way causation is likely. As discussed in Chapter 8, there almost certainly was mutual influence between organization and satisfaction. Low satisfaction probably did affect organizational mobility.

2 — Although there may have been change in causes common to both measured variables, such change was not responsible for the observed differences in cross-lagged correlations.

14. These findings have substantive implications which are summarized in terms of status incongruence in Appendix F.

Appendix D. New Organizations and Elite Jobs

At various times in this book we have suggested that the rate of expansion of elite jobs has had important consequences for political stability. Over the 1938–1957 period, the size of the bureaucracy increased five-fold, while the long-established Ministry of Interior grew by only 50 percent. This increase in size of the Turkish bureaucracy has in large part been due to the creation of state economic enterprises and the addition of ministries with new functions.

As already emphasized in the text, these jobs in new, noncentral organizations have provided particularly attractive opportunities. Thus, it seemed important to both summarize the previously cited data on the founding of new organizations and make some estimates of the number of elite jobs available. The data presented in Table D-1 suggest that new organizations have been founded at a more-or-less constant rate from 1931 on.

Table D-1 : Founding Dates of Government Organizations (up to 1965)

	1930 or before	1931– 1940	1941– 1950	1951– 1960	1961– 1965
State economic enterprises	2	11	8	13	4
Ministry	7	3	3	3	2
Directorate attached to ministry	4	2	5[a]	5	1
Organization under office of Prime Minister	4	1	2	2	4

Source: *T. C. Devlet Teşkilatı Rehberi* [A guide to Turkish state organizations] (Ankara, Başbakanlık Devlet Matbaası, 1968).

[a] All of these directorates were founded in the 1948–1950 period.

Rough estimates of several kinds of jobs were made from available data on the founding dates of state economic enterprises and on the

Table D-2: Estimated Numbers of Desirable Jobs in State Economic Enterprises

	Number of Jobs for University Graduates				Number of jobs with 1965 salary of 2001 T.L. or greater (Extrapolated backwards to 1956)			
	1956	1965	Difference (1965–1956)	Ratio (1965:1956)	1956	1965	Difference (1965–1956)	Ratio (1965:1956)
State economic enterprises employing 10 or more Political Science Faculty graduates	2,563	4,659	2,096	1.82	1,067	2,168	1,101	2.03
State economic enterprises — Total	3,951	7,841	3,890	1.98	1,680	3,612	1,932	2.15

Source: *T. C. Devlet Teşkilatî Rehberi* [A guide to Turkish state organizations] (Ankara, Başbakanlîk Devlet Matbaasï, 1968) and *Devlet Personel Sayïmï, III, Kamur İktisadî Teşebbüsleri* [State Personnel Census, III, State Economic Enterprises] (Ankara, Devlet Istatistik Enstitüsü, 1967). A number of banks were included with state economic enterprises in this calculation. The extrapolation backward using 1965 salary data was done to provide an estimate of *desirable* jobs in 1956, not to suggest that such salaries were paid at that time.

268

distribution of jobs in 1965.[1] Data were collected for all state economic enterprises and for just those enterprises employing ten or more Political Science Faculty graduates. Straight-line projections on growth from the date of founding to 1965 were used to estimate the distribution of different kinds of jobs in 1956. Since many Political Science Faculty graduates were found in these enterprises in 1965 (20 percent of the older graduates from the financial section), their expansion is tied to the well-being of the administrative elite. The various estimates reported in Table D-2 suggest that desirable jobs in the state enterprises about doubled between 1956 and 1965.

It would clearly be desirable to have information about rates of expansion of all the different types of organizations in which Political Science Faculty graduates might work. Unfortunately, these data were not readily available. Future research might concentrate upon obtaining such data and relating it more systematically to information on job mobility and job satisfaction. Models of the relationship among economic growth, political change, and the creation of new jobs would also be most useful. Although this work has stressed the linkages between economic development and elite jobs, it would be interesting to investigate the degree to which new jobs are created for purely political reasons.

1. A number of banks were included with state economic enterprises in this calculation.

Appendix E. Three Points in Time

The arguments made in this book are generally reinforced by additional data available for the Ministry of Interior in 1967. Provincial yearbooks were obtained for 40 (out of 67) provinces, and job positions in Interior were coded for all of the 1956 respondents who could be located. Thirty-five of the 1956 respondents in the Ministry of Interior were identified in 1967. If we assume that these 40 provinces represent a random sample of the universe of provinces, the sample data can be used to provide an estimate of the mobility out of the Ministry of Interior.

In 1965, 109 respondents worked in the Ministry of Interior's provincial and district administration; in 1967 we estimated that there were just 59 of these respondents in provincial and district administration. Twenty of the respondents in the Ministry of Interior in 1965 worked in the central offices rather than in provincial or district administration; it is difficult to estimate how many of our respondents were working there in 1967. If 30 of the bureaucrats were found in the Ministry's central administration in 1967, this would imply a loss of 31 percent (40 out of 129) of our respondents between 1965 and 1967.

But regardless of the exact figures, the data strongly suggest a high degree of mobility out of the Ministry of Interior in the 1965–1967 period. Since this period included years of substantial economic growth, the data provide support for one thesis advanced in this book: mobility out of the Ministry of Interior is facilitated by economic development.

Appendix F. Scientific Explanation
and Social Change

We can approach the changes resulting from a ruralizing election using the model and terminology of scientific explanation proposed by Hempel and Oppenheim. "The explanandum is the phenomenon or the observation which is to be explained." [1] The explanans contains statements of antecedent conditions ($C_1, C_2 \ldots C_k$) and general laws ($L_1, L_2 \ldots L_k$) required for the logical derivation of the explanandum.

I. Parliamentary Representation and the Bureaucracy

A. EXPLANANS

C_1 The parliamentary representation of the bureaucratic elite (particularly of less autonomous ministries) declines in a ruralizing election.

L_1 The parliamentary representation of a social group is a good indicator of its political power.

L_2 Changes in political power are reflected in changes in status.

L_3 Groups and individuals with more resources are disproportionately able to take advantage of social changes, but all groups and individuals are likely to try to take advantage of these changes.

L_4 Younger individuals are better able than other age groups to take advantage of social changes.

In Turkey (and perhaps after ruralizing elections generally): [2]

B. EXPLANANDA

E_1 The status of the bureaucracy (of less autonomus ministries) was lowered in the eyes of various groups (C_1, L_1, L_2)

---

1. Kalman J. Cohen and Richard M. Cyert, *Theory of the Firm: Resource Allocation in a Market Economy* (Englewood Cliffs, N.J., Prentice-Hall, 1965), p. 22. They refer to Carl G. Hempel and Paul Oppenheim, "Studies in the Logic of Explanation," *Philosophy of Science*, 15 (1948), 135–175.

2. The letters in parentheses after the propositions in the explananda refer to general statements in the explanans from which these propositions are derived.

E_2 The bureaucracy (the less autonomous ministries) has problems with recruitment and turnover. (C_1, L_1, L_2)

E_3 Individuals from relatively advantaged backgrounds tended to avoid and to leave the bureaucracy (the less autonomous ministries). (C_1, L_1, L_3)

E_4 Younger individuals tended to avoid and to leave the bureaucracy (the less autonomous ministries). (C_1, L_1, L_4)

E_5 Other organizations (i.e., state economic enterprises) tended to encroach on the prerogatives and privileges of the bureaucracy (the less autonomous ministries). (C_1, L_1, L_2, L_3)

E_6 Client groups (i.e., local leaders) tended to encroach on the prerogatives and privileges of the bureaucracy (the less autonomous ministries). (C_1, L_1, L_2, L_3)

II. Social Consequences of Economic Growth

A. EXPLANANS

C_1 Turkey experienced relatively rapid economic growth in the 1962–1968 period.

L_1 Economic growth leads to a rise in the number of new organizations and satisfactory positions for elite employment.

L_2 Economic growth increases the demand for technical skills.

L_3 Satisfactory positions for the elite will have a stabilizing effect on the polity.

L_4 Groups and individuals with more resources are disproportionately able to take advantage of social changes.

L_5 Younger individuals are disproportionately able to take advantage of social changes.

In Turkey:

B. EXPLANANDA

E_1 Movement of individuals into satisfactory positions in the newer organizations had a stabilizing effect on the polity. (C_1, L_1, L_3)

E_2 Individuals from relatively advantaged backgrounds tended to obtain technical training. (C_1, L_2, L_4)

E_3 Younger individuals tended to obtain technical training. (C_1, L_2, L_5)

E_4 Individuals from relatively advantaged backgrounds tended to enter new organizations and find satisfactory positions. (C_1, L_1, L_4)

E_5 Younger individuals tended to enter new organizations and find satisfactory positions. (C_1, L_1, L_5)

The line of reasoning presented above emphasized various groups' and individuals' opportunities to take advantage of social change. Some of the attitudinal and mobility patterns can also be approached in terms of status incongruence. More specifically, the argument presented here posits that Political Science Faculty graduates are faced with status incongruence if they enter the Ministry of Interior. There are problems with this line of argument, since some of the indicators of organizational stratification used in Chapter 5 are taken from the individual findings presented here as consequences of stratification. This is defensible only insofar as additional independent indicators of organizational stratification are available; the information on salaries and the survey data from other samples provide such indicators. This scheme simplifies a complicated phenomenon by emphasizing its status-related aspects, stressing the logical interrelationships between status and organizational choice.[3]

III. Status Incongruence and Political Science Faculty Graduates

A. EXPLANANS

C_1 The parliamentary representation of the Ministry of Interior declines in a ruralizing election.

L_1 The parliamentary representation of a social group is a good indicator of its political power.

L_2 Changes in political power are reflected in changes in status.

L_3 Status incongruence is an unpleasant state. Individuals will be motivated to avoid — and to escape from — status incongruence.

L_4 High-status individuals will suffer from status incon-

3. Several of the general propositions in the explanans have been put forward by Andrey Malewski in "The Degree of Status Incongruence and its Effects," in Reinhard Bendix and Seymour Martin Lipset, eds. *Class, Status, and Power* (New York, Free Press, 1966), pp. 303–308.

gruence working in low-level jobs in a low-status organization (the Ministry of Interior).

L_5 Attendance at — and graduation from — a highly selective faculty (the Political Science Faculty) implies high status in a society.

L_6 Being from a relatively privileged social background implies high status in a society.

L_7 Education and social background combine in at least an additive manner to partially determine an individual's social status.

In Turkey:[4]

B. EXPLANANDA

E_1 Political Science Faculty students will tend to avoid courses of study which may lead to status incongruence. Faculty students will therefore tend to avoid courses of study (the administrative section) leading to entry-level jobs in a low-status organization (the Ministry of Interior). Because such jobs would produce disproportionate status incongruence, Faculty students from more privileged backgrounds will especially avoid such courses of study.

E_2 Political Science Faculty graduates will suffer status incongruence (as partially measured by job dissatisfaction) in low-level jobs in a low-status organization (the Ministry of Interior). Faculty graduates from more privileged backgrounds will suffer disproportionate status incongruence (job dissatisfaction) in such jobs.

E_3 Status incongruence (as partially measured by job dissatisfaction) leads to job mobility.

E_4 Political Science Faculty graduates will tend to leave jobs in which they suffer status incongruence. Faculty graduates will therefore tend to leave low-level jobs in a low-status organization (the Ministry of Interior). Because of their disproportionate status incongruence, Faculty graduates from more privileged backgrounds will be particularly likely to leave such jobs.

E_5 In order to avoid status incongruence, Political Science

4. The propositions that follow generally depended upon all the statements in the explanans; individual statements were therefore not referenced.

Faculty graduates will tend to enter jobs in higher-status organizations (new, noncentral organizations). Because of their higher status as individuals, Faculty graduates from more privileged backgrounds will disproportionately enter such jobs.

E_6 Political Science Faculty graduates will suffer less status incongruence (less job dissatisfaction) in higher-status organizations (new, noncentral organizations). Because of their higher status as individuals, Faculty graduates from more privileged backgrounds may suffer some status incongruence even in these jobs. (Note: there was so little dissatisfaction in new, noncentral organizations that this could not be tested.)

Selected Bibliography

THEORETICAL AND COMPARATIVE STUDIES

Aitken, Hugh, ed., *The State and Economic Growth* (New York, Social Science Research Council, 1959).

Ashford, Douglas E., *National Development and Local Reform* (Princeton, N.J., Princeton University Press, 1967).

Befu, Harumi, "The Political Relation of the Village to the State," *World Politics,* 29 (July 1967), 601–620.

Bendix, Reinhard, and Seymour Martin Lipset, eds., *Class, Status, and Power* (New York, Free Press, 1966).

Edinger, Lewis, ed., *Political Leadership in Industrialized Societies* (New York, Wiley, 1967).

Eisenstadt, S. N., *Essays on Comparative Institutions* (New York, Wiley, 1965).

Eldersveld, Samuel J., "Bureaucratic Contact with the Public in India," *Indian Journal of Public Administration,* 11 (April–June 1965), 216–235.

Hanson, A. H., *Public Enterprise and Economic Development* (London, Routledge & Kegan Paul, 1965).

Harris, Richard L., "The Effects of Political Change on the Role Set of the Senior Bureaucrats in Ghana and Nigeria," *Administrative Science Quarterly,* 13 (December 1968), 386–401.

Holt, Robert T., and John E. Turner, *The Political Basis of Economic Development* (Princeton, N.J., Van Nostrand, 1966).

Hopkins, Raymond, "The Role of the M.P. in Tanzania," *American Political Science Review,* 64 (September 1970), 754–771.

Huntington, Samuel P., *Political Order in Changing Societies* (New Haven, Conn., Yale University Press, 1968).

Hyman, Herbert H., Gene N. Levine, and Charles R. Wright, *Inducing Social Change in Developing Communities* (New York, United Nations Research Institute for Social Development, 1967).

Keller, Suzanne, *Beyond the Ruling Class* (New York, Random House, 1968).

La Palombara, Joseph, ed., *Bureaucracy and Political Development* (Princeton, N.J., Princeton University Press, 1963).

Pye, Lucian W., *Aspects of Political Development* (Boston, Little, Brown, 1966).

276

Quandt, William B., "The Comparative Study of Political Elites," *Sage Professional Papers in Comparative Politics,* 1 (1970).

Riggs, Fred W., *Thailand: The Modernization of a Bureaucratic Polity* (Honolulu, Hawaii East-West Center Press, 1966).

———, *Administration in Developing Countries* (Boston, Houghton Mifflin, 1964).

Roos, Leslie, L. Jr., and Noralou P. Roos, "Bureaucracy in the Middle East: Some Cross-Cultural Relationships," *Journal of Comparative Administration,* 1 (November 1969), 281–300.

Rustow, Dankwart A., "The Study of Elites: Who's Who, When, and How," *World Politics,* 18 (July 1966), 690–717.

Searing, Donald D., "The Comparative Study of Elite Socialization," *Comparative Political Studies,* 1 (January 1969), 471–500.

Smelser, Neil J., and Seymour M. Lipset, eds., *Social Structure and Mobility in Economic Development* (Chicago, Ill., Aldine Press, 1966).

Swerdlow, Irving, ed., *Development Administration: Concepts and Problems* (Syracuse, N.Y., Syracuse University Press, 1963).

Weiner, Myron, ed., *Modernization* (New York, Basic Books, 1966).

ORGANIZATION THEORY

Bennis, Warren G., *Changing Organizations* (New York, McGraw-Hill, 1966).

Blau, Peter M., and W. Richard Scott, *Formal Organizations* (San Francisco, Chandler, 1962).

Cohen, Kalman J., and Richard M. Cyert, *Theory of the Firm: Resource Allocation in a Market Economy* (Englewood Cliffs, N.J., Prentice-Hall, 1965).

Collins, Barry E., and Harold Guetzkow, *A Social Psychology of Group Processes for Decision-Making* (New York, Wiley, 1964).

Cyert, Richard M., and Kenneth R. MacCrimmon, "Organizations," in Gardner Lindsey and Elliot Aronson, eds., *Handbook of Social Psychology* (Reading, Mass., Addison-Wesley, 1968), I, 568–611.

Downs, Anthony, *Inside Bureaucracy* (Boston, Little, Brown, 1967).

Etzioni, Amitai, *A Comparative Analysis of Complex Organizations* (New York, Free Press, 1961).

Hage, Jerald, "An Axiomatic Theory of Organizations," *Administrative Science Quarterly,* 10 (December 1965), 289–320.

Haire, Mason, Edwin E. Ghiselli, and Lyman W. Porter, *Managerial Thinking: An International Study* (New York, Wiley, 1966).

Herzberg, Frederick, Bernard Mausner, and Barbara B. Snyderman, *The Motivation to Work* (New York, Wiley, 1959).

Hirschman, Albert O., *Exit, Voice, and Loyalty* (Cambridge, Mass., Harvard University Press, 1970).

Katz, Daniel, and Robert Kahn, *The Social Psychology of Organizations* (New York, Wiley, 1966).

March, James G., ed., *Handbook of Organizations* (Chicago, Rand McNally, 1965).

Porter, Lyman W., and Edward E. Lawler, III, *Managerial Attitudes and Performance* (Homewood, Ill., Irwin, 1968).

Quinn, Robert, and Robert L. Kahn, "Organizational Psychology," *Annual Review of Psychology,* 18 (1967), 437–466.

Rourke, Francis E., *Bureaucracy, Politics, and Public Policy* (Boston, Little, Brown, 1969).

Vroom, Victor H., *Work and Motivation* (New York, Wiley, 1964).

Walton, Richard E., and John M. Dutton, "The Management of Interdepartmental Conflict: A Model and Review," *Administrative Science Quarterly,* 14 (March 1969), 73–90.

STUDIES OF TURKEY

Armaoğlu, Fahir, and Guthrie Birkhead, *Graduates of the Faculty of Political Science, 1946–1955* (Ankara, Public Administration Institute for Turkey and the Middle East, 1957).

Bent, Frederick T., and Louise L. Shields, eds., *The Role of Local Government in National Development* (Ankara, CENTO, 1968).

Çankaya, Ali, *Mülkiye Tarihi ve Mülkiyeliler* [History of the Civil Service School and its graduates], (Ankara, Örnek Matbaasï, 1954), vol. II.

Davison, Roderic H., *Reform in the Ottoman Empire 1856–1876* (Princeton, N.J., Princeton University Press, 1963).

Dodd, C. H., *Politics and Government in Turkey* (Berkeley, University of California Press, 1969).

Frey, Frederick W., *The Turkish Political Elite* (Cambridge, Mass., M.I.T. Press, 1965).

——, "Surveying Peasant Attitudes in Turkey," *Public Opinion Quarterly,* 27 (Fall 1963), 335–355.

278

Giritli, Ismet, "Turkey Since the 1965 Elections," *Middle East Journal,* 23 (Summer 1969), 351–363.

Hershlag, Z. Y., *Turkey: The Challenge of Growth* (Leiden, E. J. Brill, 1968).

Hyland, Michael P., "Crisis at the Polls: Turkey's 1969 Elections," *Middle East Journal,* 24 (Winter 1970), 1–16.

Hopper, Jerry, R., and Richard I. Levin, eds., *The Turkish Administrator: A Cultural Survey* (Ankara, US AID Public Administration Division, 1967).

Hyman, Herbert H., Arif Payaslıoğlu and Frederick W. Frey, "The Values of Turkish College Youth," *Public Opinion Quarterly,* 22 (Fall 1958), 275–291.

Karpat, Kemal, "Society, Economics, and Politics in Contemporary Turkey," *World Politics,* 17 (October 1964), 50–74.

——, "The Military and Politics in Turkey, 1960–64: A Socio-Cultural Analysis of a Revolution," *American Historical Review,* 75 (October 1970), 1654–1683.

Kazamias, Andreas M., *Education and the Quest for Modernity in Turkey* (Chicago, The University of Chicago Press, 1966).

Keleş, Ruşen and Cevat Geray, *Türk Belediye Başkanları* [Turkish mayors] (Ankara, Ayyıldız Matbaası, 1964).

Kerwin, Robert W., "Private Enterprise in Turkish Industrial Development," *Middle East Journal,* 5 (Winter 1951), 21–38.

Kolars, John F., *Tradition, Season, and Change in a Turkish Village* (Chicago, Ill., University of Chicago Press, 1963).

Lewis, Bernard, *The Emergence of Modern Turkey* (London, Oxford University Press, 1961).

Mardin, Şerif, "Opposition and Control in Turkey," *Government and Opposition,* 1 (May 1966), 375–387.

Matthews, A. T. J., *Emergent Turkish Administrators* (Ankara, Political Science Faculty, 1955).

Mears, Eliot G., *Modern Turkey* (New York, Macmillan, 1924).

Mıhçıoğlu, Cemal, *Üniversiteye Giriş Sınavlarının Yeniden Düzenlenmesi* [An investigation of the new university entrance examinations] (Ankara, Sevinç Matbaası, 1962).

Pasyalıoğlu, Arif, *Türkiyede Özel Sanayi Alanındaki Müteşebbisler ve Teşebbüsler* [Entrepreneurs and enterprises in the private sector in Turkey] (Ankara, Political Science Faculty-Financial Institute, 1961).

Robinson, Richard D., *The First Turkish Republic* (Cambridge, Mass., Harvard University Press, 1963).

Roos, Leslie L., Jr., Noralou P. Roos, and Gary R. Field, "Students and Politics in Contemporary Turkey," in S. M. Lipset and P. G. Altbach, eds., *Students In Revolt* (Boston, Houghton Mifflin, 1969), pp. 257–282.

Rustow, Dankwart A., "Atatürk as Founder of a State," *Daedalus,* 97 Summer 1969), 793–828.

——, "The Army and the Founding of the Turkish Republic," *World Politics,* 11 (July 1959), 513–552.

——, and Robert E. Ward, eds., *Political Modernization in Japan and Turkey* (Princeton, N.J., Princeton University Press, 1964).

Şenel, Turhan A., *"The Ministry of Interior and the Role of the Kaymakam in Turkey"* (Ankara, Çeviri Yayĭnevi, 1965).

Sherwood, W. B., "The Rise of the Justice Party in Turkey," *World Politics,* 20 (October 1967), 54–65.

Simpson, Dwight, "Development as a Process — The Menderes Phase in Turkey," *Middle East Journal,* 19 (Spring 1965), 141–152.

Stycos, J. Mayone, "The Potential Role of Turkish Village Opinion Leaders in a Program of Family Planning," *Public Opinion Quarterly,* 29 (Spring 1965), 120–130.

Szyliowicz, Joseph S., *Political Change in Rural Turkey-Erdemli* (The Hague, Mouton, 1966).

——, "Elite Recruitment in Turkey: The Role of the *Mülkiye,"* *World Politics,* 33 (April 1971), 371–398.

Tachau, Frank, "Local Politicians in Turkey," in *Regional Planning, Local Government and Community Development in Turkey* (Ankara, Sevinç Matbaasĭ, 1966).

——, with assistance of Mary Jo Good, "The Anatomy of Political and Social Change: Turkish Parties and Parliaments 1960–1970," *Comparative Politics,* forthcoming.

——, and A. Haluk Ülman, "Dilemmas of Turkish Politics," *The Turkish Yearbook of International Relations* (Ankara, Ankara Üniversitesi Basĭmevi, 1964).

Ülman, A. Haluk, and Frank Tachau, "Turkish Politics: the Attempt to Reconcile Rapid Modernization with Democracy," *Middle East Journal,* 19 (Spring 1965), 153–168.

SOCIAL SCIENCE METHODOLOGY

Blalock, H. M., Jr., "A Causal Approach to Nonrandom Measurement Errors," *American Political Science Review,* 64 (December 1970), 1099–1111.

——, "Estimating Measurement Error Using Multiple Indicators and Several Points in Time," *American Sociological Review,* 35 (February 1970), 101–111.

Campbell, Donald T., "Factors Relevant to the Validity of Experiments in Social Settings," *Psychological Bulletin,* 54 (1957), 297–312.

——, "Reforms as Experiments," *American Psychologist,* 24 (April 1969), 409–429.

——, and Julian C. Stanley, *Experimental and Quasi-Experimental Designs for Research* (Chicago, Rand McNally, 1967).

Costner, Herbert L., "Theory, Deduction, and Rules of Correspondence," *American Journal of Sociology,* 75 (September 1969), 245–263.

Cronbach, Lee J., and Lita Furby, "How We Should Measure 'Change' — Or Should We?" *Psychological Bulletin,* 74 (1970), 68–80.

Duncan, Otis Dudley, "Some Linear Models for Two-Wave, Two-Variable Panel Analysis," *Psychological Bulletin,* 72 (1969), 177–182.

Lazarsfeld, Paul F., ed., *Mathematical Thinking in the Social Sciences* (New York, Free Press, 1954).

Mosteller, Frederick, "Association and Estimation in Contingency Tables," *Journal of the American Statistical Association,* 63 (March 1968), 1–28.

Nie, Norman H., Dale H. Bent, and C. Hadlai Hull, *Statistical Package for the Social Sciences* (New York, McGraw-Hill, 1970).

Pelz, Donald C., and Frank M. Andrews, "Detecting Causal Priorities in Panel Study Data," *American Sociological Review,* 29 (December 1964), 836–848.

Przeworski, Adam, and Henry Teune, *The Logic of Comparative Social Inquiry* (New York, Wiley, 1970).

Rozelle, Richard M., and Donald T. Campbell, "More Plausible Rival Hypotheses in the Cross-lagged Panel Correlation Technique," *Psychological Bulletin,* 71 (1969), 74–80.

Scott, William A., "Attitude Measurement," in Gardner Lindzey and Elliot Aronson, eds., *Handbook of Social Psychology* (Reading, Mass., Addison-Wesley, 1968), II, 204–273.

Webb, Eugene J., et al., *Unobtrusive Measures: Nonreactive Research in the Social Sciences* (Chicago, Rand McNally, 1966).

White, Harrison, *Chains of Opportunity* (Cambridge, Mass., Harvard University Press, 1970).

Winch, Robert F., and Donald T. Campbell, "Proof? No. Evidence? Yes. The Significance of Tests of Significance," *The American Sociologist,* 4 (May 1969), 140–143.

Yee, A. H., and N. L. Gage, "Techniques for Estimating the Source and Direction of Causal Influence in Panel Data," *Psychological Bulletin,* 70 (1968), 115–126.

Index

286